AF352272

Business and Nonproliferation

BUSINESS AND NONPROLIFERATION

Industry's Role in Safeguarding a Nuclear Renaissance

JOHN P. BANKS
CHARLES K. EBINGER

editors

BROOKINGS INSTITUTION PRESS
Washington, D.C.

Library of Congress Cataloging-in-Publication data

Business and nonproliferation : industry's role in safeguarding a nuclear renaissance /
John P. Banks and Charles K. Ebinger, editors.
    p.   cm.
Includes bibliographical references and index.
Summary: "Forecasts pressure on the fragile nuclear nonproliferation regime because
of expected increases in civilian nuclear power worldwide due to global demand
and concerns over energy security and greenhouse gas emissions and addresses how
the nuclear industry can act as a responsible partner in preventing nuclear weapons
proliferation"—Provided by publisher.
  ISBN 978-0-8157-2147-5 (hardback : alk. paper)
 1. Nuclear industry. 2. Nuclear energy. 3. Nuclear nonproliferation. I. Banks, John P.
II. Ebinger, Charles K.

HD9698.A2B84 2011
327.1'747—dc23   2011034305

9 8 7 6 5 4 3 2 1

Printed on acid-free paper

Typeset in Adobe Garamond

Composition by Cynthia Stock
Silver Spring, Maryland

Printed by R. R. Donnelley
Harrisonburg, Virginia

Contents

Preface

As this book was in the final stages of preparation, the Fukushima Daiichi nuclear plant in Japan was damaged severely by a catastrophic earthquake and tsunami that left its cooling systems disabled and radioactive materials leaking into the surrounding environment. The emergency received the International Atomic Energy Agency's highest rating, a level 7, the same given to the Chernobyl disaster of 1986. At this point, the full impact remains unclear as Japanese officials continue to try to contain damage at the plant and the global nuclear energy community begins to assess the accident and lessons learned from it.

What is clear is Fukushima's immediate effect on the world's resurgent interest in nuclear power. Japan itself announced a complete reversal of its energy policy, replacing its plans for raising nuclear energy's contribution to electricity supply from 30 percent to 50 percent with a major commitment to energy efficiency and the accelerated development of renewable energy. Numerous other governments are now planning to reexamine nuclear energy policy and review the safety of their reactors and adequacy of their regulatory frameworks. On March 16, 2011, the European Union's (EU's) energy commissioner Gunther Oettinger pointed to the need for safety and "stress tests" on all 143 reactors in EU member countries. In the United States, President Barack Obama called on the Nuclear Regulatory Commission to conduct "a comprehensive safety review . . . of all our existing nuclear energy facilities." Germany has closed temporarily seven of its oldest plants and suspended a previous decision on life extensions for all of its seventeen plants. Switzerland and Italy have dropped plans to build new reactors. China, which is engaged in the world's largest nuclear reactor construction program, says it is suspending approval of new plants and conducting safety reviews at existing plants.

As all aspects of nuclear power plant construction and operation face increased scrutiny, some notable concerns will be the ability of reactors to withstand catastrophic events and seismic activity, emergency preparedness, the adequacy of backup power systems, the siting of multiple units in one location, the relicensing of older facilities, the handling and storage of spent fuel, and liability in the event of an accident. The examination of these issues and detailed assessment of the events at Fukushima will almost certainly result in new policy and regulatory revisions, which in turn will cause delays to global nuclear expansion plans in the short term.

Like the nuclear accidents at Three Mile Island and Chernobyl, Fukushima has had a strong impact on public opinion. In a U.S. poll conducted several weeks after the accident, nearly 60 percent of respondents did not think the federal government was prepared adequately to deal with a nuclear accident, and almost two-thirds did not favor building new nuclear power plants in their community (although about 70 percent thought nuclear plants in operation were safe). In Europe about half of those polled in France, Germany, Spain, and Britain were "more concerned" about nuclear safety after the accident.

Even before the Fukushima disaster, the much-heralded nuclear "renaissance" was already facing financial, regulatory, and logistical challenges in the industrialized world. High up-front capital costs had emerged as the principal obstacle in expanding nuclear capacity, especially for investor-owned utilities in the United States and Europe. Just days before Fukushima, John Rowe, chairman and chief executive officer of Exelon Corp., the largest U.S. nuclear generator, had said that nuclear energy would not become competitive in the next decade largely because of cheap natural gas. In Western Europe, the only two nuclear plants under construction are both behind schedule and over budget. Now that Fukushima has brought safety concerns to the forefront, the risk premium in the cost of nuclear power is bound to rise.

Fukushima will have less of an impact on nuclear power expansion in emerging markets, however, where three other considerations come into play. First, energy and development challenges are more daunting. According to the International Energy Agency, 80 percent of the growth in global electricity consumption between 2008 and 2035, and nearly all of the increase in global CO_2 emissions, will take place in developing countries as they endeavor to support economic modernization, population growth, urbanization, and a growing middle class. To meet rising electricity demand while also lowering CO_2 emissions, these countries will have no alternative but to keep nuclear energy on the table as a component of their economic development and energy security strategies.

Second, many developing countries are further along in their commitment to nuclear power development than those in the industrialized world. The emerging markets, especially in Asia, account for most of the current reactor construction and planned expansion in the coming decades. Of all reactors now being built, 75 percent are located in China, Russia, South Korea, and India. China alone accounts for 42 percent of total global construction. Some national nuclear plans are very ambitious: China is aiming to increase its nuclear capacity from the current 10.8 gigawatts to 90 gigawatts by 2020, South Korea hopes to export eighty nuclear power plants over the next two decades, and Russia wants to increase reactor sales from $17 billion to $50 billion in the next twenty years. Those looking to build their first nuclear reactors in the next several decades include Egypt, Indonesia, Jordan, Kazakhstan, Saudi Arabia, South Africa, Turkey, the United Arab Emirates, and Vietnam. While a change of nuclear energy policy in the United States and Europe is largely a matter of rearranging energy planners' drawing boards, emerging markets have far more to lose from a reversal of their positions.

Third, nuclear power expansion in emerging markets is led mainly by the state: governments directly plan and implement civilian nuclear energy programs, support their state-owned nuclear companies in becoming international vendors, and partner with international companies (many also state-owned). Rosatom in Russia, the China National Nuclear Corporation, and the Nuclear Power Corporation of India are examples of these nuclear "national champions." State backing lowers transaction and capital costs, and government commitments—if not outright mandates—facilitate and streamline project implementation. According to recent estimates, it costs two times as much to build a nuclear power plant in the United States and Europe as in China, while France's EPR reactor costs 2.5 times as much as South Korea's APR1400. Under such active state participation, political considerations and not purely commercial factors play a major role in determining the future of nuclear power.

In the wake of Fukushima, emerging market countries will also face increased challenges to a continued policy of civilian nuclear power expansion. Whether augmenting existing capacity or building reactors for the first time, countries will be under closer international scrutiny to ensure that appropriate infrastructure, financial resources, human capacity, and legal and regulatory frameworks are in place. These considerations apply equally to plant safety and to proliferation prevention. Countries also will face louder public opposition to nuclear power. As the events of the "Arab Spring" populist uprisings in the Middle East and North Africa demonstrate, countries that have hitherto been used to centralized decisionmaking ignore public opinion at their peril. Nongovernment groups in India, Turkey, Jordan, Malaysia, Indonesia, and elsewhere have already started to question their country's nuclear plans. Some governments are responding: partly because of public concerns, India has indicated it will seek to establish a new independent regulator to oversee the nuclear industry.

While the full impacts of Fukushima will not be known for some time, developing countries are likely to continue expanding nuclear capacity, but at a slower rate in the short term as they review safety measures at their existing plants, reexamine plans, or delay licensing, siting, and other decisions. At the same time, most have reaffirmed their long-term commitment to nuclear power. Officials in Turkey and Indonesia, both earthquake-prone countries, as well as Brazil, India, Russia, South Africa, and Vietnam have pronounced that plans for nuclear power will stay on track. Even though China's suspension of approvals for new reactors is expected to slow nuclear development for two to three years, the deputy secretary of its Nuclear Energy Association says that "in the medium and long-term China's nuclear strategy cannot be shaken."

The accident at Fukushima does not alter the fundamental theme of this volume. A global expansion of nuclear power is very likely to continue over the long term, and this expansion will require continued and enhanced proliferation prevention efforts—especially from the commercial nuclear industry.

Acknowledgments

We owe thanks to many people for their contributions to this book. First and foremost, we want to thank each of our authors—Michael Moodie, Lawrence Scheinman, and Sharon Squassoni—for their outstanding work, their patience through successive revisions, and their significant efforts and always high-quality analysis and insights.

A special thanks also goes to Govinda Avasarala, research assistant at the Energy Security Initiative, for his research, analysis, and inputs throughout this project, and to Kevin Massy, assistant director of ESI, for his substantive thinking and editorial suggestions. We are also grateful to Eleanor Cooper and Cassie Hammond for their research efforts.

We also want to thank all those organizations, companies, and individuals who participated in our research for their invaluable contributions to this volume.

Finally, we want to thank Chris Kelaher, Janet Walker, Larry Converse, Susan Woollen, and the rest of the Brookings Press staff for their patience and support.

And here we add one disclaimer to cover all of our coauthors:

Disclaimer: Views expressed in the following chapters are those of the authors alone and do not represent those of the institutions or entities of which they are a part, or for which they work.

BUSINESS AND NONPROLIFERATION

1

Introduction:
Planning a Responsible Nuclear Energy Future

CHARLES K. EBINGER AND JOHN P. BANKS

Nuclear energy is a twentieth-century innovation but until recently has not spread beyond a relatively small number of industrialized nations (see maps on pages 4 and 5). All this is about to change. With global electricity demand increasing dramatically and greenhouse gas emissions and energy security becoming national priorities, developed and developing countries alike are reexamining nuclear energy as a means of providing a reliable and scalable source of low-carbon power.

The International Energy Agency (IEA) projects that global electricity demand will increase 2.2 percent a year to 2035, with about 80 percent of that growth occurring in emerging economies outside the Organization for Economic Cooperation and Development (OECD).[1] Even if new policy initiatives are introduced to lower carbon dioxide (CO_2) emissions and combat global climate change, global energy-related CO_2 emissions are expected to increase 21 percent between 2008 and 2035.[2] Emerging market economies account for all of this projected increase in emissions. In the face of rising prices and increasing volatility in the oil market, many of these economies have shifted their attention to nuclear energy as a means of reducing dependence on oil (often a major source of their power generation), improving their balance of payments, and bolstering national energy security.[3]

Currently, 440 reactors with a total capacity of 375 gigawatts (GWe) are in operation worldwide.[4] As of March 2011, 65 nuclear reactor units, with a total capacity of 63 GWe, are under construction.[5] And as of April 2011, 158 projects are also on order or planned and 326 proposed.[6] These preparations for replacing or expanding reactor fleets and for new entries to the marketplace follow a decades-long lull in construction and suggest a "nuclear renaissance" has begun. While "renaissance" implies a revival or return to a better time, the global expansion of nuclear energy in the coming decades will differ in several respects from the way civilian nuclear power developed between the late 1950s and mid-1980s.

First, the scope and pace of this new deployment could be significantly larger than in previous periods of expansion: some recent analyses put installed nuclear capacity up at 550–850 GWe by 2035, depending on assumptions about the implementation of low-carbon energy policies.[7] In IEA projections, a 50 percent cut in energy-related CO_2 emissions by 2050 would require global capacity to reach 1,200 GWe, a net addition of 30 GWe each year over the next forty years.[8] To put this figure into perspective, during the period of nuclear power's most rapid expansion (1981–90), capacity increased by only 20 GWe a year, slowing to an annual average of 4 GWe from 1991 to 2006.[9] To achieve large-scale reductions in energy-related CO_2 emissions, nuclear capacity must therefore grow not only faster but also for several decades longer than during nuclear energy's previous "golden age." (As the preface indicates, safety concerns arising in the aftermath of the Fukushima accident will slow or scale back nuclear power expansion globally in the short term. At the same time, the longer-term impact of Fukushima on global nuclear power expansion will be less adverse, especially in emerging market countries.)

Also different today is the number of countries seeking to build their *first* nuclear power reactor. Some sixty-five countries have expressed interest in or are actively planning for nuclear power.[10] As the International Atomic Energy Agency (IAEA) points out, however, most of these countries are merely "considering" the range of issues involved in nuclear power development. Many of them cannot realistically afford the large costs associated with civilian nuclear power programs. According to some analyses, countries with a GDP of less than $50 billion could not spend several billion dollars building a reactor.[11] In addition, many aspirant countries still lack the electricity grids required for nuclear power: electricity systems with a capacity below 10 GWe are unlikely to be able to accommodate a nuclear reactor.[12] Some countries could address this issue by expanding electricity interconnections with neighboring states or developing power export arrangements; however, these alternatives are not widely available and in any case would take time to implement.

At the same time, a number of countries have credible plans to become new nuclear energy states (NNES). The IAEA has indicated that ten to twenty-five countries might begin operating their first plants by 2030, whereas since Chernobyl only three—China, Mexico, and Romania—have brought nuclear plants online for the first time.[13] The following list shows the stages of progress of eleven emerging market countries in their efforts to develop a civilian nuclear energy program:[14]

—Power reactors under construction: Iran.[15]

—Contracts signed, legal and regulatory infrastructure well developed: United Arab Emirates (UAE), Turkey.

—Committed plans, legal and regulatory infrastructure developing: Vietnam, Jordan.

—Well-developed plans but commitment pending: Thailand, Indonesia, Egypt, Kazakhstan.

—Developing plans: Saudi Arabia, Malaysia.

Emerging market nations entertaining the construction of new nuclear power capacity face several critical issues. Domestically, each must establish strong institutions and viable regulatory frameworks addressing health, safety, proliferation, and environmental concerns while ensuring that adequate human and financial resources are available for these tasks. Even if a state is willing to buy a nuclear reactor on a "turnkey" basis (paying for an outside operator to build and run the system), it must still train its own nationals in these various respects and establish a strong academic and industrial culture in all aspects of commercial nuclear operations in order to achieve a sound, sustainable program. The NNES will need to build these capabilities in a sufficient and timely manner.

New States and Nonproliferation

One of the biggest challenges in any expansion of the civilian nuclear sector is that of maintaining and strengthening the global regime for nuclear nonproliferation. The changing geopolitical and security environment, combined with the political instability of many regions and countries that aspire to develop civilian nuclear reactor technology, has already raised proliferation concerns. Nuclear power reactors could become attractive targets for terrorists, who might also seek access to fissile material for radiological dispersal devices ("dirty bombs") or for nuclear weapons. With such materials more widely available, the proliferation risks could mount. As commercial enrichment and recycling programs multiply, countries may be tempted also to develop latent nuclear weapons capabilities, especially if they aspire to attain regional predominance, international standing, or the capabilities of regional rivals.

An expansion of nuclear energy could further tax an already stressed nonproliferation regime. In light of Article IV of the Nuclear Nonproliferation Treaty (NPT), which states that the treaty shall not affect the "inalienable right . . . to develop research, production and use of nuclear energy for peaceful purposes without discrimination . . . and the right to participate in, the fullest possible exchange of equipment, materials and scientific and technological information

Nuclear Power Plants in Operation

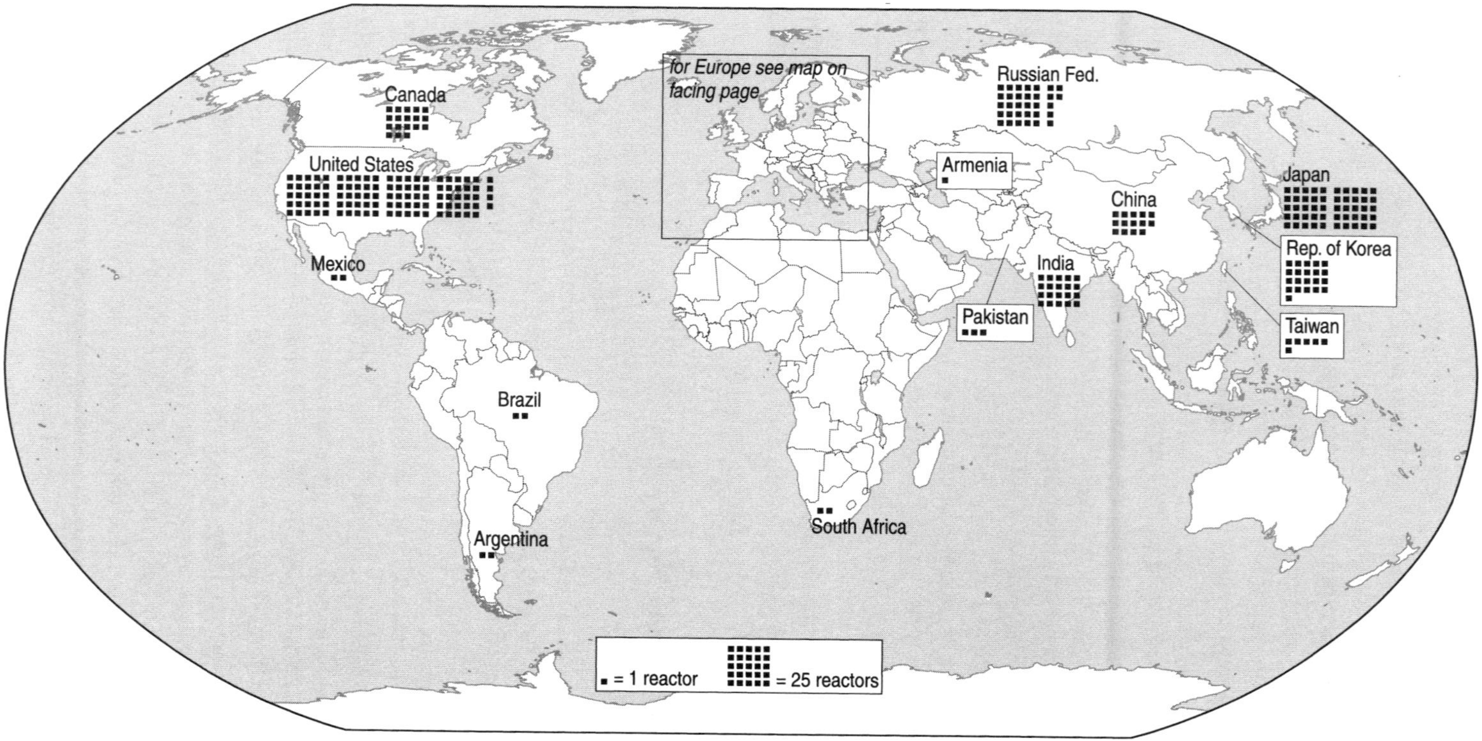

Source: Power Reactor Information System, IAEA, as of July 2011.

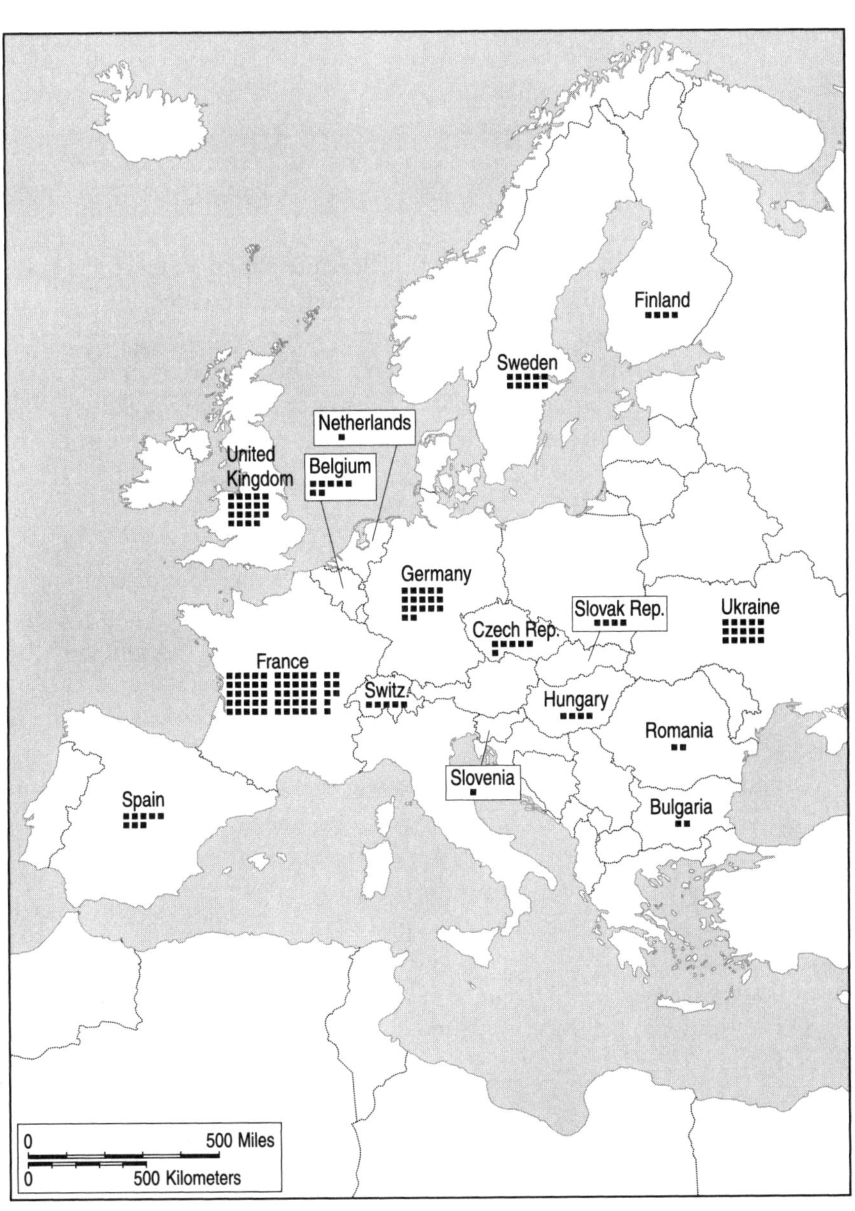

Finland
Sweden
Netherlands
United Kingdom
Belgium
Germany
Slovak Rep.
Ukraine
Czech Rep.
France
Switz.
Hungary
Romania
Spain
Slovenia
Bulgaria
0   500 Miles
0   500 Kilometers

for the peaceful uses of nuclear energy, " some nations are considering acquisition of fuel cycle capabilities as a way to avoid further dependence on foreign suppliers when they develop nuclear power.[16] The NPT contains no provisions to restrict acquisition of such capabilities, although members of the Nuclear Suppliers Group (a voluntary group of nations that restricts nuclear exports) have long practiced restraint on technology transfers of sensitive components of the fuel cycle.

A sharp increase in the demand for nuclear fuel could enhance the commercial attractiveness of uranium enrichment and reprocessing, enticing new entrants into the market.[17] Nations with large uranium resources might seek to add value to their uranium exports by moving further up the chain of production or by expanding current capabilities (Australia, Canada, Kazakhstan, and South Africa have all discussed this option recently). Even if the high cost of fuel cycle activities proves to be a disincentive to their development, the NNES—especially in emerging markets—may consider fuel supply security and exercising sovereign rights under Article IV of the NPT more relevant than economic drivers in their decisions about enrichment or reprocessing.[18] With governments playing an increasing role in securing and meeting nuclear contracts, political motivations might also enter into assessments of the nuclear capabilities necessary for recipient countries. The great danger in the race to build out new capacity is that some new players may not take proliferation concerns as seriously as existing service providers.

To address these issues, there has been a reinvigorated discussion of multilateral nuclear approaches (MNAs). MNAs establish a framework to safeguard Article IV rights, specifically by limiting the diffusion of sensitive nuclear materials and technologies while concurrently guaranteeing long-term supply of nuclear fuel to civilian nuclear power programs. Some steps in this direction include two recently approved fuel banks: the Russian-backed International Uranium Enrichment Center in Angarsk and the IAEA Nuclear Threat Initiative Fuel Bank.[19]

The institutional challenges to the nonproliferation regime are compounded both by the actions of rogue states such as Iran's clandestine nuclear program and North Korea's nuclear weapons testing and new uranium enrichment program, and by non-state activities such as the operations of black market nuclear networks arranged by Pakistani scientist A. Q. Khan. Confidence in the regime's ability to respond to and resolve proliferation threats has thus fallen. New technologies may put further stress on the nonproliferation system. Particularly worrying are the expansion of centrifuge technology, commercialization of the laser enrichment process, development and deployment of next-generation reprocessing techniques that require advanced safeguards, and the potential spread of fast reactors.

Although the impact of these dynamics is difficult to foresee, the nonproliferation regime needs to keep pace with the rapidly changing, complex nuclear market, especially those developments and activities that facilitate the expansion of uranium enrichment and spent fuel reprocessing. This is a major challenge for a nonproliferation regime already under stress.

A Renaissance and Industry

The nuclear nonproliferation regime is based on inspections, export controls, and physical protection implemented at the national and international levels through laws, treaties, agreements, regulations, protocols, and other mechanisms. Companies operating in the civilian nuclear industry serve as a lynchpin in this system. It cannot work unless they comply with the nonproliferation framework and communicate and cooperate with governments, regulators, and regional and international bodies. Industry's views of the costs and benefits of a significant expansion of nuclear energy must factor into assessments of the potential impact of such an expansion on the nonproliferation regime.

For the nuclear industry, a renaissance offers new commercial opportunities. According to the World Nuclear Association (WNA), "There is a tiger-like market out there right now of aggressive capitalist activity that is occurring in anticipation of a huge growth in the global nuclear industry. . . . In the 21st century, the nuclear industry will build hundreds, then thousands of power reactors worldwide."[20]

Many high-level industry leaders have confirmed repeatedly their commitment to nonproliferation, and companies are aware that "the nuclear industry, as well as the arms control and nonproliferation communities, must join governments in ensuring that the nuclear renaissance takes place under conditions that minimize the risk of proliferation."[21] Industry concurs that any major breach of safety, security, or proliferation safeguards could prove fatal. At the same time, the general view in the industry is that a renaissance does not pose a threat to the nonproliferation regime, and that the current legal and regulatory framework is working well—albeit with some need for improvement.[22] While the industry acknowledges and accepts the importance of its role in maintaining the integrity of and strengthening the nonproliferation regime, it sees rogue states and illicit networks, not commercial entities, as the main threats to the nonproliferation regime. Accordingly, it usually looks to government to take the lead in resolving these problems. Fearing potential market disruptions and adverse effects on its own commercial interests, industry tends to be wary of relying on multilateral mechanisms to ensure the security of fuel supplies and limit the spread of sensitive fuel cycle technologies.

As new countries enter the civilian nuclear sector and challenges to the non-proliferation regime become more acute, it is imperative to reexamine many existing assumptions on the part of industry and governments in the interests of closer cooperation in meeting those challenges. How, for example, can the commercial opportunities associated with a nuclear renaissance be reconciled with the need to strengthen the nonproliferation regime? If industry is the "first line of defense," as prominent analysts of nuclear security matters have suggested, how can industry play a more active and enhanced role alongside governments in strengthening the nonproliferation regime as new states begin nuclear power development?[23] Are there better ways to balance business and nonproliferation objectives in the twenty-first century?

The Brookings Study

To explore these questions, the Brookings Institution turned to major stakeholders in the civilian nuclear industry for their views on the existing nonproliferation regime, particularly its weaknesses, the challenges of an expansion in nuclear power, and the role of industry in strengthening the regime. Opinions were compiled from in-depth interviews, discussions, and an anonymous survey of three sets of stakeholders in the nuclear community: commercial nuclear industry entities, including uranium mining companies, reactor vendors, enrichment and reprocessing service providers, and nuclear power utilities; nongovernment organizations; and government agencies and nuclear regulators.

The written survey consisted of two parts. The first asked participants their general views on the nonproliferation regime, and the second asked participants to evaluate the effectiveness and feasibility of ten MNAs pertaining to various aspects of the nuclear fuel cycle and six proposals for industry self-regulation. "Effectiveness" refers to the likelihood that the nonproliferation regime will be strengthened; "feasibility" refers to the logistical and political ease of implementation (for details of the implementation and results of the survey, see the appendix).

This book presents and assesses the results of this research and offers recommendations. The discussion is organized in two parts: part 1 examines the changing proliferation dynamic through the shifting landscape of nuclear energy and nonproliferation. It opens in chapter 2 with Sharon Squassoni's discussion of the emerging challenges for the nuclear nonproliferation regime. Despite many improvements since the early 1990s in response to discoveries of clandestine programs and networks in Iraq, Iran, North Korea, and Pakistan, significant institutional, structural, and operational problems remain to be addressed. Some of these are long-standing issues inherent in the framework of the NPT, such as the tensions surrounding peaceful uses of nuclear energy (Article IV) and disarmament obligations (Article VI). To add to these concerns, political expedience at times overrides nonproliferation objectives, and the resources needed to improve IAEA capabilities remain in short supply. A dramatic expansion of civilian nuclear energy programs may generate new challenges surrounding the increased production, storage, and transport of nuclear materials; the potential spread of enrichment and recycling facilities; and the development of new fuel cycle and reactor technologies.

In chapter 3, Sharon Squassoni and John P. Banks turn to the commercial dimensions of the so-called renaissance, focusing on the nuclear fuel cycle and possible effect of commercial trends on the nonproliferation regime. In their view, the high capital costs and technical specialization required for most stages of the fuel cycle (especially enrichment and reprocessing) provide significant economic disincentives for *new* market entrants for the foreseeable future. Overall, the nuclear industry has consolidated but also become globalized, with many parts of the fuel cycle—including mining, enrichment, and reactor construction—resting in several global companies. Squassoni and Banks argue for close scrutiny of the potential impact of new technologies such as laser enrichment and next-generation recycling techniques on the nuclear nonproliferation regime.

In chapter 4, Charles Ebinger and Sharon Squassoni explore the unique challenges of expanding nuclear power capacity in emerging economies, especially in some of the key supplier countries and those likely to become NNES in the coming decades. As they point out, countries decide to pursue nuclear power for various reasons: skyrocketing electricity demand, energy security, concern about dependence on imported fossil fuels as well as declining export revenues from sales of oil and natural gas, climate change, national prestige, balance of power with respect to regional rivals, among others. Acquisition strategies range from relying on foreign firms to run an entire nuclear program to purchasing equipment and services on a turnkey basis. Each instance depends on detailed training and assistance.

Part 2 of the volume presents the results of our research into industry's views, beginning in chapter 5 with Sharon Squassoni, who analyzes the first half of our survey, in which industry and nonindustry participants were asked broad questions about current challenges to the nuclear nonproliferation regime and possible solutions. In general, industry respondents did not view a nuclear renaissance as a threat to the nonproliferation regime. They believe that the current legal and regulatory framework is sufficient and working, and that the major weaknesses and threats emanate from political actors, namely, "rogue" governments or non-state actors engaged in illicit or illegal activities. According to one industry respondent, "Commercial entities are not where the risk lies." Rather, most pointed to the spread of enrichment and reprocessing capabilities, and the lack of enforcement mechanisms in the regime. Industry is by and large optimistic about the role that technology can play in strengthening the nonproliferation regime, acknowledging, however, that technology alone is not the solution.

Nonindustry responses reflected similar concerns about enforcement and the risks associated with the spread of sensitive nuclear technologies but pointed out a broader range of threats, including terrorist access to nuclear materials, weapons, and highly enriched uranium (HEU) stockpiles, along with the challenge of ensuring that NNES develop a comprehensive regulatory infrastructure. Here, too, respondents said technology—including new recycling methods— could reduce proliferation risks, but like those in industry saw some risks in laser enrichment and fast breeder reactors.

Industry's perspective on MNA proposals is elaborated in chapter 6, where Lawrence Scheinman and Govinda Avasarala provide historical context illustrating that since the dawn of the NPT the international community has struggled to guarantee the Article IV rights of non–nuclear weapon states to develop nuclear energy for peaceful purposes, while also preventing the spread of nuclear weapons. Various multilateral concepts have emerged to allow these states to gain access to nuclear fuel, sensitive fuel cycle technologies, or both. In light of the impending nuclear renaissance—particularly the potential large-scale expansion in nuclear power capacity and addition of many NNES—a number of recent MNA proposals have suggested diverse ways to multilateralize the fuel cycle. As Scheinman and Avasarala point out, however, these ideas reflect a growing schism between nuclear weapons states that want to impose conditions on access to sensitive fuel cycle technologies and states without such weapons that view this as an infringement on their sovereignty and a denial of their Article IV rights. When asked to rank the effectiveness and feasibility of ten MNA proposals (encompassing nuclear fuel banks, centralized facilities, lease/take-back programs, international storage or repositories, fuel guarantees, and market mechanisms), industry respondents found all the proposals unfeasible, with the exception of an IAEA-administered international enriched-uranium fuel bank accessible to all countries in compliance with NPT regulations (proposal 2). Their foremost concern was the commercial impact of MNAs, particularly possible disruptions to what the industry views as a well-functioning and efficient market. Second, many expressed reservations about the financial and technical mechanics and logistics of implementation and raised questions about location, financing, ownership, and liabilities connected with new multilateral facilities or arrangements. Third, participants questioned the ability of some MNAs to stop determined proliferators. Finally, industry cited the political hurdles in implementation, especially in dealing with the back end of the fuel cycle.

Nevertheless, industry recognized the potential value, indeed even the necessity of MNAs in order to strengthen the nonproliferation regime while facilitating a nuclear renaissance. Companies need to be assured that any MNA approach fortifies and complements the current market, rather than weakens it with new untried mechanisms. Research feedback leads Scheinman and Avasarala to argue for further development and implementation of a "black-box" approach, granting operators the use of fuel cycle technologies but without access to critical design and technical information supporting those technologies. This concept offers a certain comfort level since it is already in operation in the Enrichment Technology Corporation, a joint venture between AREVA and URENCO, as well as in EURODIF. For example, AREVA and URENCO are applying it in the United States in the establishment of two new enrichment facilities. Such an arrangement, say the authors, could be a template for an NNES, or possibly a private utility, to become an investor or partner with an established commercial entity in the creation of a multilateral fuel cycle center of either global or regional dimensions. All parties could share in the benefits of the venture, Article IV rights would be respected, and nonproliferation objectives would be met by limiting the number of facilities capable of producing weapons-usable material.

In chapter 7, Michael Moodie and John P. Banks evaluate industry's response to self-regulatory approaches to strengthening the nonproliferation regime. These include more proactive steps by industry to prevent the proliferation of weapons as well as existing national and international compliance obligations under the global nonproliferation framework. When asked to rank the effectiveness and feasibility of a code of conduct, whistle-blower programs, black-box technology, accreditation of sensitive fuel cycle materials and technology, and a government-industry conference to enhance cooperation, industry respondents tended to view these proposals with skepticism and caution. Their primary concerns were the potential adverse commercial impacts, questionable added value given existing legal and regulatory requirements, need for more information on how self-regulation approaches would function, and assurances that they could be implemented uniformly and fairly across the industry.

Since the self-regulatory concepts were not uniformly rejected by industry (with the exception of the whistle-blower proposal), they may offer a way forward. For one thing, industry is familiar enough with several of the approaches to view them as feasible. As already mentioned, this is the case with the black-box concept. Some proposals are also acceptable to the nonindustry group. Moreover, both industry and nonindustry respondents seem to think that an enhanced partnership between industry and government is needed to strengthen the nonproliferation regime. Moodie and Banks thus explore how the model of the sustained government-industry dialogue used in negotiating the Chemical Weapons Convention could serve not only as a template for sustained dialogue in the nuclear industry but also as a mechanism for reaching a consensus on the development and implementation of effective self-regulatory and MNA schemes.

Conclusion

With commercial activity now gearing up in the global nuclear fuel cycle, access to nuclear fuel cycle activities and materials is on the brink of expanding, posing serious proliferation risks. Most notably, enrichment and recycling can produce the fissile material required for nuclear weapons, while experience in civilian nuclear power can be used as a platform for developing nuclear expertise useful for a weapons program.

The world needs to be assured that nonproliferation objectives are receiving adequate attention, through stronger institutions, legal and regulatory frameworks, human capabilities, and appropriate infrastructure designed to meet these objectives. To be sure, many countries and companies are already engaged in nonproliferation activities. However, given the weakened state of the regime, the new threats it faces, and the dire consequences of weapons proliferation in a post–cold war world, much more needs to be done to safeguard a nuclear renaissance. With industry at the center of this increased commercial activity, it is reasonable to assume that it should have an increased role in preventing proliferation, or at least in helping shape future civilian use of nuclear energy in a way that mitigates proliferation.

Just as a sufficient safety infrastructure and culture needs to be established to support a rapid build-out of new reactors, nonproliferation also needs to be a priority for all parties while a global expansion takes place. Industry and nonindustry alike must not shy away from the seminal issues in this regard—to ensure that proliferation prevention remains front and center, that industry is balancing nonproliferation and commercial objectives, that government-owned companies do not place commercial or political objectives first, and that industry and government work together, with due respect for each other's goals and concerns.

Past proliferation shocks have prompted new approaches to combating proliferation. A resurgence of nuclear commerce may provide an opportunity to draw upon the strengths of the nuclear industry to help shore up commercial, national, and international efforts to reduce proliferation risks. This book offers insights into some trends in industry thinking and reactions to some of the critical challenges, along with suggestions for ensuring that peaceful nuclear energy remains just that.

Notes

1. International Energy Agency (IEA), *World Energy Outlook 2010* (Paris, 2010). The 2.2 percent figure is under the IEA's New Policies Scenario, "which assumes the introduction of new measures (but on a relatively cautious basis) to implement the broad

policy commitments that have already been announced, including to reduce greenhouse gas emissions and . . . phase out fossil energy subsidies."

2. Ibid.

3. Natural gas in the form of liquefied natural gas (LNG) is used extensively in the power sector in several large Asian economies, typically purchased under long-term contracts with prices indexed to oil.

4. World Nuclear Association (WNA), "World Nuclear Power Reactors and Uranium Requirements" (London, April 1, 2011).

5. Data from the Power Reactor Information System, International Atomic Energy Agency (www.iaea.org/cgi-bin/db.page.pl/pris.reaucct.htm). Note: 1GWe = 1,000 MW, which is about the size of a typical nuclear power plant. We use GWe throughout to denote electric gigawatts.

6. WNA, "World Nuclear Power Reactors and Uranium Requirements."

7. See IEA, *World Energy Outlook 2010*. This is the IEA's range for three scenarios. Several other organizations, including the IAEA and the WNA, have developed high-end growth scenarios with projections of global nuclear capacity reaching nearly 750 GWe by 2030.

8. IEA and OECD Nuclear Energy Agency, "Technology Roadmap: Nuclear Energy," 2010, p. 17.

9. Keystone Center, "Nuclear Power Joint Fact-Finding" (Keystone, Colo., June 2007), p. 25.

10. International Atomic Energy Agency (IAEA), "International Status and Prospects of Nuclear Power" (Vienna, September 2, 2010), p. 10. Of these, twenty-one countries are in the Asia Pacific region, twenty-one in Africa, twelve in Europe (predominately in Eastern Europe), and eleven in Latin America.

11. Jose Goldemberg, "Nuclear Energy in Developing Countries," *Daedalus* (Journal of the American Academy of Arts and Sciences) 138 (Fall 2009): 72.

12. IAEA, "International Status and Prospects of Nuclear Power" (Vienna, September 2008), p. 35.

13. IAEA, "International Status and Prospects of Nuclear Power" (Vienna, September 2010), p. 11.

14. Adapted from the World Nuclear Association, with the focus on developing countries.

15. The details of Iran's nuclear program are a matter of enormous international discussion and debate. While it is clear that the country has made significant progress in building a nuclear power reactor, most attention on the country's nuclear activities relate to the ambiguity of its intentions and the security implications of the development of an Iranian nuclear weapons capability. The political and security-related complexities of Iran's nuclear program are beyond the scope of this volume. Similarly, given the clandestine nature of the development of the Iranian nuclear program and the lack of ongoing involvement in the program by the established commercial nuclear industry, it is the authors' view that the case of Iran is of limited relevance to this study.

16. For the full text of the NPT, see IAEA, "Treaty on the Non-Proliferation of Nuclear

Weapons," INFCIRC/140 (April 22, 1970) (www.iaea.org/Publications/Documents/ Infcircs/Others/infcirc140.pdf).

17. "Nuclear Choice: Time to Invest in Uranium?" *Financial Times,* March 25, 2010.

18. In the case of reprocessing, the extent of economically recoverable uranium resources also plays a role. The Massachusetts Institute of Technology (MIT) recently concluded that "uranium resources will not be a constraint for a long time," even with uranium costs increasing 50 percent as a result of "a world with ten times as many LWRs [light-water reactors] and each LWR operating for 60 years." See MIT, "The Future of the Nuclear Fuel Cycle" (Cambridge, Mass., 2010), p. 4.

19. These are discussed in chapter 6.

20. John Ritch, director general of the World Nuclear Association, as quoted in "The Tough Sell of Nuclear Investing," *MarketWatch,* May 20, 2010 (www.marketwatch.com/ story/nuclear-investing-a-tough-sell-but-can-pay-off-2010-05-20?pagenumber=1).

21. Anne Lauvergeon, "The Nuclear Renaissance: An Opportunity to Enhance the Culture of Nonproliferation," *Daedalus* 138 (Fall 2009): 93.

22. For the purposes of this study, industry is defined as uranium mining companies, reactor vendors, enrichment and reprocessing service providers, and nuclear power utilities.

23. See Gretchen Hund and Amy Seward, "Broadening Industry Governance to Include Nonproliferation" (Richland, Wash.: Pacific Northwest Center for Global Security, August 21, 2008), p. 3; and David Albright, *Peddling Peril, How the Secret Nuclear Trade Arms America's Enemies* (New York: Free Press, 2010), pp. 227–43.

PART I

Changing Proliferation Dynamic

2

Nuclear Energy and Nonproliferation: Today's Challenges

SHARON SQUASSONI

For nuclear security writ large, a major expansion of nuclear energy could present both traditional and new challenges. Although the nuclear nonproliferation regime provides assurances that nuclear power is not misused for weapons purposes, the dual-use nature of the technology means that regardless of intent, some nuclear capabilities could provide a baseline from which a nuclear weapons program could proceed. Traditional concerns about the expansion of nuclear power reactors are minor compared with concerns about the expansion of other capabilities, including uranium enrichment, spent fuel reprocessing, fast breeder reactors, and heavy-water production.

New challenges will arise from the geopolitics of nuclear energy. Much of the projected growth in global electricity demand will occur in countries outside the Organization for Economic Cooperation and Development (OECD). Introducing nuclear energy in these countries will require significant efforts to meet international safety, physical protection, and nonproliferation standards. In regions with terrorist activity, nuclear power plants could be perceived as attractive targets for sabotage.[1] In recent years, there have been a few terrorist plots against nuclear facilities, including the alleged plot by a group of Pakistani Americans to attack the Karachi nuclear reactor, initial plans by al Qaeda to crash an aircraft into a U.S. nuclear facility, and the 2006 "Toronto 18" plot by an Islamic fundamentalist group to use a truck bomb to attack a nuclear power facility in Ontario, Canada.[2] Analysts maintain that terrorist attacks, efforts to purchase a nuclear weapon, or efforts to purchase materials to make a nuclear bomb or radiological device are not idle threats. This contention is highlighted by former International Atomic Energy Agency (IAEA) director general Mohamed ElBaradei's declaration: "The gravest threat the world faces today . . . is that extremists get hold of nuclear or radioactive materials."[3]

A second challenge is how nuclear power is perceived within politically volatile regions. Nuclear power is concentrated in Europe, North America, and Northeast Asia, not spread across the globe. There are many regions that have no nuclear power plants or just one or two. While some maintain that nuclear power is no longer prestigious, in areas like the Middle East, this may not be the case. The fundamentally dual-use nature of nuclear material could cause some regional rivals to assume that their neighbors are acquiring equipment and expertise in support of a latent nuclear weapons capability. Such a process could develop over time and change as politics evolve. For example, little outcry was raised against plans to build many nuclear power reactors in Iran under the shah in the 1970s, but this is not the case today.[4]

This problem could become more acute if capabilities expand to sensitive fuel cycle facilities. Iran is the most notable case right now, but other countries have not ruled out acquiring sensitive capabilities. From a nonproliferation perspective, uranium enrichment and spent fuel reprocessing facilities are the most sensitive parts of the fuel cycle. These facilities could produce fissile material for use in peaceful fuel or for bombs. Only a handful of countries operate these facilities—mostly nuclear weapon states and a few advanced nuclear states such as Japan, Germany, and the Netherlands. Brazil will soon commercialize its uranium enrichment capabilities, which were developed under its clandestine nuclear program. The Nuclear Nonproliferation Treaty (NPT) contains no prohibitions on acquiring uranium enrichment or spent fuel reprocessing capabilities, as long as they are safeguarded.

Renewed interest in acquiring commercial uranium enrichment, reprocessing facilities, or both—prompted either by perceived commercial opportunities or energy security concerns about relying on other nations for the provision of these services—coupled with a projected build-out rate of new reactors not seen since the 1960s, makes a coherent response all the more important.

Charting the Path for Nonproliferation: The NPT and Nuclear Energy

When the NPT was opened for signature in 1968, the United States and the Soviet Union were locked in an arms race that deployed more than 60,000 nuclear weapons across the globe. Although efforts had begun some twenty years earlier to control both the nuclear weapons and the facilities and materials to produce them, progress was slow, and the treaty that emerged from the Eighteen

Nation Disarmament Conference in Geneva was clearly a compromise. The NPT was not a disarmament treaty, but a nonproliferation treaty. The states that had nuclear weapons at the time—the United States, the Soviet Union, China, France, and the United Kingdom—pledged to enter into good faith negotiations on general and complete disarmament, and the states that joined the treaty and did not have nuclear weapons at the time pledged never to acquire them.

As today, there was great enthusiasm then about the potential for vast growth of nuclear energy. In this spirit, many negotiators were loath to interfere with an emerging market, and those from states without nuclear weapons were keen to ensure that they would not be denied the peaceful uses of nuclear energy. It is also likely that during the negotiations, the verification challenges of the NPT were underestimated. There are no verification measures detailed in the treaty itself, beyond the obligation for non–nuclear weapon states to enter into an agreement with the IAEA to accept safeguards on all nuclear material and the obligation of all parties not to export unsafeguarded material or equipment to non–nuclear weapon states. There was optimism that clandestine construction of reactors and reprocessing facilities could be detected in time, and that major uranium enrichment facilities were beyond the technical and economic grasp of most states.

Although the NPT contains no restrictions on enrichment or reprocessing, nuclear supply in this area has been strongly restrained. India's 1974 nuclear test, using plutonium produced in a peaceful research reactor, CIRUS, prompted creation of the Nuclear Suppliers Group (NSG). Another impetus for creation of that group was concern about proposed trade in nuclear fuel cycle facilities. In the mid-1970s, the United States was influential in persuading Western suppliers like France and Germany to halt planned sales of fuel cycle facilities to Pakistan, South Korea, Brazil, and others. The NSG adopted the following policy in paragraph 6 of the guidelines in 1978:

> Suppliers should exercise restraint in the transfer of sensitive facilities, technology and weapons-usable materials. If enrichment or reprocessing facilities, equipment or technology are to be transferred, suppliers should encourage recipients to accept, as an alternative to national plants, supplier involvement and/or other appropriate multinational participation in resulting facilities. Suppliers should also promote international (including IAEA) activities concerned with multinational regional fuel cycle centres.

The situation today is in some respects unchanged, and in other respects vastly different. Non–nuclear weapon states continue to insist that their right, as described in Article IV of the NPT, to the peaceful uses of nuclear energy includes sensitive nuclear technology.[5] Today, however, this insistence may require more attention if an expansion in nuclear energy leads to more states with sensitive fuel cycle capabilities, despite the sober acknowledgment of the damage wrought by the Khan network and Iran's development of uranium enrichment.

Structural Challenges: Adaptation of a Civilian Program,
Illicit Procurement, or Both

Because of the inherently dual-use nature of nuclear technology, there is the potential for a country to adapt a civilian nuclear power program for weapons purposes. Nuclear proliferation experts are concerned about three basic scenarios: (1) the diversion of nuclear material for weapons purposes from declared facilities (either undeclared production or diversion of safeguarded material); (2) the clandestine production of nuclear material at undeclared facilities; and (3) the acquisition of capabilities by a state under the NPT, which are then used for weapons purposes after withdrawing from the treaty.

Many observers are optimistic that diversion of safeguarded material and undeclared production at declared facilities can be detected in time by IAEA inspectors, but they are less optimistic about detecting clandestine production facilities, particularly with respect to centrifuge enrichment plants. This issue has gained widespread public attention because of the activities of Iran, which many people suspect of using a peaceful nuclear power program as a cover to develop a covert weapons program within the NPT. Although some observers argue that no country with a nuclear weapons program has diverted material from a civilian program, the example of Iran's transfer of its "civilian" capabilities to the undeclared Qom enrichment plant suggests that such an outcome is possible.

The potential risk of misuse of a state-sponsored civilian nuclear program can also be more subtle. Development of a civilian nuclear program involves the establishment of a wide-ranging knowledge base and the training of a body of nuclear professionals. These capabilities may not constitute direct inputs into a nuclear weapons program, but they provide a more solid foundation on which such a program could be established. While past weapons programs have been characterized by an "intent drives capability" dynamic, future programs could see a situation in which technical and managerial capacity acts as a platform for the creation of a weapon. If a country is witnessing the deterioration of its security environment, another dynamic—"capability shapes intent"—could also come into play.

Lastly, concern remains that a state could legitimately develop sensitive capabilities under the NPT and then withdraw from the treaty without having to give up the infrastructure, technology, and expertise gained during the time it was a treaty member. To date, only North Korea has withdrawn from the NPT, and its capabilities were largely acquired before it joined the treaty. The fact remains, however, that in the future some states could avail themselves of the same opportunity. As currently configured, international law allows for withdrawal from the treaty, and no practical way exists to prevent the technology from being applied to a weapons program.

A second major structural challenge is the existence of illicit procurement networks outside of treaty and control regimes. Export controls in the nuclear sector are governed largely by:

—the Nuclear Exporters Committee (Zangger Committee), established by supplier states party to the NPT in order to implement NPT provisions requiring signatories not to export nuclear materials, equipment, and certain nonnuclear materials to non–nuclear weapon states unless subject to safeguards, and

—the Nuclear Suppliers Group, established in the wake of India's 1974 nuclear test, which used facilities and materials provided for exclusively peaceful purposes, to create a common set of guidelines regarding export of nuclear materials, equipment, and technology.

Over time, these export controls have evolved to keep pace with technological innovations and political developments including risks presented by enrichment and reprocessing activities. However, these, too, face challenges: a lack of universal adherence by all suppliers, leaving gaps in the system; keeping export controls current with novel technology changes and developments; and the appearance of being a cartel aimed at controlling international markets and depriving developing states equal opportunities.

The illicit supply network developed by Pakistan's Abdul Qadeer Khan and used first for Pakistan's nuclear weapons program and then expanded to supply North Korea, Libya, and Iran, represents one of the most flagrant and damaging breaches of the nonproliferation regime to date. Such networks—operating either with or without the complicity of a state's leadership—present a serious proliferation risk in the form of "one-stop shopping" through which rogue states or non-state actors can obtain the technology, expertise, or both necessary to produce a nuclear weapon. Strengthened export controls worldwide can hamper the activities of such networks.

Operational Challenges: Security of Operations and of Fissile Material

Linked to the formation of illicit networks is the risk of proliferation through lack of adequate security procedures, regulation, or both in respect of the handling of sensitive dual-use technology by companies in the commercial nuclear industry. Particular concern has been expressed about smaller companies in the supply chain for sensitive technology, such as suppliers of components for gas centrifuges used to enrich uranium. Regulation and enforcement of export controls in supplier countries are critical. New risks could emerge if a "plutonium economy" is pursued in the future, with closed fuel cycles and fast breeder reactors.

At the heart of all this is the critical hurdle in any nuclear weapons program: acquiring sufficient fissile material. Successful diversion or interception of unsecured fissile material, especially by non-state actors (whether terrorists or illicit networks), presents a grave threat to international security. Aside from the potential dissemination of sensitive technologies, the physical security and accounting of fissile materials are critical to nonproliferation efforts. The expansion of the global civilian nuclear energy industry, a potential increase in the use of the plutonium fuels (for example, mixed plutonium-uranium oxide, or MOX), and the possible adoption of multinational approaches to fuel provision could increase the transportation and transshipment of fissile materials. The construction of new reactors in countries not hitherto in possession of a nuclear energy program provides an additional challenge with regard to security standards and procedures, especially in the storage and handling of spent fuel.

Institutional Challenges: Funding, Responsibilities, and Enforcement

Three institutions—the IAEA, the NSG, and the United Nations Security Council (UNSC)—are vital to the effectiveness and viability of the nuclear nonproliferation regime anchored on the NPT.

The IAEA is responsible for implementing international safeguards. Such safeguards are a central pillar of the nonproliferation regime, a sine qua non for cooperative development of civilian nuclear energy, and essential for practicable international nuclear commerce. To date the IAEA has faced financial, technical, and political challenges.

Financially, the agency has tended to operate on a chronically underfunded safeguards budget while the scope of its responsibilities continues to grow, potentially compromising its ability to detect diversion of nuclear material, undeclared nuclear activities, or both. Technically, it has a continuous need to develop and implement new analytical technologies and staff with specialized skills capable of addressing novel developments in nuclear science and engineering. Politically, it needs to strengthen its safeguards authority to enable it to pursue leads, examine suspect sites, make special inspections more routine, and develop guidelines for board of governors referrals of noncompliance findings to the UN Security Council.

There are still eighteen countries party to the NPT that have yet to conclude a comprehensive safeguards agreement (largely because they have no nuclear activity to report or control). Fifty-six states have not agreed to the Additional Protocol, which provides for more information and more access to the IAEA, thus adding significantly to its verification authorities. Another thirty-seven states have signed but not implemented the Additional Protocol.[6]

Finally, the Small Quantities Protocol (SQP), which effectively holds in abeyance most of the operative provisions of standard safeguards agreements, is in force in more than ninety states. This protocol was designed for states that had such extremely limited nuclear operations that they did not hold a significant quantity of nuclear material to be subject to safeguards. In 2005 the IAEA Board of Governors took steps to modify the SQP, requiring initial reports on all nuclear material and early design information for planned nuclear facilities and reinstating the IAEA's right to conduct inspections in SQP states. It is likely that many of these SQPs will be suspended for states that actually move forward with nuclear energy plans and have significant quantities of nuclear material on their territory.

Enforcement of compliance is often hampered when it conflicts with other foreign policy and security interests. The unwillingness to impose consequences for noncompliance is in part motivated by the lack of a principled approach to enforcement, with certain key stakeholders placing geopolitical concerns above the interests of the nonproliferation regime. Examples of such political expediency include the failure to coordinate an international response to the withdrawal of North Korea from the NPT and to maintain international cohesion in applying pressure on Iran for its violation of its NPT obligations. The UN Security Council is often the "actor of last resort," and its failures reflect differences in the wider international community. Without strong action by the UN Security Council setting up a range of consequences in advance of violations, it is doubtful that anything less than a blatant violation could evoke a strong, prompt response. Lack of political will is also manifested in the chronic problem of insufficient funding, which hampers the IAEA's ability to fulfill its missions.

Experience of the Past Few Decades

The current nonproliferation regime has enabled the development of peaceful nuclear energy for the past four decades. The NPT forms the basis of the nonproliferation regime, but the entire effort is layered with multilateral and bilateral agreements, initiatives, organizations, unilateral political and economic actions, and recourse to military operations should they become necessary. Cooperation and coercion are used to restrict both the supply of and demand for nuclear weapons and their components and technologies. Over the years, greater attention has been paid to harmonizing national laws, regulations, and policies to reflect established norms of nonproliferation.

The twin proliferation shocks of Iraq and North Korea in the 1990s prompted new approaches in inspecting and monitoring nuclear activities in states. In 1991 Iraq was discovered to have been pursuing a mini–Manhattan Project to develop nuclear weapons, relying on dual-use imports from many nations and hiding its activities from the IAEA at both declared and undeclared sites. Coupled with difficulties verifying North Korea's nuclear program as it joined the NPT, member states of the IAEA decided to develop new monitoring techniques, which eventually became the Additional Protocol to safeguards agreements. The Additional Protocol expands the monitoring capabilities of the IAEA, including new information requirements, enhanced access, and new techniques of inspection. Today the voluntary protocol is implemented in many member states of the NPT, but not all.

More recent shocks have included discovery of Iran's clandestine nuclear program in 2003, discovery of the A. Q. Khan nuclear black market network, North Korean nuclear tests, and revelations about Syrian–North Korean cooperation to build a clandestine plutonium production reactor.

The regime has responded to the threats described above by strengthening export controls, limiting technology transfers, promoting a nuclear test ban treaty, urging the negotiation of a fissile material production cutoff treaty, and strengthening IAEA safeguards. Sanctions for violations have also been part of the mix. There has also been an increased effort to harmonize national laws, regulations, and policies. Improvements in the past two decades are summarized in table 2-1.

Current Debate on These Challenges

In particular, the sale of sensitive nuclear technology and nuclear weapon designs by Pakistani A. Q. Khan to states such as North Korea, Libya, and Iran prompted specific proposals to enhance the nonproliferation regime, including those related to the nuclear fuel cycle. In 2004 then director general of the IAEA Mohamed ElBaradei proposed seven steps to strengthen the nonproliferation regime:

1. A five-year moratorium on building enrichment and reprocessing plants;

2. Conversion of nuclear reactors using highly enriched uranium (HEU) to low-enriched uranium;

3. Making the Additional Protocol the verification norm of the NPT;

4. Revisiting UN Security Council actions in response to a state's withdrawal from the NPT;

5. Universal implementation of UN Security Council Resolution 1540;

6. Acceleration of Article VI actions by nuclear weapons states (toward nuclear disarmament); and

7. Resolution of regional security tensions that give rise to proliferation, including a Middle East nuclear weapon–free zone.

The five-year moratorium on construction of uranium enrichment and spent fuel reprocessing facilities was not taken up (particularly by the nuclear weapon states), but the Group of Eight (G-8) agreed to ban sales of uranium enrichment and spent fuel reprocessing equipment to additional states from 2004 to 2008.[7] The Nuclear Suppliers Group spent seven years discussing, since 2004, ways to

Table 2-1. *Efforts to Improve the Nuclear Nonproliferation Regime, 1990 to Present*

Date	Program	Target	Elements
1991–present	Cooperative Threat Reduction	Weapons of mass destruction (WMD) activities in the former Soviet Union and beyond	Arms control implementation, physical protection, and material accounting and control of nuclear material; other WMD activities; reorientation of weapons scientists, as well as Science Centers.
2002–present	G-8 Global Partnership	WMD activities in the former Soviet Union and beyond	$10 billion over 10 years toward nonproliferation, disarmament, counterterrorism, nuclear safety, submarine dismantlement, chemical weapons destruction.
1993–present	Strengthened safeguards	Better detection capabilities for undeclared nuclear activities	Additional Protocol (INFCIRC/540), includes enhanced access, information, techniques, and authorities for IAEA.
2005		Closing loophole for monitoring states that have only small quantities of fissile material	Modified small quantities protocol
2002	Nuclear Suppliers Group	Gaps in controlling nuclear supply	Require full-scope safeguards for all significant nuclear supply; revise control lists regularly.
2005+	Physical protection of nuclear material		Amend the Convention on the Physical Protection of Nuclear Material to include domestic controls; serial revisions of INFCIRC/225; creation of World Institute for Nuclear Security.
2004	Legal reforms	Access of non-state actors to WMD-related materials	UNSCR 1540 obliges all UN members to establish and enforce effective measures to prevent non-state actors, terrorist groups, and illicit traffickers from gaining access to WMD-related technologies, equipment, and materials.
2003	Multilateral initiatives	Improve interdiction of WMD-related items	Proliferation Security Initiative improves voluntary cooperation on interdiction.
2006		Shore up antiterrorist controls	Global Initiative to Combat Nuclear Terrorism.
2010		Enhance nuclear security	Nuclear Security Summit.
2010	Arms control	U.S.-Russian strategic nuclear weapons reduction	New START treaty ratified by U.S. Senate
		Halting nuclear tests	Comprehensive Test Ban Treaty signed in 1998—U.S. commitment to ratify soon.

strengthen its restraint on such transfers, culminating in a 2011 decision that accomplished little beyond requiring the Additional Protocol for such transfers.

The United States has accelerated its decades-long program to convert domestic and foreign research reactors from using HEU to LEU, and hosted the 2010 Nuclear Security Summit to promote this objective, among others. The United States is also pursuing NSG adoption of the Additional Protocol as a condition of nuclear supply, but reportedly this awaits resolution of further restrictions on enrichment and reprocessing. During those discussions, Argentina and Brazil, which are the only NSG members not to sign the Additional Protocol, objected to a straightforward inclusion of that criterion in the new restrictions, citing a conflict with their bilateral inspection protocols under the Brazilian-Argentine Agency for Accounting and Control of Nuclear Material (ABACC). With respect to the potential withdrawal of a country from the NPT, efforts are focused on ensuring that safeguards on all nuclear material continue after withdrawal.

In particular, efforts to accelerate nuclear disarmament and discussions on a weapons-of-mass-destruction-free zone in the Middle East were prominent on the agenda of the May 2010 NPT Review Conference. Inevitably, the political debate always returns to the balance of three pillars of the NPT—nuclear disarmament, nuclear nonproliferation, and the peaceful uses of nuclear energy. The 2010 Review Conference was able to produce a final document with sixty-four action items. Unfortunately, the desire to produce a consensus document in 2010 after what most experts agree was an unsuccessful review conference in 2005 resulted in less progress on some of these issues than might have been hoped.

With respect to fuel cycle issues, the report and action items give a nod to the need for safeguards, safety, and security but also reiterate long-standing language that the parties should "respect each country's choices and decisions in the field of peaceful uses of nuclear energy without jeopardizing its policies or international cooperation agreements and arrangements for peaceful uses of nuclear energy and its fuel-cycle policies."[8] Even the brief reference to multinational approaches to the fuel cycle contains a caveat about not affecting states' rights.

This relatively new focus on "nuclear sovereignty" stems from several sources. One source is economic, although many—if not most—analysts dismiss such economic justifications, arguing that for many countries now interested in civilian nuclear power it would be more expensive to develop their own capabilities than to purchase what they need from existing nuclear suppliers. Another argument a country might make is that developing its own enrichment and reprocessing capabilities is part of a broader national policy of investing in advanced technology to promote development. Still another argument, albeit usually unstated, is national prestige. This argument, too, is rejected by some industry leaders such as Anne Lauvergeon, the chief executive officer of AREVA, who has argued, "Potential AREVA customers are not interested in enrichment and reprocessing. . . . Why? Because the era of prestige is over."[9]

A final argument in favor of a nation establishing a complete fuel cycle on its own soil is security of supply. The argument goes that depending on external sources of supply for the nuclear material needed to power its nuclear reactors creates a vulnerability to supply or price disruptions motivated by political or other reasons. No country can accept such vulnerability; therefore it must have its own entire fuel cycle in order to guarantee supply.

Those interested in limiting the spread of enrichment and reprocessing capabilities point out that no country has yet encountered major problems in supply specifically because of commercial disruption,[10] and they suggest that alternative arrangements can be established that guarantee the availability of nuclear fuel supplies for those countries that forgo enrichment and reprocessing. A variety of proposals for such arrangements have been offered, most of which entail multinational or multilateral control of the stocks of enriched uranium or plutonium to be used.[11] In essence, these proposals are intended to provide an incentive to states interested in nuclear energy not to pursue indigenous enrichment and reprocessing capabilities.

Some countries will continue to oppose restrictions because they want ultimately to become players in the commercial market. A few, like Argentina, Australia, Brazil, Canada, Kazakhstan, South Africa, and Ukraine, have indicated that they may be interested in establishing enrichment plants in the future and have no desire to relinquish, or even dilute, their right to do so.[12] A few others may be more ambiguous about their reasons.

The expansion of fuel cycle capabilities—both enrichment and reprocessing, discussed below—is still a theoretical concern because no country beyond the current technology holders has begun work on such a plant (barring Iran) and because the Nuclear Suppliers Group has not yet changed its long-standing policy of restraint on such technology transfers. Efforts by the United States to get individual countries to forswear domestic development of uranium enrichment and spent fuel reprocessing, with the exception of the United Arab Emirates, have not yet yielded the desired results.

On the back end of the fuel cycle, the arguments are slightly different. Energy security concerns tend to focus on the long-term availability of uranium, and the fact that recycling can free a country from uranium sources. The prospect of spent fuel accumulating as nuclear energy expands has also led countries to consider recycling as part of a spent fuel waste management program, if only to put off the difficult political decisions accompanying final disposal of nuclear waste.

Leaving aside the difficulty of calculating the "energy security" benefits of recycling, the current economics of recycling remain controversial because of sharply divergent assessments of the following issues:

—the adequacy of uranium reserves to fuel upper range projections for the expansion of commercial nuclear reactors with forty- to sixty-year operational lives through utilization of a once-through fuel cycle with no recycling;

—the need for geologic repositories for waste and the costs associated with allowing for the future retrieval of spent fuel;

—the degree to which recycling can be made more proliferation-resistant; and

—the role that recycling plays in the long-term management of spent fuel.

A recent Massachusetts Institute of Technology report, *The Future of the Nuclear Fuel Cycle,* concluded that "there is no shortage of uranium resources that might constrain future commitments to build new nuclear plants for much of this century at least" and that "the benefits to resource extension and to waste management of limited recycling in LWRs using mixed oxide fuel as is being done in some countries are minimal."[13] Nonetheless, advocates for recycling consistently point to its ability to recover over 95 percent of the uranium used in the generation of a conventional nuclear reaction.

The potential nuclear renaissance raises the prospect that many more countries (from thirty to fifty or more) could require their own geologic waste repositories, whether or not they decide to dispose of spent nuclear fuel directly, recycle it themselves, or have another country recycle it. Encouraging individual repositories is not cost-effective and in the short to medium term, many countries store spent fuel above ground and on site. However, in the long term, more individual repositories may be inevitable without bilateral or multilateral agreements covering nuclear fuel repositories or take-back agreements for spent fuel from those nations originally providing the nuclear fuel that do not require return of high level waste if the spent fuel is reprocessed. These approaches could raise other risks inherent in increased transportation of spent fuel, whether to be reprocessed, stored indefinitely, or put into deep geological storage. The potential for new back-end approaches compelled by a doubling of the numbers of countries with nuclear power reactors, and new entrants into front-end services will have a direct bearing on the industry and on the management of global non-proliferation policies and concerns with some in the industry actively engaged in this new nuclear commerce.

There has been much recent debate on the proliferation resistance of new recycling technologies. Recycling spent fuel using the current PUREX process raises proliferation concerns because it separates plutonium-239 from the proliferation barrier of fission products. All countries that have commercially reprocessed spent fuel use the PUREX process and have stockpiles of this separated plutonium, which could be used for nuclear explosives. The existing plants—in France, the United Kingdom, Russia and Japan—are large, complex industrial undertakings and have been expensive to build. Japan's Rokkasho reprocessing plant has been under construction for twenty years at a cost of $20 billion; an estimated additional $13 billion will be required to decommission it at the end of its life.[14]

Other recycling processes, such as COEX and UREX, are still under development.[15] The UREX process, developed in the United States, only separates out depleted uranium, which can then be recycled, leaving the plutonium mixed with the fission products and other actinides in a more "proliferation-resistant" form.[16] In the case of COEX (co-extraction of actinides), which was developed in France, small amounts of depleted uranium are comingled with the plutonium so that the plutonium is never available in a pure stream that might be subject to diversion.[17]

While recycling and vitrification can reduce the volume of high-level waste that is placed in a repository, they produce other waste streams that must be managed, and they do not eliminate the need for a repository, whose costs are not proportional to the volume of waste. One potential savings would be the avoidance of IAEA safeguards on spent fuel for long periods of time. Vitrified waste does not require safeguards because it does not pose a proliferation threat.[18] Although the reuse of plutonium recovered during recycling in light-water reactors has not been proven to be very cost-effective, the development of fast reactors would allow for plutonium recycle and burn-up of actinides in spent fuel. It could also entail significant proliferation risks, depending on how it is managed.[19]

The spread of dual-use enrichment and spent fuel reprocessing facilities, the growth in the amounts of fissile material and spent fuel requiring protection and storage, and the larger volumes of sensitive nuclear materials in international commerce place new burdens on an international regime struggling to cope with long-standing institutional and structural constraints. International nuclear industry leaders can help reduce this burden by supporting nuclear security, nonproliferation, and nuclear safety initiatives in partnership with governments and international organizations. Such collaboration is essential in creating a sustainable nuclear future.

Notes

1. Jeffrey Goldberg, "The Point of No Return," *Atlantic Monthly,* September 2010 (www.theatlantic.com/magazine/archive/2010/09/the-point-of-no-return/8186/).

2. On Toronto, see "Attacking Parliament, Devastating Canada at Heart of Toronto 18 Plot, Jury Hears," *CP24.com,* April 12, 2010 (www.cp24.com/servlet/an/local/CTVNews/20100412/100412_toronto_18_trial/20100412/?hub=CP24Home). On Pakistan, see "Detained Americans Had Nuclear Power Site Map, Say Pakistan Police," *The Guardian,* December 27, 2009. On al Qaeda, see the 9/11 Commission Report, chap. 5 (www.9-11commission.gov/report/911Report_Ch5.htm).

3. Steven E. Miller and Scott D. Sagan, "Alternative Nuclear Futures," *Daedalus* 2 (Winter 2010): 127–28.

4. On the other hand, in the mid-1970s, despite Iran being a close ally of the United States, U.S. officials were skeptical of Iran's nuclear intentions—particularly its interest in reprocessing—and sought multinational reprocessing agreements with France and West Germany to prevent proliferation of reprocessing capabilities.

5. Article IV of the NPT states, "Nothing in this Treaty shall be interpreted as affecting the inalienable right of all the Parties to the Treaty to develop research, production, and use of nuclear energy for peaceful purposes without discrimination and in conformity with Articles I and II of this Treaty."

6. For the latest status of safeguards agreements, see www.iaea.org/OurWork/SV/Safeguards/index.html.

7. Both France and the United States signed nuclear cooperation agreements with India in 2008 that included a provision for enrichment and reprocessing cooperation (with caveats in the U.S. case). However, the G-8 ban unraveled in 2008 because of Canadian objections.

8. "Review of the Operation of the Treaty, as Provided for in Its Article VIII (3), . . . Conclusions and Recommendations for Follow-on Actions," final draft for the 2010 Review Conference of the Parties to the Treaty on the Non-Proliferation of Nuclear Weapons, NPT/CONF.2010/L.2 (New York, May 27, 2010).

9. Anne Lauvergeon, "Nuclear Industry's Role in Nonproliferation," paper presented to the Carnegie International Nonproliferation Conference, April 6, 2009.

10. Erwann O. Michel-Kerjan and Debra K. Decker, "Insure to Assure: A New Paradigm for Nuclear Nonproliferation and International Security," *Innovations* 4 (Spring 2009): 144.

11. See, for example, Yury Yudin, *Multilateralization of the Nuclear Fuel Cycle: Assessing the Existing Proposals* (Geneva: UN Institute for Disarmament Research, 2009).

12. Tariq Rauf and Soryana Vovchok, "Assurance of Supply: A New Framework for Nuclear Energy," *Innovations* 4 (Spring 2009): 195.

13. Massachusetts Institute of Technology, "The Future of the Nuclear Fuel Cycle," Summary Report (Cambridge, Mass.: September 2010), p. x.

14. Frank von Hippel, "The Costs and Benefits of Reprocessing," paper prepared for the Nonproliferation Policy Education Center, January 2009, p. 9.

15. Other recycling technologies are also under development, including DIAMEX-SANEX, GANEX, and pyroprocessing. See chapter 3 for more discussion.

16. Charles McCombie and Thomas Isaacs, "The Key Role of the Back-End in the Nuclear Fuel Cycle," *Daedalus* 139 (Winter 2010): 35.

17. Ibid., p. 33.

18. Ibid. Vitrified waste is the vitrified blocks that are produced when waste that contains fission products is treated. These vitrified blocks incorporate most of the highly radioactive materials and other low- and intermediate-level radioactive technological wastes. Vitrified waste is a high-quality standardized product well suited for geological disposal. This definition is adapted from McCombie and Isaacs, "The Key Role of the Back-End of the Nuclear Fuel Cycle," p. 33.

19. For more information on fast reactors, see chapter 3.

3

Commercial Nuclear Markets
and Nonproliferation

JOHN P. BANKS AND SHARON SQUASSONI

A dramatic increase in demand for nuclear power could have a large impact on the commercial nuclear industry. Existing companies might see expanded commercial opportunities, while new private sector entrants might be dissuaded by high capital costs, required degree of specialization, and regulatory hurdles. At the same time, governments have shown significant interest in helping promote their national firms' export capabilities, facilitating entrance into new markets. To provide the context necessary to understand the results of the Brookings survey discussed in later chapters, the following discussion provides an overview of the technical activities and commercial operations of the nuclear fuel cycle, as well as important market trends and their implications for nonproliferation.[1]

Fuel Cycle Overview

The nuclear fuel cycle is commonly divided into two broad stages: the front end, in which uranium is prepared for use in reactors; and the back end, which encompasses how spent nuclear fuel is handled after it is removed from the reactor (see figure 3-1).[2] The activities of each stage can be summarized as follows.[3]

Front End
—*Uranium exploration, mining, and milling.* Uranium ore is mined and processed to produce uranium ore concentrate (U_3O_8, or yellowcake).

Figure 3-1. *The Nuclear Fuel Cycle*

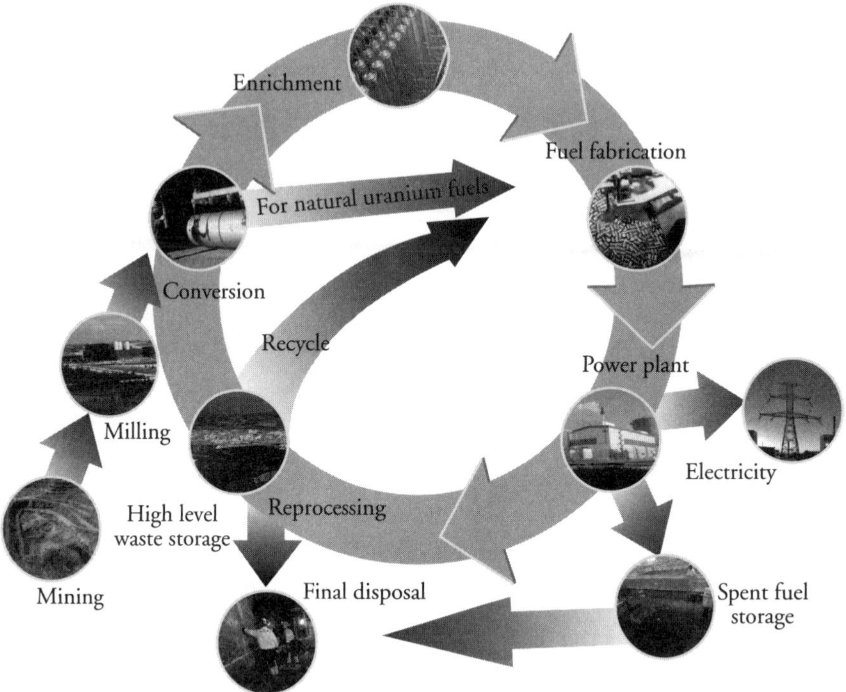

Source: Reprinted with the permission of the International Atomic Energy Agency.

—*Conversion.* The concentrate is converted to uranium hexafluoride gas (UF_6).

—*Enrichment.* The UF_6 is enriched up to 5 percent U235 in the enriched uranium product (EUP).

—*Fuel fabrication.* The EUP is made into pellets that are encased in tubes to form a fuel assembly for use in a reactor.

Back End

—*Spent fuel interim storage.* Spent fuel is temporarily stored in cooling pools and dry storage casks at and away from the reactor.

—*Reprocessing and recycling.* Spent fuel is treated to extract usable fertile and fissile materials for further use as fuel in a reactor.

—*High-level waste disposal.* Spent fuel or high-level wastes are placed in a permanent geologic repository.

The nuclear fuel cycle can operate in two fashions: as an "open" or "once-through" cycle, and as a "closed" cycle. In the open cycle, nuclear fuel is used once in a reactor, and the resulting irradiated spent fuel is disposed of directly in a long-term geologic repository. The majority of countries with existing civilian nuclear power programs have opted for this approach, although none has yet opened a geologic repository for spent nuclear fuel. A few countries have chosen to "close" the nuclear fuel cycle, reprocessing the spent fuel and recycling it as reactor fuel. At present, such countries have succeeded in reusing the fuel once more in light-water reactors, and research and development into multiple recycles of fuel in fast reactors is under way.

Reactors and the Nuclear Fuel Cycle

The type of reactor in large part determines the details of the nuclear fuel cycle. Light-water moderated reactors (LWRs)—which account for about 90 percent of all reactors in operation worldwide—require enriched uranium. The common version of the LWR uses uranium that is enriched in the isotope U235 to 5 percent weight or less. Part of the remaining 95 percent weight, the U238, is converted into plutonium (Pu239) in the reactor. Part but not all of this Pu239 is also consumed in the reactor. The result is a reactor that uses a fresh fuel that is unattractive for use in weapons and, after a year or more of operation, yields spent fuel that contains recoverable Pu239, but that is radioactive and mixed with other isotopes, making it unattractive for weapons production.

At the other end of the spectrum are heavy-water moderated reactors. They do not require enriched uranium fuel, and the continuous, online refueling reduces the time the fuel spends in the reactor. Heavy-water reactors have been used to produce plutonium for weapons, but newer models use low-enriched uranium, which makes the plutonium in the spent fuel less suitable for weapons.

Although some smaller reactors, such as those used on ships and submarines, use highly enriched uranium, the trend is to move away from such fuels. These reactors can operate for long periods of time without refueling but pose a proliferation risk because their fresh fuel would be attractive to divert for weapons. Floating reactors that Russia recently proposed to sell, for example, would use fuel 20 percent enriched in U235, but the concern is that they could also use higher levels of enriched uranium.[4] In addition, some fast reactors would be fueled with either highly enriched uranium or plutonium.[5]

Generally, the irradiated fuel that comes out of the power reactor must cool for five years in fuel storage pools before it can be transferred to dry storage casks. After a sufficient cooling period, it can be packaged for direct disposal underground. Currently, no spent fuel from the commercial nuclear power industry is placed in geological repositories for permanent disposal, although work on such repositories is progressing in several countries.

Closing the Nuclear Fuel Cycle

Several countries have opted to reprocess their spent nuclear fuel. France and the United Kingdom offer reprocessing services to other countries, while Russia and Japan will take back spent fuel that may be reprocessed. China is also exploring recycling, as well as fast reactors.

In fully closing the nuclear fuel cycle, both the uranium and plutonium in the spent fuel could be recycled, not just in thermal reactors but also in fast reactors. Fast reactors, which require no moderation of the neutron flux, can use a wider range of fuel types, including those embedded with fission products.[6] Thus they reduce the requirement for "fresh" uranium. A type of fast reactor called a burner reactor can fission a larger range of the minor actinides and transuranics, helping to eliminate the most harmful fission products.[7] Fast reactors can be configured to "breed" plutonium—producing more fuel than they consume—thereby offering the possibility of an endless fuel supply.

At present, only a limited amount of fuel from commercial power reactors has been reprocessed to recover the unused uranium and plutonium. Such material is fabricated into mixed oxide (MOX) fuel and burned in light-water reactors.[8] Inventories of separated plutonium are vastly larger than the amount used in fuel and now amount to about 250 tons worldwide.[9] Compared with the open fuel cycle, spent fuel reprocessing has been shown to be largely uneconomic.[10]

Market Overview

The high degree of requisite technical specialization, enormous capital costs, security, proliferation and environmental concerns, along with considerable government involvement and regulation, have helped to keep the nuclear fuel cycle industry relatively small (for industry leaders, see table 3-1). Several companies are active in multiple activities of the fuel cycle, principally AREVA, Rosatom, China National Nuclear Corporation (CNNC), General Electric, and Hitachi. Several existing companies (especially government-owned entities) are attempting to expand their global commercial fuel cycle activities.

U.S. companies are no longer leading participants in the international nuclear fuel cycle. In the past few decades, the development of U.S. nuclear reactors has stagnated, while nuclear energy has expanded elsewhere, particularly in China, France, Russia, Japan, and Korea. Because its production costs are high, the United States mines only limited amounts of uranium. ConverDyn, the country's major uranium conversion company, serves mainly U.S. nuclear power plants, though it also is engaged in international nuclear commerce. The gaseous diffusion process for enrichment originally developed in the United States is becoming obsolete, while the gas centrifuge process developed in Europe and Russia

Table 3-1. *Major Nuclear Fuel Cycle Companies*

Company	Ownership[a]	Mining	Conversion	Enrichment	Fabrication	Reactors	Reprocessing
AREVA	G, France	X	X	X	X	X	X
AECL	G, Canada					X	
Babcock & Wilcox	P					X	
BHP Billiton	P	X					
Cameco	P	X	X	X[b]			
Converdyn	P		X				
CNCC	G, China		X	X	X	X	
ENUSA	G, Spain				X		
GE[c]	P			X[b]	X	X	
General Atomic	P	X					
Global Nuclear Fuel	P				X		
Hitachi	P			X[b]	X[d]	X	
IPEN	G, Brazil		X				
INB	G, Brazil				X		
JNFL	P[e]			X			X
Kazatomprom	G, Kazakhstan	X		X	X[f]		
KEPCO-KHNP[g]	G, Korea					X	
KNF	G, South Korea				X		
Mitsubishi	P				X	X	
Navoi	G, Uzbekistan	X					
NPCIL	G, India					X	
Nuclear Fuels Complex	G, India				X		
Nuclear Fuel Industries	P				X		
Paladin	P	X					
Rio Tinto	P	X					
Rosatom[h]	G, Russia	X	X	X	X	X	X
Sellafield	G, P						X
Toshiba-Westinghouse	P				X	X	
Uranium One	G, Russia	X					
URENCO	G, P[i]			X			
USEC	P			X			

Sources: See Tables 3-2 to 3-7. Also Kazatomprom (www.kazatomprom.kz/en/); Atomic Energy of Canada Limited (www.aecl.ca/); "Nuclear Power in India," *World Nuclear Association* (www.world-nuclear.org/info/inf53.html).

a. G = government-owned corporation, P = private. Additional notes and details are provided in separate tables for each fuel cycle stage. Some entities engage in activities not checked in this table given the limited global impact of that activity currently.

b. GE, Hitachi, and CAMECO announced a joint ownership venture in 2008 involving the Silex laser enrichment process.

c. Now in partnership with Hitachi.

d. Hitachi is an owner in Global Nuclear Fuel with GE and Toshiba.

e. JNFL is jointly owned by ten Japanese utility companies.

f. Joint venture announced with AREVA.

g. Korea Electric Power Corporation owns Korea Hydro and Nuclear Power; Doosan is equipment supplier.

h. In Russia, Atomenergoprom (Atomic Energy Power Corporation) is the integrated holding company that oversees numerous enterprises operating throughout the fuel cycle, such as ARMZ for uranium mining, TENEX for enrichment, and TVEL for fuel fabrication. It is 100 percent owned by Rosatom, the State Atomic Energy Corporation.

i. URENCO's ownership is split evenly between the governments of the United Kingdom and the Netherlands and publicly traded German utility companies RWE AG and E.ON AG.

is now predominant.[11] The fuel fabrication business in the United States is led by Westinghouse, a company owned by a consortium headed by Toshiba. The other major historic U.S. vendor, General Electric, has become GE Hitachi. The French company AREVA is also a major fuel fabricator in the United States, while other foreign companies are exploring similar opportunities there. Mitsubishi and AREVA are competing to sell nuclear power plants in the United States. Toshiba's Westinghouse subsidiary is the only company successfully selling U.S. reactor technology in the international market.

At the back end of the nuclear fuel cycle, the United States has not engaged in civilian spent fuel reprocessing for decades. Once the Ford and Carter administrations stopped government support of such activities, industry efforts languished. For many years, the Department of Energy pursued the construction of a geological repository at Yucca Mountain, but in 2009 the Obama administration halted the licensing procedures—for what many believe to be political reasons—after successive administrations had spent $15 billion on its development. This policy reversal has raised questions about how the United States will manage its nuclear waste in the future. In response, in March 2010 the Obama administration appointed the Blue Ribbon Commission on America's Nuclear Future to study new policy options for spent fuel. The U.S. government conducts research into both the open and closed fuel cycle, as well as the "modified open fuel cycle," which includes partial recycling of actinides.

Impact of U.S. Policy

Current U.S. law contains significant restrictions on how other countries may use or transfer U.S. nuclear technology, know-how, materials, and equipment. These restrictions are incorporated into bilateral nuclear cooperation agreements. Many restrictions—such as the requirement for full-scope safeguards—have been adopted by other countries, but others have not. The U.S. Atomic Energy Act seeks to ensure that peaceful nuclear cooperation does not inadvertently contribute to another country's ability to misuse or divert sensitive nuclear material. Therefore other countries may not transfer, alter in form or content, enrich, or reprocess nuclear material of U.S. origin without explicit permission. Requirements are especially stringent for sharing sensitive nuclear technology such as uranium enrichment and spent fuel reprocessing. As a rule, the United States does not engage in such transfers and has been attempting to persuade new nuclear cooperation partners to forswear acquiring uranium enrichment or spent fuel reprocessing capabilities. There is such a provision in an agreement with the United Arab Emirates, but it is unclear whether other countries—notably Saudi Arabia, Jordan, and Vietnam—will follow suit.

The United States has been a leader in crafting rules for nuclear commerce, chiefly within the Nuclear Suppliers Group, established in 1975. Despite decades of attempts to harmonize export controls, gaps remain. Different rules and terms for sharing nuclear technology can distort competitiveness in the nuclear energy market, of which the nuclear energy industry is keenly aware.

Fuel Cycle Stages and Suppliers

This discussion of market trends follows the fuel cycle from the front end to the back end. If a country is procuring a reactor for the first time, it must first choose a reactor design, which then dictates which suppliers and services may be involved. Typically, the contractual arrangements at each stage of the front end of the fuel cycle are undertaken by the reactor owner. For example, utilities usually purchase the uranium concentrates and arrange for conversion, enrichment, and fabrication under separate, long-term contracts for each service. Increasingly, however, fuel services may be bundled. In other words, a reactor supplier, such as Russia, will provide completed fuel assemblies, and the buyer will not have to mix and match services.[12] Some suppliers carry this approach even further, offering a "cradle-to-grave" fuel service, not only leasing the fuel but also taking it back at the end of its life. Such an arrangement has significant benefits for the nonproliferation regime, although there are only a few instances in which this has occurred (for example, in Russia's leasing of fuel to Iran's Bushehr reactor).

Uranium Mining

Uranium ore is mined in many countries and by a variety of techniques: open-pit mining for low-grade deposits, underground mining for higher-grade deposits, and in situ leaching (extracting uranium with chemicals), which is becoming more widespread.[13]

Five countries account for about 72 percent of known, "reasonably assured" uranium resources, and three (Australia, Canada, and Kazakhstan) account for 60 percent of total global uranium production (see figure 3-2). Ten companies accounted for 89 percent of all uranium mined in 2009 (see table 3-2).

Many firms in this market are active in other aspects of the fuel cycle. Major players include private and government-owned entities, and there are many partnerships, joint ventures, and other investment or ownership arrangements. For example, the Akdala mine in Kazakhstan is 70 percent owned by the Russian government's ARMZ through its subsidiary Uranium One, with the remaining 30 percent owned by Kazatomprom.[14]

Unlike other commodities and precious metals, uranium (U_3O_8) is not a publicly traded good. A spot price is determined by a group of private businesses that monitor transactions, offers, and bids. The price is then reported each week, and this provides a benchmark (although there are some daily price updates now).[15] Long-term, take-or-pay contracts of five to six years' duration

Figure 3-2. *Uranium Production, 2008*

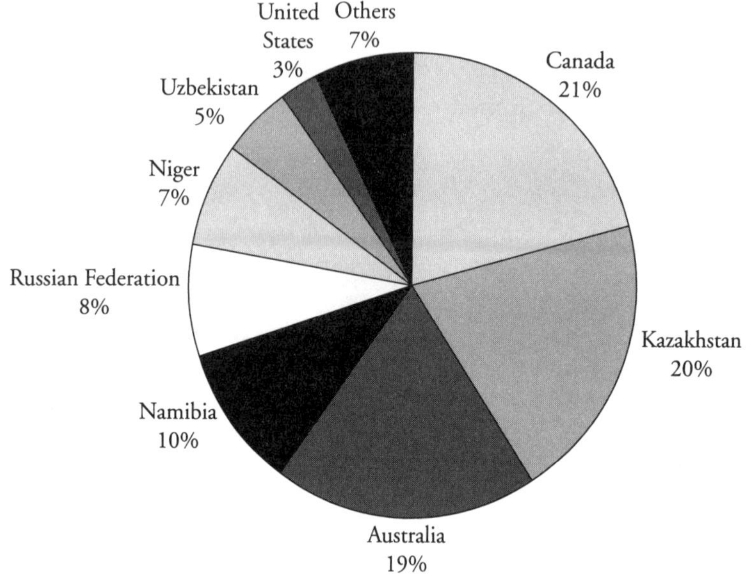

Source: OECD Nuclear Energy Agency and IAEA, "Uranium 2009: Resources, Production and Demand" (2010), p. 45.

make up over 90 percent of the uranium trade.[16] The contractual process is fairly straightforward: utilities sign a U_3O_8 contract for the mining and processing of uranium that requires the mining company to meet product specifications (as to its purity and isotopic composition) that are generally accepted throughout the industry. Miners are responsible for transporting the U_3O_8 to the conversion facility. To diversify supply sources, most utilities, as the end-users of uranium, enter into several long-term contracts with various companies from different regions.[17]

With the decline in nuclear reactor construction in the 1980s and 1990s, the demand for fuel decreased, the prices for uranium and its production decreased, and mining, exploration, and milling markets correspondingly shrank. Since 2004, demand and exploration have increased, suggesting an upturn in this market.[18] One possible reason is the increasing involvement of governments to secure uranium assets around the world. For instance, India, a country with limited domestic uranium resources to fuel its expanding reactor fleet, recently signed a memorandum of understanding with Mongolia for access to its potentially vast uranium deposits. In early 2010 France obtained an agreement granting AREVA a twenty-five-year concession for mining 1,469 square kilometers of land in the central part of Jordan.[19]

Table 3-2. *Uranium Mining Activities by Company, 2009*

Company	Ownership	Country of operation	Production (tU)	Percent of global market
AREVA	Government: France	Australia, Canada, Namibia, Niger, South Africa	8,623	17
BHP Billiton	Private	Australia	2,955	6
Cameco	Private	Canada, United States, Kazakhstan	8,000	16
General Atomic	Private	Australia, United States	583	1
Kazatomprom	Government: Kazakhstan	Kazakhstan, Russia	7,467	15
Navoi	Government: Uzbekistan	Uzbekistan	2,429	5
Paladin	Private	Australia, Malawi, Namibia	1,210	2
Rio Tinto	Private	Australia, Namibia	7,963	16
Rosatom (ARMZ)	Government: Russia	Kazakhstan, Russia	4,624	9
Uranium One	Majority owned: ARMZ	Australia, Kazakhstan	1,368	3
Other		10	5,550	11
Total			50,772	100[a]

Sources: http://www.kazatomprom.kz/en/Kazatomprom; Paladin Resources (www.paladinresources.com.au/); General Atomic (www.ga.com/index.php); "World Uranium Mining," *World Nuclear Association,* May 2010 (www.world-nuclear.org/info/inf23.html).

a. Figures here and in the remaining tables of this chapter may not total owing to rounding.

Governments also play an important role in the uranium-mining sector through regulations on access to resources and the supply of U_3O_8. In recent years, some countries have relaxed trade regulations, potentially enhancing access to supplies to meet demand. Australia, for instance, changed its policy in 2007 to allow increased mining and exploration, Canada revised foreign ownership rules in 2010, and the United States permitted larger imports of Russian military fuel to begin in 2008. At the same time, some countries continue to regulate the use of any exported uranium. Australia, for one, requires all uranium mined in the country to be used only for "peaceful nonexplosive" purposes and allows it to be exported only to countries that, at a minimum, are "party to the NPT and have concluded a full-scope safeguards Agreement with the IAEA [International Atomic Energy Agency]."[20]

TRENDS

A critical question is how a significant surge in demand for uranium will be met— with primary sources (newly mined uranium) or secondary sources (from downblended uranium, weapons, or recycled uranium)?[21] Developing new mines takes years, which may affect the ability to meet demand. On the other hand, the uncertainty of Russian highly enriched uranium (HEU) will affect secondary markets.

Around 2003 renewed interest in nuclear power began pushing the price of U_3O_8 up, taking it to a high of $138 a pound in 2007 from a level less than a tenth of that at the beginning of the decade.[22] From 2010, however, prices have retreated to about $60 a pound of U_3O_8 in response to the global economic recession. Other factors include overselling in the uranium spot market and a surplus of nuclear fuel on the market.

Despite the recent decline in uranium prices, most analysts expect future reactor construction to again drive up the demand for uranium. According to Nuclear Energy Agency (NEA) projections, the demand for uranium should increase 20 to 25 percent by 2015,[23] with additional supply likely to come from several sources. As of 2009, the NEA's "Red Book" of known uranium resources estimates that 5.4 million tons are recoverable at $130 a pound of U_3O_8.[24] With the growth of global interest in uranium production, uranium assets are attracting more attention, particularly in Africa, Asia, Australia, and the United States. In January 2009 the NEA stated that global uranium exploration activity was already triple that of 2004–06 and "identified and undiscovered resources [appeared] sufficient for 100 years of current consumption [with] mine production capability projected to be adequate to meet even high case uranium requirements through 2030 and beyond ."[25] Some substantial resources are not economically recoverable at current prices but may become so as demand increases. Nevertheless, the production of uranium would still have to double to meet this growing demand.[26]

Advances in technology may be a great help in this respect. Expanded use of in situ leaching, given its operational flexibility and lower capital costs, may make the uranium mining market more responsive to demand, while declining costs for uranium extraction from seawater could also help boost uranium supplies.[27]

Uranium Conversion

Before it can be fed into enrichment plants, yellowcake (U_3O_8) needs to be converted into a gas (uranium hexafluoride, or UF_6). Of the principal conversion companies worldwide (table 3-3), four—AREVA, Rosatom, Cameco, and Conver-Dyn—export their services rather than concentrating just on domestic markets.[28]

Most conversion contracts consist of long-term agreements between nuclear power plant operators and the major conversion firms. Some vertically integrated companies (such as AREVA and Rosatom) have conversion capabilities, allowing operators to purchase bundled services. However, conversion and other front-end services are typically priced separately.

Table 3-3. *UF$_6$ Conversion Suppliers, 2010*

Company	Ownership	Location	Nameplate capacity (tU as UF$_6$)	Percent of global market
AREVA	Government: France	France	14,000	19
Cameco	Private	Canada	17,500	23
ConverDyn	Private[a]	United States	15,000	20
CNCC	Government: China	China	3,000	4
IPEN	Government: Brazil	Brazil	90	—
Rosatom (Atomenergoprom)	Government: Russia	Russia	25,000	34
Total			74,590	100

Source: EURATOM Supply Agency, "Annual Report 2010" (European Union, 2011), table 3, p. 17. See also: www.ga.com/index.php; www.nukeminc.com/; www.cameco.com/; www.westinghousenuclear. com/ProductLines/Nuclear_Fuel/springfields_site.shtm.

a. Converdyn is a 50-50 joint venture between General Atomics and Honeywell.

Conversion services have relied on secondary sources and Russian HEU to support the primary enriched uranium market. In fact, most of the secondary sources and Russian HEU are delivered in the form of UF$_6$, thus reducing the demand for both mined uranium and conversion services. In turn, the slump in demand for traditional conversion services has depressed conversion prices.[29] Currently, conversion capacity exceeds demand for conversion services by 15,000 tU.[30]

Trends

Given current projections for the global expansion of civilian nuclear energy, conversion services may be able to meet demand only until 2013.[31] Furthermore, the lack of investment in developing new capacity will put pressure on the long-term supply of UF$_6$.[32] In the past several years, some firms, including AREVA, have announced plans to develop greater conversion capacity to meet long-term increases in demand.

Although greater fuel demand could bring new entrants into the conversion market, it is more likely to motivate existing conversion service providers to increase capacity. Unlike the mining sector, which is of interest to a number of aspirant nuclear states, fuel conversion tends to be unattractive to new entrants because it is a relatively uneconomic activity in its own right. In a consolidated market, the easiest and cheapest route is to expand existing conversion capacity.[33] Another disincentive for new entrants is the strong noncommercial advantage enjoyed by the incumbents. The few conversion facilities in operation are a well-established gateway for the delivery of uranium and also provide storage facilities for uranium concentrate and UF_6. Thus they serve as "clearinghouses" for uranium transactions, which makes it difficult for newcomers to gain a foothold in the market.[34]

Enrichment

For light-water reactors, uranium fuel needs to be "enriched" in the isotope U235, a fissile uranium isotope, to about 3–5 percent. Six companies enrich uranium (see table 3-4), with the market highly concentrated among four providers: USEC, EURODIF (which is 59 percent owned by AREVA), URENCO, and Rosatom). Although Argentina, China, Japan, India, Pakistan, and Brazil all have domestic enrichment capacities, they currently have minimal impact on the global commercial market.[35] The amount of enrichment effort involved in separating the U235 atoms from the U238 atoms is measured in separative work units (SWUs).[36]

Most uranium is enriched under long-term (five years or more) contracts with some enrichment for a very small spot market. The movement toward centrifuge technology will reinforce this trend as the development of centrifuge capacity will likely depend on assured demand. Enrichment service providers will only want to boost new centrifuge capacity if long-term enrichment contracts are in place.[37] Suppliers therefore have as much interest in long-term contracts as recipients.

Trade policy also plays a major role in enrichment markets. In the European Union, an informal quota system imposed by EURATOM limits the supply of Russian EUP to approximately 20 percent of all EUP used in order to protect domestic producers.[38] In 2008 the United States and Russia came to an agreement allowing U.S. utilities to import enriched uranium directly from Russia.[39] The compromise allows for small amounts of imports until 2013, after which an import quota mechanism will be in effect up to 2020.[40]

Trends

The supply of enrichment capacity currently exceeds enrichment demand, largely because of Russia's surplus HEU from the cold war era.[41] The U.S. Megatons to Megawatts program paid Russia to convert its HEU into fuel for U.S. civilian nuclear power stations, but this program will end in 2013. Without renewal, the supply of enrichment services to the U.S. market will be reduced by 5.5 million SWUs a year.[42] To compensate for this and to meet the growing demand fed by an expansion of nuclear power, enrichment capacity will need to be substantially increased. The United States is building three enrichment plants on its soil to provide the needed services, including a URENCO centrifuge plant in New Mexico, an AREVA centrifuge plant in Idaho, and a USEC

Table 3-4. *Enrichment Companies, 2010*

Company	Ownership	Location and name	Process	Name-plate capacity (thousand SWU)	Percent of global market
AREVA (EURODIF)	Government: France	France: Georges Besse I and II[a]	Gaseous diffusion	10,800	18
CNNC	Government: China	China: Lanzhou 2, Shaanxi	Centrifuge	1,300	2
Japan Nuclear Fuel Ltd. (JNFL)	Private: consortium of Japanese utilities	Japan: Rokkasho	Centrifuge	150	0
Rosatom (Atomenergoprom)	Government: Russia	Russia: Sverdlovsk-44, Seversk, Krasnoyarsk, Angarsk	Centrifuge	27,500	45
URENCO	Government: United Kingdom and Netherlands Private: E.ON (Germany), RWE (Germany)	United Kingdom: URENCO UK Limited Netherlands: URENCO Neth. Germany: URENCO Deutchland United States: National Enrichment Facility/ New Mexico[b]	Centrifuge	13,000	21
U.S. Enrichment Corp. (USEC)	Private	United States: Paducah, Kentucky	Gaseous diffusion	8,000	13
Total				60,750	100

Source: EURATOM Supply Agency, "Annual Report 2010" (European Union, 2011), table 4, p. 18; Congressional Research Service, "Managing the Nuclear Fuel Cycle" (Washington, March 2010).

a. Georges Besse I uses a gaseous diffusion process and is being phased out; Georges Besse II is a centrifuge plant and will be fully operational within a year or two.

b. URENCO USA's enrichment facility operates through its subsidiary, Louisiana Energy Services.

centrifuge plant in Ohio. Elsewhere, EURODIF's Georges Besse I gaseous diffusion enrichment facility is expected to be decommissioned in the next few years, making way for the Georges Besse II centrifuge plant that began construction in September 2008.

Some countries are interested in acquiring or expanding domestic enrichment capabilities for export. Should countries like Brazil, China, and Japan—all of which operate enrichment plants to serve domestic needs—get into the enrichment services market, there could be larger market consequences. Brazil's Nuclear Energy Commission predicts that by 2012 the country will be producing enough enriched uranium to supply its Angra 1 reactor and 20 percent of its Angra 2 needs, greatly reducing dependence on URENCO, the current source of its enriched uranium.[43] Similarly, CNNC and Japan Nuclear Fuel Limited are expected to increase their market share of the global enrichment market by 2013 through capacity additions.[44]

The most transformative enrichment trend in the short and medium term will be the development of centrifuge technology. More efficient use of uranium could help alleviate any capacity shortages. Since 2000 the European gas centrifuge developed by URENCO has become the leading technology in the West and is now being used by AREVA under a "black-box" arrangement (see chapter 7). At the same time, Russian centrifuge technology is now successfully competing with URENCO technology.

Because of the high costs of entry and sensitive nature of the technology, private sector investment in enrichment has been limited. At present, only General Electric is looking into entering the enrichment business. It has partnered with Hitachi of Japan and Cameco of Canada to form Global Laser Enrichment (GLE), a company attempting to commercialize its Separation of Isotopes by Laser Excitement (SILEX) technology.[45] This new technology could be commercialized as early as 2015.[46] Such a breakthrough would provide further efficiencies and cost reductions in the enrichment of uranium. However, laser enrichment facilities pose proliferation risks because their small physical footprint makes them more difficult to detect (see the section on proliferation later in the chapter).

Interest in multinational investment in national enrichment capabilities is also growing. EURODIF was the first, but the Russian International Uranium Enrichment Center in Angarsk has moved forward rapidly, attracting several investors.

Fuel Fabrication

Fabrication is a more specialized engineering process than mining, conversion, and enrichment, because fuel rods must be tailored to the specific needs of each reactor. Reactor vendors or their affiliates are the major fuel fabricators. Most fuel contracts require the fuel fabricator to provide sufficient information to develop a detailed design for the reactor. The design development takes about five years and involves a conceptual design followed by years of testing and then at least a year's effort to acquire a license for use of the new design. This specialization of product has led to increased consolidation, with the market dominated by fewer reactor vendors, or subsidiaries or licensees of vendors (see figure 3-3).

A profile of the main fuel fabrication companies is provided in table 3-5. Each supplier specializes in a specific type of fuel and therefore competes with no more than three other producers. Although some new firms have entered the fabrication sector in recent years, these are all government-owned operations and were developed to improve energy security rather than serve economic purposes.[47]

Consolidation has also been abetted by the overcapacity of fabricated product. In the West alone, fabrication capacity exceeds demand by nearly 40 percent.[48]

Fabricated fuel is generally not brokered but sold through long-term agreements. End-users rarely switch fabricated fuel suppliers because of the technical complications involved. The plant would have to be operated under a "mixed-core" system for two to three years, using fuel from old and new suppliers together. Such a system is harder to license, requires separate and more complicated regulatory approvals, and may also require modified warranties on behalf of both fuel fabricators.

TRENDS

Since the mid-1990s, fuel fabrication has evolved from a regional market to an international one. More than sixteen suppliers (with twenty-five or more fuel designs) consolidated down into four dominant ones: AREVA, Westinghouse, Global Nuclear Fuel, and TVEL (Rosatom).[49] Undoubtedly, consolidation in the reactor sector triggered proportional consolidation among fuel fabricators because fuel assemblies reflect the reactor type. This trend is expected to continue—and thus discourage new market entrants—as long as significant overcapacity exists.

High up-front costs and technical sophistication of fuel fabrication are further barriers to new private sector market entrants. However, government-owned vendors are becoming increasingly active, as their governments underwrite the costs associated with their market entry.

Domestic fabrication is protected to some extent by import tariffs. The United States, for instance, levies a 3 percent import tariff on fabricated fuel, forcing the leading foreign fuel fabricators to set up separate fabrication plants in the United States to serve their nuclear plants.[50] This competition is aggravated by the design of new fuel assemblies, which can last two or more years in the reactor and thus reduce the need for fuel fabrication facilities.

Figure 3-3. *Evolution of the Nuclear Reactor Industry*[a]

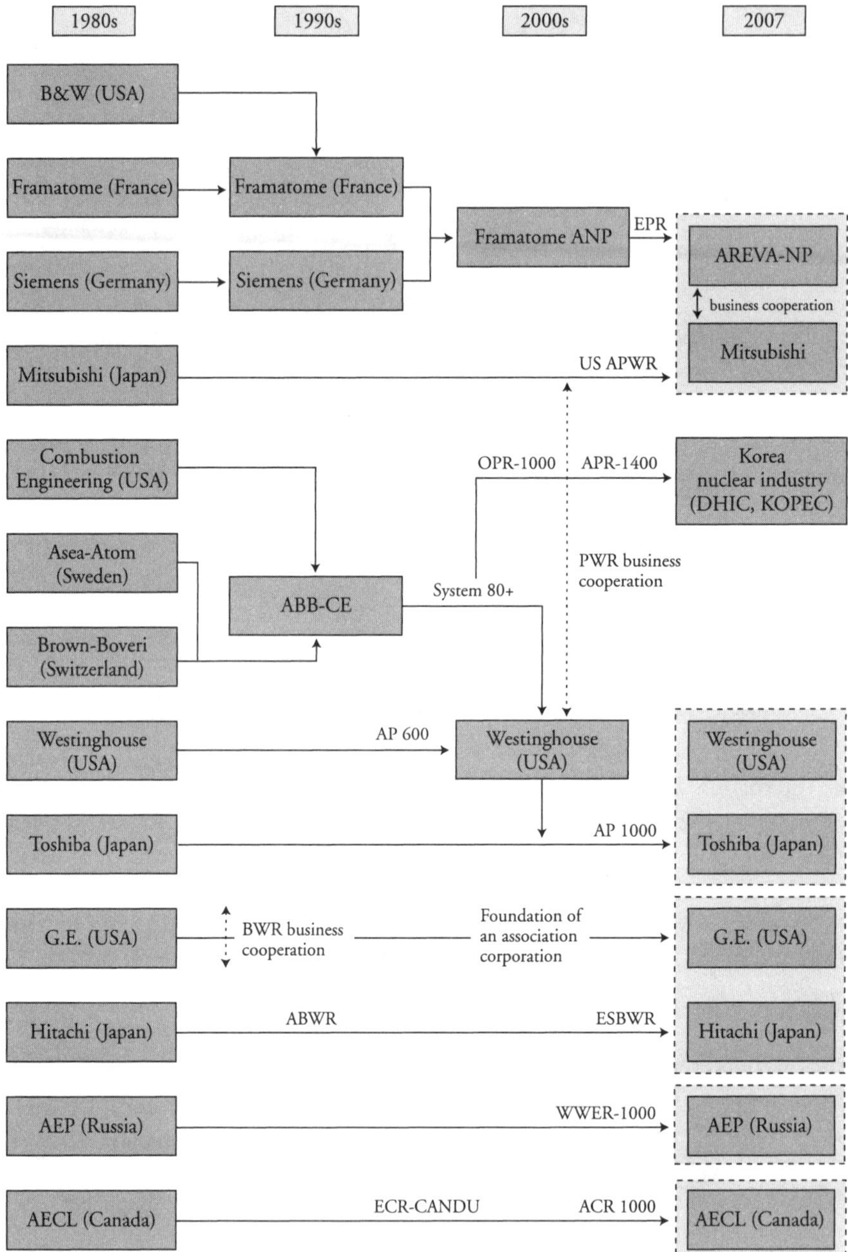

Source: International Atomic Energy Agency.

a. ABWR, Advanced Boiling Water Reactor; APWR, Advanced Pressure Water Reactor; EPR, European Pressurized Water Reactor; ESBWR, Economic Simplified Boiling Water Reactor.

Table 3-5. *Fuel Fabrication Companies, 2008*

Company	Ownership	Location	Capacity (tHM/ year)	Percent of global market
AREVA	Government: France	France, Germany, United States, Belgium	3,600	31
CNNC	Government: China	China	200	2
ENUSA	Government: Spain	Spain	400	3
Global Nuclear Fuel	Private: GE-Hitachi-Toshiba	Japan, United States	1,950	17
Nuclear Fuel Complex	Government: India	India	24[a]	...
Industrias Nucleares do Brasil (INB)	Government: Brazil	Brazil	240	2.0
Korea Nuclear Fuel (KNF)	Government: South Korea	Korea	400	3
Mitsubishi Nuclear Fuel	Private[b]	Japan	440	4
Nuclear Fuel Industries	Private[c]	Japan	534	5
Rosatom (TVEL)	Government: Russia	Russia	1,620	14
Westinghouse	Private	United States, United Kingdom, Sweden	2,080	18
Total			11, 488	100

Sources: IAEA, "Nuclear Fuel Cycle Information System," 2nd ed., 2009, table 22, p. 56. Data depict commercial LWR fuel fabrication capacities. In addition, there are eight facilities in Argentina, Canada, China, India, South Korea, Pakistan, and Romania with 4,060 tHM/year capacity for PHWR fuel fabrication. See also ENUSA (www.euronuclear.org/e-news/e-news-28/enusa.htm); AREVA (www.areva.com/EN/operations-57/operations-the-entire-nuclear-cycle-and-renewable-energy-sources.html); General Electric (www.gepower.com/prod_serv/products/nuclear_energy/en/nuclear_fuel.htm); Korea Nuclear Fuel (www.knfc.co.kr/eng/); Industrias Nucleares do Brasil (www.inb.gov.br/inb_eng/WebForms/Interna2.aspx?secao_id=4); Mitsubishi Nuclear Fuel (www.mnf.co.jp/); Nuclear Fuel Industries (www.nfi.co.jp/e/company/outline.html); Rosatom (www.tvel.ru/en/); and Westinghouse (www.westinghousenuclear.com).

a. Production is for BWRs.

b. Mitsubishi Nuclear Fuel is jointly owned by Mitsubishi Heavy Industries, Ltd. (35 percent), Mitsubishi Materials Corporation (30 percent), AREVA NP (30 percent), and Mitsubishi Corporation (5 percent).

c. NFI is jointly owned by Westinghouse Electric Company (52 percent), Sumitomo Electric Industries, Ltd. (24 percent), and the Furukawa Electric Co., Ltd. (24 percent).

Nuclear Reactors

A nuclear power plant is comprised of a nuclear island, which includes everything inside the containment structure, and the balance of the plant, which is the conventional equipment that generates electricity from the reactor such as steam turbines, electricity generators, and condensers. For the most part, first-, second-, and third-generation reactors are pressurized light-water reactors, boiling water reactors, and heavy-water moderated reactors. Most models now being proposed are Generation III and Generation III+ reactors. These include GE/Hitachi/Toshiba's advanced boiling water reactor (ABWR), Westinghouse's AP-1000, AREVA's European pressurized water reactor (EPR), Mitsubishi's advanced pressure water reactor (APWR), and GE/Hitachi's economic simplified boiling water reactor (ESBWR).[51]

The evolutionary Generation III+ reactors are designed to enhance safety and reduce costs. Of the five designs, the AP-1000 and the ESBWR offer passive safety features. Only one, AREVA's double containment structure for the EPR, includes aircraft hazard protection. Passive safety systems incorporate natural processes like gravity, condensation, and evaporation alongside features such as battery-powered valves. Given their lower expected failure rates, these systems should require less redundancy, and thus should incur lower capital, operations, and maintenance costs.

Generation IV reactors include a mix of technologies. Four of the six are fast neutron (or simply "fast") reactors: gas-cooled fast reactors (GFRs), lead-cooled fast reactors, molten salt reactors, and sodium-cooled fast reactors (SFRs). Supercritical water-cooled reactors (SCWRs) can operate either in the thermal or fast neutron spectrum and very high temperature reactors (VHTRs) in the thermal spectrum.[52]

Although some prototypes of the Generation IV reactors have been built, they are unlikely to reach the market for decades to come. Some of these reactors may require highly enriched uranium and plutonium and therefore will depend on some kinds of recycling. If they could be fueled with low-enriched uranium, some of the proliferation implications of closing the nuclear fuel cycle could be avoided.[53] Research into these reactors is being carried out under the auspices of the Generation IV International Forum, an international research partnership that includes Argentina, Brazil, Canada, France, Japan, the Republic of Korea, South Africa, the United Kingdom, the United States, Switzerland, China, and Russia. EURATOM also participates.

Nuclear reactor construction in Western nations has traditionally been dominated by Toshiba/Westinghouse, AREVA, General Electric, and Rosatom, which in 2008 collectively accounted for nearly 75 percent of the reactors under operation at the time.[54] Since then, previously smaller suppliers, such as South Korea's

Table 3-6. *Nuclear Power Plant Vendors, 2008*

Company	Reactors in operation	Percent of global market	Type of reactor
AREVA	96	22.1	PWR
AECL	34	7.8	PHWR
Babcock & Wilcox	7	1.6	PWR
CNNC	7	1.6	PWR
GE[a]	54	12.4	BWR
Hitachi	10	2.3	BWR
KEPCO-KHNP[b]	9	2.1	PWR
Mitsubishi	19	4.4	PWR
Nuclear Power Corp. of India, Ltd. (NPCIL)	16	3.7	PHWR
Rosatom (Atomenergoprom)	52	12.0	VVER
Skoda Praha	10	2.3	VVER
Toshiba-Westinghouse	120	27.6	BWR, PWR[c]
Total	434	100	

Source: NEA, "Market Competition in the Nuclear Industry," p. 29, table 1.

a. GE and Hitachi now have a joint venture.

b. Korea Electric Power Corporation owns Korea Hydro and Nuclear Power; Doosan is equipment supplier.

c. Before Toshiba bought Westinghouse in 2006, Westinghouse was the largest provider of BWR-type nuclear reactors, while Toshiba specialized in PWR-type reactors. Toshiba-Westinghouse now produces both reactor types for commercial sale. See "Toshiba Completes Westinghouse Acquisition," PR Newswire, October 17, 2006 (www.prnewswire.com/news-releases/toshiba-completes-westinghouse-acquisition-56540472.html).

KEPCO, the Nuclear Power Corporation of India Ltd., China's Guangdong Nuclear Power Corporation, and the China National Nuclear Corporation have gained significant market share. Table 3-6 lists the major reactor vendors.

South Korea, China, and India are all expanding their domestic nuclear energy capacities and now account for 57 percent of all reactors currently under construction.[55] The majority are being built by domestic suppliers such as the firms just mentioned, but U.S., French, Russian, and Japanese suppliers are clearly intent on entering these developing markets.

Over time, alliances have shifted among vendors, with a trend toward multinational ownership as entities from different countries have merged (figure 3-3). Less obvious, however, is the extent of multinational collaboration on big reactor projects, in which several entities cooperate on reactor design, engineering, procurement and construction, equipment manufacture, and fuel provision. Several large firms offer many of the services along this chain. Among its services, Westinghouse, one of the world's leading reactor vendors, offers development, licensing, detailed engineering, project management, component manufacturing, and startup support for new nuclear power plants. It also manufactures nuclear fuel.

For particular projects, the mix of services and service providers can vary. For the Shin Kori and Shin Wolsong plants in South Korea, Westinghouse provided reactor coolant pumps, reactor vessel internals, and control element drive mechanisms.[56] For the AP-1000, a third-generation reactor being built by Westinghouse, the company either manufactures reactor vessel internals itself or purchases them from one of four suppliers. Westinghouse purchases reactor pressure vessels, control rod drive mechanisms, steam generators, steam turbine generators, and condensers from other manufacturers. Some of its partners include Doosan Heavy Industries, Mitsubishi Heavy Industries, Ansaldo Camozzi, Equipos Nucleares, S.A., and other major equipment providers.[57] As for nuclear fuel, Westinghouse collaborates with Korea Nuclear Fuel, among others.

Bids for reactors are often judged as "package deals." Even if a particular reactor design is preferable, countries or utilities are more likely to purchase reactors in a package they consider most cost-effective. Engineering experience and project-management skills are also a critical factor in the reactor industry; longer construction times lead to escalating costs, not just for construction but also financing, which can total between 20 and 80 percent of the cost of a reactor.

Trends

Consolidation of vendors has been a slow trend over the past twenty years, although increased demand for nuclear energy, if it materializes, could bring Korean, Chinese, and Indian competition into the global nuclear market. Vendors like AREVA and Rosatom may offer vertically integrated contracts, including fuel services.

To reduce costs, some firms are turning to off-site modular construction, thereby limiting the need for on-site skilled labor. Japanese plants have employed modular construction with success. All the designs currently being considered, except the EPR, employ modular construction. Another way to cut costs is to simplify designs and thus reduce the required amount of steel and concrete. Here too, modular designs, apart from the EPR, boast lower costs than first- and second-generation reactors.

Some of the research and development for Generation III, III+, and IV reactors has focused on passive safety features, better containment, and better physical protection. The U.S. government has sponsored research into "safeguards by design," the aim of which is to incorporate safety, security, and safeguards concerns into the actual design of nuclear power plants (and other facilities) in collaboration with vendors.

It is difficult to generalize the costs of nuclear power, since variables such as capital, labor and materials, the regulatory environment, and the availability and costs of alternative generating technologies differ widely among countries. Another important factor to consider is the liberalization of electricity markets, which can have a significant impact on the competitiveness of nuclear power. In North America, the costs of new nuclear power plants have made financing unrealistic and dampened interest in construction, even when loan guarantees and other subsidies are available.[58] Although some form of carbon pricing might make nuclear power more competitive in the United States, it may still not be able to vie with natural gas. Costs appear to be far lower in other parts of the world, although any estimation should take care not to equate reactor pricing with the true cost of construction and financing. Dramatic cost overruns, as in the case of AREVA's fixed-price EPR in Finland, could discourage other vendors from providing fixed-price contracts. Some vendors may submit lower bids initially, accepting "loss leaders" to build up export credentials. South Korea's KEPCO, for instance, reportedly promised the United Arab Emirates $10 billion in loans to help finance the cost of four reactors—a subsidy of about 50 percent.[59]

Reprocessing and Recycling

Two fuels are currently produced for commercial use from reprocessed LWR spent fuel: reprocessed uranium (RepU) and mixed oxide fuel. The PUREX process is the only means of fuel separation in commercial use. It chemically separates uranium and plutonium in aqueous solution from fission products and other radioactive by-products (see table 3-7 for a profile of reprocessing companies).[60]

According to its proponents, reprocessing makes it possible not only to extract the remaining usable energy in spent fuel but also to reduce the volume and toxicity of waste materials required for storage. In some estimates, recycling recovered uranium and plutonium can reduce the use of natural uranium by 25 percent, reduce waste toxicity by 90 percent, and lower the volume necessary for final disposal by 75 percent in comparison with the direct disposal of spent fuel.[61] About a quarter of the 12,000 tons of nuclear waste generated globally each year is currently being reprocessed.[62]

Opponents, however, raise proliferation concerns, since reprocessing recovers plutonium in a separate stream, making it easier for dedicated use in weapons production. In addition, critics of reprocessing argue that there is no economic justification for reprocessing, since the once-through fuel cycle is cheaper.[63] By one estimate, at a reprocessing price of $1,000 per kilogram of heavy metal (kgHM), "reprocessing and recycling plutonium in existing light-water reactors (LWRs) will be more expensive than direct disposal of spent fuel until the uranium price reaches over $360 per kilogram of uranium (kgU)."[64] Furthermore, there are no assurances that it will be less expensive to dispose of packaged

Table 3-7. *Reprocessing Companies*

Company	Ownership	Location	2007 nominal capacity	2006 production (tHM)	Percent of global market (production)
AREVA	Government: France	France	1,700	1,015	91.0
JNFL	Private: Japanese utilities	Japan	800	0	0
Rosatom (Atomenergoprom)	Government: Russia	Russia	400	100	9.0
NDA/Sellafield[a]	Government: (NDA)	United Kingdom	900	0	0
Total			3,800	1,115	100

Source: NEA, "Market Competition in the Nuclear Industry," p. 82.

a. Sellafield is owned by the Nuclear Decommissioning Authority (NDA), which has contracted out management and operations to Nuclear Management Partners (owned by AREVA, Amec, and URS).

high-level waste than a spent fuel bundle. Finally, spent fuel and final MOX fuel product must be transported long distances, creating a proliferation concern and increasing the cost.

The uranium recoverable from spent fuel must undergo conversion again before it can be reenriched for use as fresh fuel. The enrichment and fabrication of reprocessed uranium fuel are essentially the same as for fresh uranium and are carried out by the same companies that supply these services during the once-through nuclear fuel cycle.[65] Owing to differences in isotopic composition, however, reprocessed uranium requires greater enrichment than natural uranium in order to produce fresh fuel.[66]

Reprocessed uranium commands a much larger share of the reprocessing market than MOX fuel. The World Nuclear Association estimates that MOX accounts for only 2 percent of new nuclear fuel used globally. Unlike plutonium trade, the reprocessed uranium market is not governed by stringent legal restrictions and thus is open to greater commercial involvement from both a supply and demand standpoint: the utility that produces the spent fuel is not obligated to conduct the uranium reprocessing, but it cannot sell the right to reprocess its plutonium stock.

MOX fuel is a combination of plutonium and uranium dioxides and can be used in LWRs as well as in fast reactors. MOX fuel has the advantage of capturing some of the potential fissile energy that would otherwise be considered waste in the once-through cycle. Nuclear power reactors designed to accept low-enriched uranium can sustain up to a third of their core capacity as fresh MOX fuel with the simple addition of more control rods, but beyond this fraction the power plant must undergo more significant retrofitting, for example, in fuel-handling and refueling facilities.[67]

Individual utilities retain ownership over all of the materials produced during the recycling and reprocessing stage (including wastes). These products are eventually returned to the country in which the fuel was initially irradiated. Given the large amount of time between the unloading of spent fuel rods and the fabrication of new fuel, reprocessing agreements usually take the form of long-term contracts.

AREVA has been the leader in developing the international market for reprocessing spent fuel. However, its plants are now operating at only half capacity and have few new customers.[68] Commercial reprocessing for the international market occurs primarily at AREVA's facility in La Hague in France (90 percent of all global fuel reprocessing in 2007 took place at this site). India, China, Russia, and Japan have all indicated that they are planning to expand or develop commercial reprocessing facilities.[69] Commercially available MOX fuel is fabricated on a large scale principally at the MELOX plant in France. Japan has plans for a MOX production facility, and the United States is constructing a facility in South Carolina to produce MOX from weapons-grade plutonium.

Trends

State-controlled nuclear fuel companies are the only facilities to offer reprocessing on the international market, in large measure owing to proliferation concerns and the high cost and long lead times for construction of facilities. Government involvement is also necessitated by the special regulations for the handling of MOX, with the result that some governments are instituting policies to eliminate its use. Belgium and Germany, for example, have not allowed new reprocessing contracts to be signed by utilities in those countries, and Switzerland has implemented a moratorium on the use of MOX fuel.[70] Low uranium prices also have made reprocessing a less attractive option, but this could change in light of increasing demand following on expanded reactor construction and potential increases in uranium prices.

New reprocessing technologies being developed along with the next generation of reactors may provide more proliferation resistance than existing processes. These include variations on the PUREX process that do not separate out plutonium in a separate stream, or electrometallurgical processes that do not dissolve the Pu in a liquid but use a metal reduction method, as in pyroprocessing. However, none of these would provide greater proliferation resistance than direct disposal of spent nuclear fuel in a repository.

Spent Fuel Storage and Disposal

Spent fuel storage is often classified into interim storage and long-term disposal.

Interim

Since most countries do not reprocess spent fuel and do not have long-term disposal sites, dry storage casks are widely used as an interim solution. Both reprocessed fission products and spent fuel can be kept in dry storage facilities. The U.S. Nuclear Regulatory Commission considers dry cask storage safe and environmentally sound.[71]

Long term

Most countries have policies for placing the spent fuel directly in a repository rather than reprocessing it and separating out high-level waste. However, no country has yet placed civilian nuclear spent fuel in a permanent repository. Although Canada, Finland, Germany, South Korea, Spain, Sweden, and the United States all have direct disposal policies, Finland and Sweden have made the most progress in this direction as they have identified permanent geological disposal sites and have begun licensing and other activities. As noted earlier, the U.S. Department of Energy was creating a geological repository at Yucca Mountain, but in 2009 the Obama administration halted the licensing procedures and is reexamining spent fuel policy.

The handling and final disposal of radioactive waste is governed by both national laws and international agreements such as the Joint Convention on the Safety of Spent Fuel Management and the Joint Convention on the Safety of Radioactive Waste Management. While the commercial industry is responsible for low-level and intermediate-level waste (the latter category is used in Europe but not in the United States), the government is responsible for permanent disposal of high-level waste.[72]

High-level waste from reprocessing is first vitrified—mixed with molten glass, sealed, and solidified in special containers—to allow for safe transport, long-term storage, and eventual disposal. It is transported in vitrified form from reprocessing facilities to storage facilities, where it can be safely stored until a subterranean disposal site is constructed. Subterranean disposal sites at depths of 250–1,000 meters are considered the safest and most likely depositories for vitrified HLW in the future. Since disposal of this waste is handled by national governments, no commercial organizations compete for the task.[73]

International and regional nuclear waste sites have received increasing attention in recent years following an endorsement in 2003 from Mohamed ElBaradei, formerly head of the IAEA. On a regional level, fourteen European countries have expressed interest in developing a safe and cost-efficient multinational site in response to the European Union's Strategic Action Plan for Implementation of European Regional Repositories (SAPIERR).[74] Southeast Asian countries are exploring regional cooperation in this regard as well. Although most concepts for geologic repositories have focused on a centralized underground repository reached through tunnels, it may be useful to consider other approaches, including deep borehole technology.

Technology and Nonproliferation

The preceding discussion illuminated some technology trends that need to be placed in the context of their impact on proliferation. Some, if widely deployed, would pose a considerable proliferation risk, as in the case of laser enrichment of uranium and fast reactor recycle technologies. Others could reduce such risks, as in the case of reactor designs with built-in safeguards or recycle technologies that do not separate out plutonium. The proliferation impact of technologies should be measured against specific proliferation risks as well as the marginal improvement over current systems and standards (see chapter 5 for industry views on particular technologies).

Technological improvements can reduce the proliferation risks of nuclear energy but in themselves cannot ensure the peaceful uses of nuclear energy. The best hopes for proliferation resistance rest on a combination of technological, operational, institutional, and monitoring improvements. The IAEA defines proliferation resistance as "that characteristic of the nuclear energy system that impedes the diversion or undeclared production of nuclear materials or misuse of technology by the host states in order to acquire nuclear weapons or other nuclear explosive devices. The degree of proliferation resistance results from a combination of, inter alia, technical design features, operational modalities, institutional arrangements and safeguards measures."[75]

Measures of proliferation resistance can be divided into two categories: those intrinsic to the technology and those extrinsic to it. Physical and engineering characteristics of nuclear technology are examples of intrinsic features, and safeguards and physical barriers are examples of extrinsic ones.[76] Any state decisions and actions related to nuclear energy systems, such as forswearing domestic enrichment and reprocessing, can also enhance extrinsic proliferation resistance.

Intrinsic proliferation-resistance features can result from the technological approach, or can be facilitated by efforts to design safeguards into the construction of new facilities—an approach called safeguards by design. Not only are new technologies deployed, but the actual construction also takes into account safeguards modalities.

More broadly, certain technologies developed to accomplish similar tasks can either diminish or add to proliferation risks. Laser enrichment technology, according to many observers, is likely to increase proliferation risks because uranium enrichment can be performed in small facilities that have few signatures for detection. The benefits of SILEX—described as "low power consumption and

capital costs and modular technology providing versatility in deployment"[77]—
are precisely the characteristics that make this technology more difficult to detect
and monitor than current enrichment processes. Indeed, most industry and
nonindustry participants in our survey believe laser enrichment poses a strong
challenge to the nonproliferation regime.

Proliferation Resistance and the Fuel Cycle

Most observers agree that a nuclear fuel cycle without recycle of spent fuel has
higher proliferation resistance than its alternatives, primarily because spent fuel
is largely protected from theft or diversion by its intense radiation. Such a fuel
cycle still has the risk of clandestine reprocessing and diversion or theft of highly
enriched uranium.

In broad terms, technologies that help maintain open (no recycle) nuclear
fuel cycles without the use of plutonium or highly enriched uranium for fresh
fuel promote nonproliferation. Although the dominant technology, as noted
earlier, is light-water reactors that use low-enriched uranium, other options are
possible: thorium can be used in a variety of reactors, natural uranium or low-
enriched uranium in heavy-water reactors, and low-enriched uranium in high-
temperature gas-cooled reactors.

At the front end of the fuel cycle, uranium recovery technologies, such as in
situ leaching and extraction from seawater, could help make spent fuel reprocessing unnecessary and uneconomic; the perceived scarcity of uranium was one
of the early factors behind the drive to reprocess spent fuel to extract both the
uranium and plutonium for recycle. Advances in the thorium fuel cycle could
similarly eliminate the need for recycling to extract more resources from spent
fuel, since thorium is quite abundant in the earth's crust. (See table 3-8 for the
different reactor options for different fuel cycles.)

The predominance of light-water reactors means that uranium enrichment
will be required, so any expanded deployment of these designs would increase
the demand for enrichment services, potentially encouraging its spread beyond
those countries with enrichment facilities at present. Two open-cycle options—
thorium and high-temperature gas-cooled reactors (HTGR)—could require fuel
enrichment of 19.9 percent and 14.0 percent, respectively, raising proliferation
risks.[78] The composition of HTGR fuel, however, makes reprocessing difficult.

Heavy-water reactors raise a different set of proliferation concerns. Because
these reactors are fueled with natural uranium, which has a relatively short burn-
up phase, the resulting plutonium is less contaminated with poisoning isotopes
and is thus attractive for use in weapons. India used such reactors to produce its
weapons plutonium. Although technical improvements such as remote monitoring of online refueling and the use of low-enriched uranium have lessened the

Table 3-8. *States of Reactor Development for Different Fuel Cycles*[a]

| | Open cycle | | Open/closed cycle | | Closed cycle | |
| | Uranium | | | | Plutonium | |
Reactor type	Natural	Enriched	Thorium	Plutonium	Breeder	Burner
Thermal	X	X	F	X		
Fast		XP	XP	XP	F	F

Source: Adapted from Scott DeMuth and others, "Increased Proliferation Resistance for 21st Century Nuclear Power," LA-UR-07-0461 (Los Alamos, N.M.: Los Alamos National Laboratory, 2007).

a. X = deployed now; F = future; XP = pilot-scale.

risk associated with these reactors, they are still more open to proliferation than light-water reactors.

Thorium-fueled reactors, according to some observers, are more proliferation resistant than those fueled with uranium. Thorium232 transmutates into U233, which then decays into U232. Although U233 can be used in weapons, it is essentially poisoned by the U232, and some experts believe the two cannot be chemically separated, unlike plutonium and uranium. A handful of thorium-fueled reactors have been in use over the past few decades, but the technology did not catch on because uranium was widely available, and in the early years because the nuclear weapon states favored the uranium cycle for the plutonium that it bred for use in weapons. Table 3-9 summarizes the results of a 2008 U.S. Department of Energy assessment of some of the proliferation risks associated with different fuel cycle alternatives.

Conclusions

A key concern for nonproliferation analysts is that increased interest in nuclear power will result in more states acquiring capabilities that could aid a nuclear weapons program. The chief concerns are the acquisition of uranium enrichment and spent fuel reprocessing technologies because of their dual-use nature. The increased interest in nuclear energy has led some countries (many for the first time) to consider expanding their own domestic nuclear fuel cycle capabilities, or at least not to dismiss the option. These countries are as diverse as Canada, Jordan, South Africa, South Korea, and Mongolia.

Beneath the discussion of rights and future options are practical considerations that argue against acquiring domestic fuel cycle capabilities for energy security or cost-effectiveness reasons. The uranium market is global, although the largest and cheapest-to-recover resources are in a handful of states—Australia, Canada, and Kazakhstan. Still, shares in uranium mines can be purchased

Table 3-9. *Policy Assessment of Fuel Cycle Alternatives*

Impact on proliferation	*Once-through*	*Full actinide recycle*	*Partial actinide recycle*
Can technology be used directly or with modifications to produce weapons-usable materials?	*Lowest risk:* Does not create technical basis for separating weapons-usable material from spent fuel. HWRs have higher risk of misuse.	*Highest risk:* Capable of separating weapons-usable material, though some modification may be needed, depending on the separation technology used.	*Highest risk:* Capable of separating weapons-usable material, though some modification may be needed, depending on the separation technology used. DUPIC has low risk because it involves limited separation, although HWRs have higher risk of misuse.
Can it avoid accumulations of separated plutonium and draw-down of existing stocks?	*No improvement:* Reactors could use existing plutonium stocks in MOX fuel but are not currently licensed to do so.	*Potential significant reduction:* Recycling creates a market for plutonium-bearing fuel. Fast reactor startup would require large quantities of plutonium.	*Potential reduction:* Recycling separated plutonium creates a market for plutonium-bearing fuel. DUPIC alternative is no improvement since it would not reduce separated plutonium stocks.
Can materials in fuel cycle be used in nuclear weapons?	*Lowest risk:* Spent fuel is bulky and highly radioactive, although radioactivity decays over many decades. HWR spent fuel bundles are smaller and radioactivity decreases more quickly. HTGR spent fuel is difficult to reprocess. Enrichment of fresh fuel varies, but all is LEU.	*Highest risk:* Removal of fission products and separation of actinides greatly reduce barriers to theft, misuse, or further processing, even without separation of pure plutonium. Fast reactor fuels have higher concentration of weapons-usable materials.	*Highest risk:* Removal of fission products and separation of actinides greatly reduce barriers to theft, misuse, or further processing, even without separation of pure plutonium. Thermal reactor fuels have lower concentration of weapons-usable materials. Low for DUPIC, which has limited removal of fission products.
Is it difficult for international safeguards to verify that nuclear materials are not diverted and facilities misused?	*Lowest cost and difficulty:* Spent fuel assemblies tracked as items. Costs are significantly higher for HWRs. Low to medium cost and difficulty for thorium or HTGR, which requires new safeguards approach.	*Highest cost and difficulty:* Separation processes require continuous monitoring to guard against diversion; novel bulk materials present new measurement challenges. Novel processes may provide new opportunities to detect misuse.	*High cost and difficulty:* Separation processes require continuous monitoring to detect diversion; bulk material measurement presents familiar challenges.

Source: Adapted from National Nuclear Security Administration, "Draft Nonproliferation Impact Assessment for the Global Nuclear Energy Partnership Programmatic Alternatives" (Washington: Department of Energy, December 2008), p. 106, table 1.

and uranium can be stockpiled. For those countries considering nuclear power that have identified uranium resources, it may still be cheaper to purchase uranium abroad, particularly at current prices. Overall, uranium resources do not appear to be a bottleneck for new nuclear supply.

When it comes to conversion and fuel fabrication, the choices narrow. New nuclear states are unlikely to find it cost-effective to develop their own capabilities and so will have to rely on the relatively small number of conversion service providers and fuel fabricators in existence. Given that the cost of conversion is a small portion of the price of fuel, there are few economic incentives for new suppliers in a consolidated market where it is easier and cheaper to expand existing capacities. New nuclear states will be dependent on fuel fabricators, not only because specific types of fuel are available from only about three major suppliers, but also because specific reactors require specific fuel. Alternative suppliers will be difficult and costly to find. Ironically, many of the leasing schemes designed to provide fuel assurances make states almost wholly dependent on a particular fuel supplier. Nonetheless, commentators are quick to point out that no nuclear power reactor has ever shut down for lack of fuel.

Enrichment and reprocessing capabilities are still tightly controlled by national governments and in most cases are wholly or partly owned by them. States that are concerned about energy security can procure enrichment services from several suppliers, as the United States does. Note, too, that multinational investment in enrichment capabilities is on the rise. Although EURODIF may have been the first, there will likely be more. AREVA, for one, is seeking foreign investment from Japan, Kuwait, Qatar, and others. Of the four new enrichment plants planned or under construction in the United States, three will be foreign owned. Of course, doubling or tripling reactor capacity could put a strain on uranium resources, but it would have to get very expensive before recycling becomes economical.

While there is more diversity in parts of the nuclear fuel cycle that require less capitalization, the suppliers mainly developed to respond to domestic needs. Several of these suppliers now are seeking to supply foreign markets. For example, Korea Nuclear Fuel is seeking to expand its market share by supplying Westinghouse's PWRs in the United States.[79] The firm will also supply fuel for Korean reactors built for export.

Non–nuclear weapon states tend to view suppliers as a "nuclear cartel" because of their concentration and consolidation. Yet the technological support required by nuclear power necessitates long-term relationships between recipients and fuel suppliers. Where liability and convenience are a concern, reactor vendors may supply the first few cores for the reactor, but a contract can also stipulate that they supply cores over the life of the reactor, which suggests that there is little need for fuel assurances. Of course, countries that are concerned about fuel supply over the life of the reactor may feel more secure if fuel assurance arrangements are in place.

Since its early days, the nuclear industry has undergone several structural changes: it began with a few dominant suppliers (like General Electric and Westinghouse) that provided turnkey plants; then, with the diffusion of technology, national companies emerged in France, Japan, and Korea; eventually reactor vendors became consolidated on a global scale. As a result, many current reactor projects are global affairs—reactor vendors have teamed up on designs, and contracts often include foreign suppliers. The limited demand for nuclear reactors over the past two decades and the highly specialized nature of the nuclear power industry are the primary reasons for this consolidation. The emergence of new nuclear suppliers, discussed in chapter 4, may change the landscape to enhance competition and supply.

Notes

1. This summary does not cover dual-use suppliers, brokers, or other equipment and service vendors. It concentrates on uranium as the starting point and waste products as the end of the fission process. Efforts related to weapons production are not discussed except where the civilian nuclear process may cross over to the fabrication of nuclear weapons, and the decommissioning of fuel cycle facilities is not covered either.

2. Nuclear fuel includes both fissile and fertile material. Fissile material can sustain a chain reaction, while fertile material can be converted to fissile material in a reactor. Uranium isotopes U235 and U233, as well as plutonium isotope Pu239, are fissile materials that are used in generating civilian nuclear power. Uranium 238 (U238) and thorium 232 (Th232) are fertile material. Both U235 and U238, as well as Th232, are mined. Pu239 results from the neutron bombardment of U238 in a reactor, and U233 results from the neutron bombardment of Th232.

3. Adapted from International Atomic Energy Agency (IAEA), *Nuclear Fuel Cycle Information System: A Directory of Nuclear Fuel Cycle Facilities* (Vienna, April 2009), pp. 9–11.

4. Russia is planning to build several floating nuclear power plants to serve isolated regions, especially in the Arctic. The plant design is a KLT-40S light-water reactor similar to that used on Russian nuclear icebreakers, with a capacity of 30 megawatts (MW) (www.nti.org/e_research/e3_floating_nuclear_power_plants.html).

5. A few reactors have also used thorium in conjunction with uranium. Thorium is fertile and requires U235 or some other fissile material. The combination of uranium and thorium makes it more difficult to recover plutonium from reprocessing. The thorium fuel cycle also produces U233, a weapons-usable isotope of uranium that is equally difficult to recover via reprocessing.

6. A thermonuclear reactor requires a moderator to slow down the neutrons released during fission, and thereby maintain the chain reaction that produces nuclear energy.

7. Minor actinides and the transuranics are components of spent nuclear fuel that can be further used as fuel in a reactor. In a fast reactor, neutrons are not moderated, or

slowed down, and thus are less efficient in inducing fission. However, the "fast" neutrons can create a fission reaction with a wider range of isotopes, specifically transuranics and minor actinides.

8. MOX fabrication is also being used to dispose of excess weapons plutonium. The facility under construction in Savannah River, South Carolina, will serve this purpose.

9. International Panel on Fissile Materials, "Global Fissile Material Report 2010: Balancing the Books: Production and Stocks" (Princeton University, 2010).

10. Matthew Bunn and others, "The Economics of Reprocessing vs. Direct Disposal of Spent Nuclear Fuel" (Harvard University, Belfer Center for Science and International Affairs, December 2003).

11. Two large gaseous diffusion plants are still in operation: USEC's plant in Paducah, Kentucky, is running at full capacity, and the Georges Besse I facility in France is operating until AREVA's Georges Besse II centrifuge facility comes online in the next year or two.

12. In the Russian example, reactor owners can also buy Russian EUP even if the owner does not have Russian-made reactors. Russia may soon be providing complete fuel assemblies for Western-style reactors. AREVA can also offer completed nuclear fuel assemblies, as well as a full range of intermediate products.

13. In situ leaching—used predominantly in Australia, Kazakhstan, the United States, and Uzbekistan—extracts uranium by dissolving minerals in the ore, drawing the solution to the surface, and then reclaiming the uranium from the solution through chemical treatment, leaving the surface largely undisturbed and the radioactive waste rock underground. This is a flexible technique and requires low capital investment, but it can only be used in rock formations that are permeable to the acids used and will not contaminate nearby groundwater. See "In Situ Leach (ISL) Mining of Uranium," *World Nuclear Association,* June 2009 (www.world-nuclear.org/info/inf27.html).

14. Uranium One is now majority owned by Rosatom's mining subsidiary, ARMZ. See "Rosatom Controls Uranium One," *Financial Times,* June 9, 2010.

15. Spot contracts can be purchased to hedge against potential long-term price increases.

16. OECD Nuclear Energy Agency (NEA), "Market Competition in the Nuclear Industry" (Issy-les-Moulineaux, France, 2008), p. 48.

17. According to World Nuclear Association estimates, annual uranium requirements for the world's nuclear reactors from 2007 to 2010 averaged about 66,000 tons of uranium (tU). Newly mined uranium is said to account for 60–65 percent of this yearly reactor fuel requirement, with the remainder provided by secondary sources, including reenriched tailings from enrichment operations, commercial and government stockpiles and inventories, and military materials made available to the market.

18. Robert Vance, "Current and Future Market Trends in Nuclear Fuel Supply," Nuclear Energy Agency paper presented to the International Atomic Energy Agency, January 26, 2009. According to the NEA, uranium resources increased 15 percent in the period 2004–07.

19. From interviews with members of the Jordan Atomic Energy Commission in Amman, Jordan, February 2011.

20. Government of Australia, Department of Foreign Affairs and Trade, "Australia's Uranium Exports Policy" (www.dfat.gov.au/security/aus_uran_exp_policy.html).

21. In 2006, for example, 66,500 tU were required to fuel the global reactor fleet, of which 40,000 tU were produced and the remainder obtained from secondary sources. A typical 1,000-MW reactor uses about 200 tU a year. See Hans Forsström, "The Nuclear Fuel Cycle and Its Market: An Overview," paper presented to the International Atomic Energy Agency, Seminar on Global Nuclear Fuel Supply, February 2009 (www.mofa.go.jp/policy/energy/iaca/seminar0902/nf.pdf).

22. Data from First Uranium Corporation (www.firsturanium.com/sjfu/view/sjfu/en/page148).

23. NEA, "Market Competition in the Nuclear Industry," p. 44.

24. NEA, *Uranium 2009: Resources, Production, and Demand* (Issy-les-Moulineaux, France, 2010), p. 18.

25. Vance, "Current and Future Market Trends in Nuclear Fuel Supply."

26. Ibid.

27. See, for example, K. B. Gongalsky, "Impact of Pollution Caused by Uranium Production on Soil Microfauna," *Environmental Monitoring and Assessment,* 2003, pp. 197–219.

28. In addition to participating in the commercial fuel cycle described here, NUKEM acts as a trader, even in the downblending of former military HEU to make UF_6. For more information, see www.nukeminc.com/nf_components.cfm.

29. NEA, "Market Competition in the Nuclear Industry," p. 53.

30. EURATOM Supply Agency, "Annual Report 2010" (European Union, 2011), p. 17.

31. Vance, "Current and Future Market Trends in Nuclear Fuel Supply."

32. Jonathan Hinze, "Keys to Successful SMR Commercialization," presentation to the Platts Small and Modular Reactors Conference, Washington, D.C., June 28, 2010.

33. In a notable exception, Kazatomprom has expressed interest in establishing conversion capabilities to supplement its growing mining assets. It has signed a joint venture agreement with Cameco and may develop a facility in Kazakhstan using Cameco technologies. It is expecting to enter the market by 2016–17. "Cameco, Kazakhstan Eye Conversion Plant in 2016, 2017," Dow Jones Newswires, June 4, 2010.

34. NEA, "Market Competition in the Nuclear Industry," p. 10.

35. Brazil has a small enrichment facility and has expressed interest in providing EUP globally for commercial power reactors, but its present capacity is about equal to its domestic needs.

36. EURATOM offers the following background on separative work units: "SWU . . . measures the effort made in order to separate the fissile, and hence valuable, U-235 isotopes from the non-fissile U-238 isotopes, both of which are present in natural uranium. As a standard indicator of enrichment services, the concept of SWU is very complex, as it is a function of the amount of uranium processed and the degree to which it is enriched, i.e. the extent of increase in the concentration of the U-235 isotope relative to the remainder. The unit is strictly 'kilogram separative work unit' or kg SWU (but in graphs is usually shown as SWU or tSWU for thousands) and measures the quantity of separative work (indicative of energy used in enrichment) when feed and product

quantities are expressed in kilograms. To produce one kilogram of uranium enriched to 3.5% U-235 typically requires 4.3 SWU if the plant is operated at a tails assay of 0.30 % or 4.8 SWU if the tails assay is 0.25 % (thereby requiring only 7.0 kg instead of 7.8 kg of natural U feed). Between 100000 and 120000 SWU are required to enrich the annual fuel loading for a typical 1000 MWe light water reactor. Enrichment costs are related to the electrical energy used. The gaseous diffusion process consumes some 2400 kWh per SWU, whereas gas centrifuge plants require only about 60 kWh/SWU." See EUR-ATOM Supply Agency, "Annual Report 2010," pp. 36–37.

37. NEA, "Market Competition in the Nuclear Industry," pp. 64–65. However, there is also evidence that this dynamic is changing, in that enrichment suppliers may be increasing capacity in order to obtain new contracts.

38. Ibid., p. 68. According to EURATOM, about 33 percent of EU utilities' purchases of EUP came from Russia in 2010. However, 7 percent of the EU's EUP imports come from long-term contracts with Russia that were signed before the creation of EURATOM and therefore must, by EU law, continue to be imported. See EURATOM Supply Agency, "Annual Report 2010," p. 28.

39. Before the agreement, and as a result of a U.S. antidumping investigation into Russian enriched fuel, the U.S. government had suspended the import of Russian uranium ore, uranium concentrates, LEU, or HEU. The only uranium product that was permitted in the United States was HEU stock from Russia's weapons program that was to be downblended. See Alexander Pavlov, "Enrichment: Present and Projected Future Supply and Demand," paper presented to the International Atomic Energy Agency, January 26, 2009.

40. U.S. Department of Commerce, "United States and Russian Uranium Agreement Reached," press release, February 1, 2008 (http://2001-2009.commerce.gov/NewsRoom/PressReleases_FactSheets/PROD01_005136).

41. EURATOM estimates global enrichment capacity at 61,000 tSWU, while demand is 47,000 tSWU. See EURATOM Supply Agency, "Annual Report 2010," p. 18.

42. International Atomic Energy Agency, "Management of High Enriched Uranium for Peaceful Purposes: Status and Trends" (Vienna, June 2005), p. 23. In addition, EURATOM reports that Rosatom will no longer reenrich uranium tailings for EU enrichers after 2011. See EURATOM Supply Agency, "Annual Report 2010," p. 17.

43. "Brazil to Start Enriching Uranium at Resende," *World Nuclear News,* January 14, 2009 (www.world-nuclear-news.org/newsarticle.aspx?id=24321).

44. NEA, "Market Competition in the Nuclear Industry," p. 63. In the wake of Fukushima, Japan's priorities in this respect no doubt will change.

45. This method relies on lasers to photo-ionize the U235, physically or chemically changing it and thus allowing it to be separated from the rest of the uranium, thereby increasing the concentration of fissionable material in the uranium. For information on specific enrichment technologies of gaseous diffusion, gas centrifuge, and laser separation, see www.nrc.gov/materials/fuel-cycle-fac/ur-enrichment.html.

46. NEA, "Technology Roadmap: Nuclear Energy" (Issy-les-Moulineaux, France, 2010), p. 22.

47. NEA, "Market Competition in the Nuclear Industry," p. 74.

48. Steve Kidd, "Fuel Fabrication—Outside of the Fuel Cycle?" *Nuclear Engineering International,* January 14, 2010.

49. See International Atomic Energy Agency, *Country Nuclear Fuel Cycle Profiles,* Tehnical Report Series 425, 2nd ed. (Vienna, 2005).

50. NEA, "Market Competition in the Nuclear Industry," p. 77.

51. In addition, Canada's AECL is marketing the Advanced Candu Reactor-1000 (ACR-1000). Second-generation reactors are also being sold, including the APR-1400 Korean reactor that is based on a Westinghouse design.

52. See Generation IV International Forum website for details of the various approaches (www.gen-4.org/index.html).

53. See Massachusetts Institute of Technology, *The Future of the Nuclear Fuel Cycle: An Interdisciplinary MIT Study* (Cambridge, Mass., 2010).

54. NEA, "Market Competition in the Nuclear Industry," p. 29.

55. As of December 7, 2010.

56. For more information, see www.westinghousenuclear.com/ProductLines/Nuclear_Power_Plants/component_manufacturing.shtm.

57. The description of Westinghouse's contracting relationships is taken from U.S. Department of Energy, "DOE NP2010 Nuclear Power Plant Construction Infrastructure Assessment" (Washington, October 21, 2005).

58. Two projects are likely to move ahead in the United States: Southern Company's two units at the Vogtle plant in Georgia, and SCANA's two units at the Summer facility in South Carolina.

59. See "S. Korea Found to Loan $10B for UAE Power Plant," *Hankyoreh* (South Korea), February 12, 2011.

60. Belgium, France, Germany, Japan, and Switzerland have used reprocessed plutonium as mixed oxide fuel, although several of these countries are phasing out its use. A number of countries use reprocessed uranium (repU), although this represents about only about 3–4 percent of the uranium fuel market. See International Atomic Energy Agency, "Management of Reprocessed Uranium: Current Status and Future Prospects" (Vienna, Austria, February 2007), p. 80 and table 22 on p. 38.

61. Alan Hanson, testimony to the Blue Ribbon Commission on America's Nuclear Energy Future, August 30, 2010.

62. See "Radioactive Waste Management," *World Nuclear Association,* June 2009 (www.world-nuclear.org/info/inf04.html).

63. Note that reprocessing is also undertaken to ensure security of supply, not for cost savings. In other words, reprocessing is intended to mitigate any risk of a supply disruption.

64. Bunn and others, "The Economics of Reprocessing vs. Direct Disposal of Spent Nuclear Fuel."

65. NEA, "Market Competition in the Nuclear Industry," p. 80.

66. For more information, see "Uranium Enrichment," *World Nuclear Association* (www.world-nuclear.org/info/inf28.html).

67. NEA, "Market Competition in the Nuclear Industry," p. 88.

68. From an interview with an industry consultant, June 24, 2010.

69. NEA, "Market Competition in the Nuclear Industry," pp. 82–83. See also Arjun Makhijani, "Plutonium End Game: Managing Global Stocks of Separated Weapons-Usable Commercial and Surplus Nuclear Weapons Plutonium" (Takoma Park, Md.: Institute for Energy and Environmental Research, January 22, 2001).

70. NEA, "Market Competition in the Nuclear Industry," pp. 89–90.

71. Nuclear Regulatory Commission Fact Sheet on Dry Cask Storage of Spent Nuclear Fuel (www.nrc.gov/reading-rm/doc-collections/fact-sheets/dry-cask-storage.html).

72. In addition to HLW, the nuclear industry generates low-level waste (LLW), which includes protective clothing, equipment, and short-term radioactive building materials from decommissioned reactors that do not require sequestration. LLW accounts for 90 percent of all radioactive nuclear waste by volume but contains only 1 percent of the radioactivity. Intermediate-level waste (ILW) includes the metal cladding and other mid-term radioactive components from decommissioned plants, chemical sludge, and resins that must be more closely monitored and stored. ILW makes up 7 percent of the waste volume and 4 percent of the radioactivity. In comparison, HLW makes up only 3 percent of the total volume but generates 95 percent of the radioactivity in nuclear waste. For more information, see "Radioactive Waste Management," *World Nuclear Association* (www.world-nuclear.org/info/inf04.html).

73. NEA, "Market Competition in the Nuclear Industry," p. 91.

74. "Europe Steps Towards Shared Repository Concept," *World Nuclear News,* February 11, 2009 (www.world-nuclear-news.org/newsarticle.aspx?id=24640).

75. "Proliferation Resistance Fundamentals for Future Nuclear Energy Systems," STR-332, Report on meeting held in Como, Italy, October 28–31, 2002.

76. "Evaluation Methodology for Proliferation Resistance and Physical Protection of Generation IV Nuclear Energy Systems," Revision 5, Generation IV International Forum, November 30, 2006.

77. See the SILEX website (www.silex.com.au/s03_about_silex/s30_1_content.html).

78. National Nuclear Security Administration, "Draft Nonproliferation Impact Assessment for the Global Nuclear Energy Partnership Programmatic Alternatives" (Washington: Department of Energy, December 2008), p. 52.

79. Meeting with Korea Nuclear Fuel officials in Daejeon, South Korea, July 20, 2010.

4

Industry and Emerging Nuclear Energy Markets

CHARLES K. EBINGER AND SHARON SQUASSONI

As mentioned previously, a notable feature of the nuclear renaissance is the widespread interest in nuclear power, especially in countries without a commercial nuclear infrastructure.[1] According to the International Atomic Energy Agency (IAEA), at least sixty-five countries have expressed such interest, most from outside the industrialized economies of the Organization of Economic Cooperation and Development (OECD), the main locus of nuclear power capacity at present.[2] Most of the capacity growth up to 2030 is expected to occur in the Middle East, South Asia, Southeast Asia, and the Far East.[3] As part of this growth, eleven developing countries are serious candidates for first reactors, although progress in carrying out their plans varies widely (see table 4-1).[4] These countries are drawing new suppliers into the nuclear market (notably China, India, and South Korea) and sparking activity among existing suppliers such as Russia and Japan. Overall, however, many countries will not be able to follow through on growth plans owing to cost, limited grid capacity, and perhaps public resistance.[5]

Countries are moving toward nuclear energy, not to mention other sources of primary fuel, in large part because of mounting demand: between 2008 and 2035 global electricity consumption is expected to increase 80 percent, and 80 percent of that growth will take place in non-OECD countries.[6] Underlying this large increase in electricity demand are population growth, urbanization, concerns about CO_2 emissions from fossil fuel combustion, energy security, and pressure from a growing middle class for goods and services using or produced

Table 4-1. *Status of Nuclear Power in Emerging Nuclear Markets*

Category	Country
Reactors currently operating	Argentina, Brazil, China, India, Pakistan, South Africa, South Korea, Taiwan
Power reactors under construction	Iran[a]
Contracts signed, legal and regulatory infrastructure well developed	United Arab Emirates (UAE), Turkey
Committed plans, legal and regulatory infrastructure developing	Vietnam, Jordan
Well-developed plans but commitment pending	Thailand, Indonesia, Egypt, Kazakhstan
Developing plans	Saudi Arabia, Malaysia

Source: World Nuclear Association, "Emerging Nuclear Energy Countries" (Paris, February 2011).

a. The details of Iran's nuclear program are a matter of enormous international discussion and debate. While it is clear that the country has made significant progress on a nuclear power reactor, most attention on the country's nuclear activities relate to the ambiguity of its intentions and the security implications of the development of an Iranian nuclear weapons capability. The political and security-related complexities of Iran's nuclear program are beyond the scope of this volume. Similarly, given the clandestine nature of the development of the Iranian nuclear program and the lack of ongoing involvement in the program by the established commercial nuclear industry, it is the authors' view that the case of Iran is of limited relevance in this study.

by electricity. Over this period, global population will rise from 6.7 billion to 8.5 billion, with 7.2 billion of the total living in non-OECD countries.[7] Most of this increase will take place in China, India, and the Middle East, with the balance in the rest of the developing world, while the share of global population in the OECD and Russia will decline.

Today nearly 1.4 billion people have no electricity, a figure that may well increase with further population growth, despite movement into the modern energy economy.[8] Urbanization will undoubtedly push demand up as well. For the first time in history, a majority of the world's population is living in urban areas, a trend likely to continue, especially in developing countries. With the movement of hundreds of millions of people from rural areas to cities, more communities will turn from traditional and often free fuels (wood, forest residues, agricultural wastes, bagasse, and dung) to modern fuels such as electricity, natural gas, and petroleum products.

The dramatic growth of the middle class in a number of emerging market nations is also having a large impact on energy consumption. The World Bank predicts that by 2030 the middle class in these nations will jump to 1.2 billion from 430 million in 2000.[9] It is estimated that in Indonesia alone, a country that before Fukushima was developing plans for nuclear power, the number of households with an annual disposal income of $5,000–$15,000 will increase from 36 percent of the population in 2010 to more than 58 percent by 2020.[10]

Climate change, too, will have some of its largest impact in developing countries, which, according to the International Energy Agency (IEA), will be responsible for nearly all of the projected global increase in CO_2 emissions by 2035. In large part, the cause of this rise is coal-fired power in China and India. The urgency of finding alternatives to coal is recognized by others as well, including Indonesia, Pakistan, Poland, South Africa, and Russia.

Compared with developed countries, developing nations rely far more on imported fossil fuels, especially oil, to generate power. When the price of oil on the world market rose to $147 a barrel in 2008, it became clear that dependence on imported fossil fuels for electricity generation can destroy a nation's economy and that fuel diversification is vital for energy security. As prices climbed beyond $100 a barrel, Jordan, a country committed to introducing civilian nuclear energy, was particularly hard hit: 99 percent of its electricity is generated from either oil or gas, 96 percent of which is imported.[11]

Developing countries also see nuclear energy as a possible source of power for desalination plants, especially in the Gulf Cooperation Council (GCC) countries and elsewhere in the Middle East. As the demand for freshwater supplies increases—along with the emphasis on limiting the use of fossil fuels to generate electricity because of the impact of emissions, price volatility, and supply disruptions—the nuclear option will be considered even more viable. Moreover, some countries with large resources of oil or gas, such as the United Arab Emirates (UAE) and Saudi Arabia, are hoping nuclear power will help reduce their domestic use of these fuels in generating power and will boost the financial benefits of exporting them.

For some developing countries, status and geopolitics are undoubtedly important factors in considering the development or expansion of a civilian nuclear energy program. In the view of Turkey's energy minister Hilmi Guler, for instance, nuclear technology is a requirement for a seat at the table with the ten most developed countries in the world.[12]

Challenges for New Nuclear States

As noted in chapters 1 and 2, the expansion of nuclear power in developing countries raises questions about whether countries with regional security concerns may acquire sensitive uranium enrichment or reprocessing technologies under the rubric of a commercial nuclear fuel cycle that gives them the technology to also build a nuclear weapon. Many aspiring nuclear energy states are located in politically volatile regions with competing national interests that contribute to ongoing tensions that can ignite into major political crises. There exists a credible possibility that states confronted with serious geopolitical security threats in the future might use a civilian nuclear energy infrastructure as a base to develop a latent nuclear weapons capability to counter them.

Some threats could arise from a regime's lack of transparency, violent non-state actors, or corrupt individuals. One such individual is Moukhtar Dzhakishev, the former head of Kazakhstan's national nuclear company, Kazatomprom, who was sentenced to fourteen years in jail in March 2010 for stealing state uranium mining assets.[13] Similarly, the former head of the China National Nuclear Corporation was sentenced in 2010 to life in prison for taking bribes.[14] More important, transnational threats and corruption increase the possibility of sabotage or theft of nuclear materials.

Needless to say, a safe and reliable civilian nuclear energy program cannot function without adequate infrastructure, financial resources, human capacity, and legal and regulatory frameworks. The IAEA has issued detailed guidelines focusing on nineteen serious issues to be tackled and a timetable for countries to follow in the conception, design, and launch of a nuclear power program.[15] As the agency points out, the dimensions of the challenge are enormous, involving "a commitment of at least 100 years to maintain a sustainable national infrastructure throughout operation, decommissioning, and waste disposal. For a country with a little-developed technical base the implementation of the first nuclear power plant would, on average, take about 15 years."[16]

A country with sufficient financial resources and a motivated leadership might even hire foreign talent to accelerate its nuclear power timetable, as demonstrated by the UAE, which is likely to have a developed program in about eight years. Although such an approach runs the risk of losing steam if the expatriate advisers leave the country before building a truly indigenous technical capacity, the UAE program should be scrutinized to see how it evolves and whether it represents a new approach for countries embarking on civilian nuclear programs.

With the growth of nuclear power capacity around the world and a commensurate increase in the demand for nuclear fuel, chances are that enrichment and perhaps recycling will also increase. Although there may be few economic incentives for domestic acquisition of these fuel cycle technologies, especially in developing countries, concerns about access to fuel suggest otherwise, especially among new nuclear energy states. Given that fuel supply is dominated by the advanced nuclear states, developing countries fear that political tensions might put their fuel supply in jeopardy. In addition, efforts to restrict fuel cycle technologies, described in other chapters, might also heighten their sensitivity to what they perceive as their sovereign rights and guarantees under Article IV of the Nuclear Nonproliferation Treaty (NPT). Some non-nuclear-weapon states that signed the treaty categorically reject any restrictions related to nuclear technology. This sentiment is particularly strong among Brazil, South Africa, Egypt, and other countries that ardently object to any prohibition against their acquiring the full fuel cycle, even if they have no intention of doing so. On the other hand, some nuclear weapons states and advanced nuclear energy states such as Japan argue that further dissemination of these technologies is actually risky since an enrichment or recycling plant can be used to produce fissile material for nuclear fuel or nuclear weapons. They point to Iran's operation as one that has possibly used commercial or energy security as a smokescreen for a clandestine weapons program. The difficult, seven-year-long discussions on new criteria for restricting enrichment and recycling transfers within the Nuclear Supplies Group (NSG), which culminated in an agreement in June 2011, suggest that even some members of the NSG resist restricting their own future opportunities in this regard.[17]

Commercial Dynamics

The commercial dimensions of expanding nuclear energy in developing countries have direct implications for nonproliferation. First, the market is potentially very large. The IEA estimates that in the period 2008–35 emerging markets will account for two-thirds of the required $16.6 trillion investment in the global electricity infrastructure.[18] Many governments, including those looking to develop civilian nuclear power for the first time, are already entering nuclear commerce at varying stages of the fuel cycle: political leaders are promoting their nuclear industries at the highest levels and some states are establishing or strengthening government-owned "national champions" (in the case of countries with existing fuel cycle activities), or entering into a wide variety of arrangements with public and private actors to support the development of a nuclear industry (in the case of emerging nuclear states). These approaches not only address economic and political concerns over fuel supply but also allow governments to take advantage of commercial opportunities. In other words, government actions to establish or strengthen a nuclear industry can serve both political and commercial ends.

By way of example, the United Arab Emirates awarded a Korean consortium a tender for four nuclear reactors valued at $20.4 billion, a price nearly 50 percent lower than the same nuclear capacity would cost in the United States.[19] The award shocked established vendors in the United States, Europe, and Japan who had lobbied heavily for the tender. While the lower cost was certainly a consideration in the award, a major determining factor was the consortium's offer, backed by the South Korean government, to establish a major training program for UAE nationals both in Korea and in the Emirates so that UAE nationals would be ready to run the first reactor when it is commissioned in

2017. Another critical factor was the assistance offered for the establishment of academic "centers of excellence," which as they evolve will become major training institutions for Emirati nationals as well as people from other GCC, Middle Eastern, and North African nations if their governments decide to embark on civilian nuclear energy programs. A third factor was the significant financing offered by the South Korean government.

This contract marked the birth of a changing international market. Before the Fukushima accident, South Korea hoped to export eighty nuclear power plants over the next two decades.[20] In addition, industry and government officials seem interested in adding uranium enrichment to South Korea's repertoire to increase its competitiveness as an exporter. Meanwhile, China recently unveiled a plan to export two power reactors to Pakistan, in contravention of NSG guidelines, since Pakistan has not signed the NPT and has nuclear weapons. India also plans to export nuclear power reactors, likely its smaller, 300 MWe heavy-water reactors. Russia, which has traditionally supplied the Eastern bloc countries, is seeking new customers for its reactors and services in the Middle East and Asia. These new suppliers will be competing with more established vendors in Europe, Japan, Canada, and the United States. In still other cases, discussed in the next section, nations as diverse as Kazakhstan, Brazil, South Africa, Jordan, and Mongolia are reevaluating their options for entering the global market as providers of uranium, take-back services for spent fuel, or commercial nuclear enrichment, or as repositories for spent nuclear fuel.

As new state actors enter the market, including government-owned companies, a top issue on the international nuclear agenda will be whether they will have and enforce the same strict standards on all aspects of nonproliferation. Clearly, no international regime governing nuclear energy will survive if one or more participants in the regime are able to increase market share by demanding less stringent safety, security, or environmental standards so as to make its commercial bid for a new reactor sale or service more financially or politically attractive.

Nuclear Capacity Growth: New Potential Suppliers

Consider now what is actually taking place in the international nuclear market. These activities are summarized in table 4-2 (p. 105).

China

Unlike many other countries, China is exceeding its plans for commercial nuclear construction. Although the accident at Fukushima prompted Chinese officials to temporarily halt construction, few experts believe this will slow down construction growth significantly. As of 2011, it is operating fourteen nuclear power plants with a capacity of about 11 gigawatts electric (GWe), and an additional twenty-seven plants are under construction.[21] According to a recent official statement, China expects to increase nuclear power from 2 percent of total electricity capacity today to 5 percent by 2020, and 10 percent by 2040–50, necessitating the construction of five or six large-scale reactors a year.[22] Various estimates project that Chinese nuclear capacity will grow to 90 GWe by 2020, 200 GWe by 2030, and 400 GWe by 2050.[23] By 2030 China hopes to add fast breeder reactors, which could significantly expand the global stockpile and transportation of plutonium.

China is a relative newcomer to commercial nuclear power, operating reactors only since the 1990s. While China has relied heavily on foreign firms to construct its current generation of reactors, this policy is changing as China moves to develop its own reactor designs even as it continues to import reactors from France, Russia, the United States, and Canada. Nuclear energy was China's first foray into inviting foreign investment for electricity projects. In the early 1980s the Guangdong provincial government and China Light and Power Company of Hong Kong negotiated the development of the Daya Bay nuclear power plant, which supplies electricity to both Hong Kong and Guangdong. Framatome, an institutional predecessor to AREVA, designed the reactors.

China's demand for energy—and electricity in particular—is growing rapidly, with the IEA projecting a 75 percent rise in primary energy consumption by 2035. Beijing will continue to meet much of that demand through coal, which in 2008 represented 70 percent of China's primary energy consumption, compared with 20 percent for oil, 6 percent for hydropower, 3 percent for natural gas, and 1 percent for nuclear. Coal is even more important in power generation, accounting for nearly 81 percent of the overall fuel mix in 2008, with hydroelectric power and nuclear constituting 17 percent and 2 percent, respectively. Although China is attempting to reduce coal consumption and increase the use of natural gas, nuclear energy, and renewables, the IEA forecasts that by 2035 coal's share in energy will fall to 53 percent, but the absolute volume of coal consumed will rise, along with CO_2 emissions.[24]

China aims to become self-sufficient in nuclear technology, as is evident from its contracts with outside suppliers, including AREVA and Westinghouse, which have included significant provisions for technology transfer. In November 2010 Westinghouse transferred much of its reactor designs in exchange for guaranteed future market sales. China is now poised to reproduce Westinghouse's AP-1000 and the French European pressurized reactor (EPR).[25]

In a step toward commercial recycling, China has constructed a pilot plant with a capacity of 100 tons of heavy metal a year, which is currently being commissioned, and is negotiating the purchase of a recycling plant from AREVA. However, Chinese officials are confident they can build their own plants with capacities of either 200 tons or 400 tons of heavy metal a year.[26] Even though

China is a nuclear weapon state, suppliers will require safeguards on foreign-supplied plants and restrict the technology transfer. For example, AREVA officials have noted publicly that they plan to supply COEX recycling to China, which does not separate out pure plutonium from fission products. In the enrichment sphere, the industry standard is to supply on a black-box basis, avoiding technology transfers. Therefore when China bought a Russian centrifuge enrichment facility in the 1990s, the assemblies were provided on a black-box basis and China was required to put the facility under IAEA safeguards.

Although domestic demand for nuclear energy will keep Chinese suppliers busy, there is no doubt that China will seek to export nuclear power reactors in the future. In 2010 China announced it would build two additional nuclear power reactors at the Chashma site in Pakistan, bending the current NSG rules requiring full-scope safeguards for all nuclear exports. Some analysts question how China will approach future nuclear cooperation agreements with other recipients, or whether this was simply an isolated response to the 2008 U.S.-India nuclear cooperation agreement.

Republic of Korea

South Korea has an advanced nuclear power program with twenty-one reactors supplying 32 percent of total power produced.[27] Five additional reactors are under construction, and six more are on order. Given that it depends almost entirely on imported oil and liquefied natural gas (LNG) to generate power, South Korea plans to expand its domestic nuclear capacity to 60 percent of generated electricity by 2030.[28] To enhance its energy security, South Korea, like others, has moved through various stages of nuclear development, from receiving turnkey projects and technology to developing the technology itself. The push for self-sufficiency will be complete in the next few years, when new construction will be entirely indigenous. South Korean reactors have some of the highest operating capacities in the world and excellent safety records.

South Korean scientists are involved in the development of the next generation of reactors under the Generation IV international program. They are also exploring fast reactor technology and recycling technologies for spent fuel, including DUPIC (direct use of spent power reactor fuel in CANDUs) and pyroprocessing. South Korea is constrained in how it can handle spent fuel by the terms of its existing nuclear cooperation agreement with the United States. All U.S. nuclear cooperation agreements with non-nuclear-weapon states require prior consent for the transfer and alteration in form or content (that is, enrichment or recycling) of nuclear material originating in the United States. About two-thirds of Korean spent fuel is of U.S. origin. The current agreement will expire in 2014, and South Korea reportedly is seeking to loosen the restrictions by requesting advance consent for the transfer and recycling of the fuel.

If granted, it would allow Seoul to ship fuel abroad for recycling or storage. Domestic pyroprocessing would be another option. U.S. and South Korean negotiations will be watched closely for the precedents they might set for managing spent fuel.

In many respects, South Korea has excellent nonproliferation credentials: it has a comprehensive IAEA safeguards agreement, and its Additional Protocol entered into force on February 15, 2004; it is a long-standing member of the Nuclear Suppliers Group and joined the Global Nuclear Energy Partnership in 2008. Nonetheless, its past nuclear weapons program (under military rule in the 1970s) as well as its undeclared activities—ranging from plutonium separation experiments in 1982 to laser enrichment activities as late as 2000—have raised questions about its nonproliferation credibility. While both North Korea and South Korea agreed in 1992 not to engage in domestic enrichment or recycling, this agreement has been undermined by North Korea's nuclear weapons activities, which include weapons testing and the recent unveiling of uranium enrichment capabilities.

South Korea is also emerging as a major commercial competitor in international nuclear commerce. Through full or partial ownership of a number of the country's industrial giants, the government is able to make competitive bids on a host of industrial construction projects. As part of its industrial policy, Seoul is willing either directly or indirectly to subsidize components of a project to win tenders, as in the case of a bid to build four power reactors in the UAE won by the Korea Electric Power Company (KEPCO) consortium. The consortium comprised Samsung, Hyundai, Doosan Heavy Industries, a number of KEPCO subsidiaries, Toshiba, and Westinghouse. As part of the contract with the UAE, the South Korean government agreed to provide a $10 billion loan through the Korea Eximbank to cover part of the $18.6 billion order.[29]

In view of its plan to export eighty power reactors over the next two decades (thereby capturing 20 percent of the export market), South Korea may well emerge as a preferred nuclear supplier for many of the countries considering nuclear power for the first time.[30] Some industry and government officials have suggested that South Korea also develop an enrichment capability to offer a broader range of fuel services. It is not clear which suppliers would agree to export enrichment technology to South Korea and under what restrictions such transfers would occur.

India

India currently operates twenty power reactors having a capacity of 4.4 GWe, which account for 2.7 percent of electricity generated in India. Coal provides 68 percent, hydropower 15 percent, natural gas 8 percent, and renewables the rest. Most are indigenous pressurized heavy-water reactors based on the CANDU design, but two are light-water reactors constructed by Westinghouse. Russia has been building another two light-water reactors at Kudankulam for several years and will likely build more.

India has ambitious plans for increasing nuclear capacity, although to what extent they can be implemented and in what time period remains to be seen. Past plans for expanding nuclear power and other parts of the electricity sector have fallen far short of their targets. However, the 2008 decision by the NSG to open nuclear trade to India may facilitate India's reaching its target goals. Currently, five reactors with a total capacity of 3,564 MW are under construction. India plans to increase its nuclear capacity to 20 GWe by 2020 and up to 63 GWe by 2050, at which time nuclear energy is expected to contribute about 25 percent of total installed electricity capacity.[31] To achieve this prodigious growth, however, India will have to overcome significant inefficiencies in its electricity transmission and distribution infrastructure. One important step will be to reduce the technical and nontechnical losses of the state electricity boards and the central institutions responsible for the power sector. Another will be to persuade state governments to relax tariffs under their control so as to reduce demand. In addition, roughly $600 billion of investment over the next decade is required to improve transmission and distribution infrastructure, and to finance the expansion of generation.[32] India will also have to contend with the political influence of the coal and hydro lobbies and a burgeoning environmental movement opposed to all new hydro, coal, LNG, and other large-scale energy projects.[33] Despite these commercial challenges, India is building vast international commercial linkages as a major exporter of wind, solar, and energy efficiency technologies that may prove invaluable once it is ready to export its commercial nuclear technology.

As for the future, India has long espoused a three-stage plan for nuclear development, which envisions moving from the pressurized heavy-water reactors available today to breeder reactors in the second stage, and eventually a thorium-based fuel cycle (India holds some of the largest thorium reserves in the world). A prototype fast breeder reactor is expected to start operating in several years.

In addition to pursuing these huge domestic plans, the Nuclear Power Corporation of India expects to market 220 MWe and 540 MWe pressurized heavy-water reactors (PHWRs) abroad. Although buyers are still to be identified, these reactors will have significant implications for proliferation since spent fuel can be removed from a PHWR without having to shut it down, so clandestine diversion is more difficult to detect.

Brazil

Faced with rising fuel costs and supply vulnerabilities, Brazil is looking to nuclear power for relief. Nuclear energy has become an important alternative because

Brazil's hydroelectric resources are being adversely affected by the deforestation of the Amazon (which is destroying valuable watersheds) and by the melting of glaciers in the Andes. With the country's extreme dependence on hydroelectricity combined with the large expense of transmitting hydropower over vast distances, nuclear energy is seen as an important component of its fuel mix, which at present consists of 84 percent hydropower and 3–5 percent each of natural gas, biomass, coal, oil, and nuclear power. [34]

Currently Brazil operates two nuclear power plants, one designed by Westinghouse and the other by Kraftwerk Union (later AREVA-NP). A third facility, also designed by Kraftwerk Union, is under construction. While current nuclear capacity is modest at about 2,000 MW, the government recently announced plans for four new reactors by 2020.[35] Brazil is one of the few NPT non–nuclear weapon states to be capable of commercial uranium enrichment, and though small, its facility at Resende is surrounded by controversy. One reason is that it was spun off from the navy's military program to enrich uranium for a bomb. Second, Brazilian officials have negotiated fiercely with the International Atomic Energy Agency to limit inspector access to protect proprietary information about the facility. Third, Brazil intends to enrich uranium for its navy submarine propulsion program, which no non–nuclear weapon state under the NPT has yet done. Such a program will require certain exemptions from IAEA inspection that have never been applied for before. Fourth, Brazil thus far has opposed signing the 1998 Additional Protocol, which is intended to help inspectors detect undeclared activities. Since Brazil does not have its own power reactor technology, it is unlikely to export reactors but may someday export enriched uranium, which it sees as opening a major commercial opportunity.[36]

Emerging Nuclear Energy Markets

Among the sixty-five countries interested in nuclear power, those in Southeast Asia and the Middle East are experiencing particularly high population growth, increased electricity demand, urbanization, and rapidly growing economies. The following discussion provides an overview of both the challenges and opportunities these countries face, supplemented by a profile of South Africa and Kazakhstan, which are also expected to play an important role in the future of international nuclear commerce.

Southeast Asia

The countries in this region have traditionally relied on oil, natural gas, coal, and hydropower for the bulk of their energy needs, and several of them are exporters of these resources. Of the ten member countries of the Association of Southeast Asian Nations, only three have not expressed an interest in nuclear power: Brunei,

Cambodia, and Laos. The others—Vietnam, Indonesia, Thailand, Malaysia, the Philippines, Singapore and Myanmar—are at different levels of commitment. Singapore is conducting a prefeasibility study, Myanmar is reportedly discussing buying a research reactor from Russia and is rumored to be secretly cooperating with North Korea on nuclear weapons, and Thailand has suspended its plans to install two large nuclear power plants by 2020 in the face of domestic opposition to nuclear power and significant political instability. The Philippines, although interested in refurbishing the abandoned Bataan reactor, is unlikely to move quickly because the project will cost about $2 billion. Vietnam, Indonesia, and Malaysia provide a general sense of the status of nuclear development in the region.

Vietnam

In 2008 Vietnam generated 36 percent of its electricity from hydroelectric power, 41 percent from gas, 21 percent from coal, and 2 percent from oil.[37] With electricity demand skyrocketing at the rate of 14 percent a year, the country has rationed electricity supplies.[38] To add to this bleak situation, in 2010 Vietnam incurred a significant power shortfall owing to a series of events across the energy sector: electricity generation was temporarily curtailed at several coal-fired power plants owing to spot coal shortages, gas supply was suspended at the PM3-Ca Mau pipeline for ten days, and hydroelectric facilities struggled with low water levels.[39] As a result, interest in commercial nuclear power quickly intensified.

This interest dates back to 2006 when Hanoi announced that it would have a 2,000 MW plant on line by 2020.[40] A detailed nuclear energy plan put forth in August 2007 set a new target of 8,000 MW by 2025 and under its high-growth scenario envisioned 15–16 GWe installed by 2030, at which time nuclear energy would account for 10 percent of the nation's electricity.[41] In mid-2008 a general law on nuclear energy was passed and work on a comprehensive legal and regulatory framework began.

In 2009 Hanoi announced that it would start construction of two 1,000 MW reactors between 2013 and 2015, with completion expected by 2020. This set off a fierce competition among reactor vendors in Japan, France, the United States, South Korea, and Russia.[42] In November 2009 the Vietnam National Assembly approved resolutions setting out a financing plan for the country's first reactor, to be built in Ninh Thaun Province. In December, after a hotly contested procurement, Hanoi announced that the contract for the first two reactors would be awarded to a consortium representing Electricité de Vietnam (EVN) and the Russian Nuclear Energy State Corporation (Rosatom). Apparently one of the primary reasons Russia won the deal was that Moscow had also agreed to provide Hanoi with submarines and aircraft, which Vietnam wanted to help bolster its claims against China over potentially resource-rich islands in the South China Sea.[43]

Vietnam's civilian nuclear energy goals create a formidable challenge for a system with total electricity production of only 18 GWe. Hanoi will have to invest large resources to upgrade and extend its electricity transmission and distribution networks—as much as $10 billion for power grid development from 2010 to 2015, according to an October 2010 statement by Vietnamese officials. It is far from certain how such a quantum leap in power sector investment can be financed. While the first two reactors, also costing $10 billion, are apparently being financed by Russia, it is unclear how the rest of the nuclear expansion program will be financed, given that Vietnam's gross domestic product (GDP) stands at only $100 billion. Moreover, Vietnam has not yet decided where to procure additional plants, whether from one or several sources, and whether to settle on one standardized design.

As part of its agreement with Moscow, once the reactors are completed an Atomic Research Institute will be built to train Vietnamese and develop a cadre of personnel. Vietnam also has signed nuclear cooperation agreements with China, India, South Korea, and Argentina. Japan, too, is keen to build nuclear power plants in Vietnam, especially after losing the international tender in the UAE. In October 2010 the newly formed International Nuclear Energy Development of Japan Company (JINED) signed an agreement with the government of Vietnam to cooperate on nuclear power technology and materials.[44] JINED will coordinate proposals from the electric utilities, manufacturers, financial institutions, and the government to "develop comprehensive packages to support power plant projects in countries planning new deployments."[45] France and the United States also see Vietnam as a potential new nuclear market. France has been working with Vietnam on the peaceful uses of nuclear energy since 1996, when France's Atomic Energy Commission and the Vietnam National Atomic Energy Commission (Vinatom) signed an agreement—renewed in 2007—to cooperate on nuclear energy application strategies, reactor technology and fuels, and radioactive waste management and safety. In September 2010 French officials agreed to help Vietnam establish two nuclear laboratories.[46]

Also in 2010 U.S. officials signed a multifaceted memorandum of understanding with Hanoi including plans to develop the human resources related to nuclear energy, a requisite safety and security infrastructure providing access to reliable fuel supply, and a plan for managing spent nuclear fuel and radioactive waste technologies. An official nuclear cooperation agreement is still under negotiation. Vietnam has expressed no commercial interest in developing a uranium enrichment or recycling capability but reportedly wants to leave open the possibility of developing a full fuel cycle. The United States finds this stance vexing since it had hoped that its so-called 123 Agreement with the UAE, which contains an explicit prohibition on domestic enrichment and recycling, might serve as a model for other nations.

INDONESIA

Like many other countries, Indonesia benefited from the Atoms for Peace program, under which it inaugurated nuclear research in 1954. With no nuclear power plants, however, Indonesia's 237 million people rely on just 31 GWe of electricity from brown coal (44 percent), oil (29 percent), natural gas (15 percent), and hydro (7 percent) and geothermal (5 percent) energy. As a result, 80 million people still have no access to electricity. Furthermore, electricity consumption is expected to increase from 130 tWh in 2009 to 160 tWh in 2014.[47] Reserve margins are already razor thin, power plant availability is extremely low, and blackouts are frequent. Although opposed by a significant environmental movement, in official circles nuclear power is considered critical for the country's economic future. Moreover, the government believes that the development of nuclear energy can free up oil and gas for export and thus generate valuable foreign exchange earnings.

With 8.7 billion barrels of proven oil reserves, Indonesia was the only Asian member of the Organization of Petroleum Exporting Countries (OPEC) until 2008, when it switched from exporting to importing oil under the pressure of a growing population, subsidized pricing, and thus increased demand. From 2002 to 2007 electricity demand in Bali and Java grew 11 percent a year. Despite its sagging oil production, Indonesia possesses the world's tenth largest proven natural gas reserves, amounting to 185 trillion cubic meters. Indonesia also has extensive coal resources (5.3 billion tons) and has emerged as a major exporter in the Asian and world market. Despite this wealth of resources, only 64 percent of Indonesian households have access to electricity. With the economy expected to sustain its strong growth, electricity supplies will fall short of demand, and the development of alternative energy sources such as nuclear power will become a strategic priority for the government.

In 1989 the National Atomic Energy Agency (BATAN) launched a study of the Muria Peninsula in central Java as a possible site for a nuclear power reactor. A major feasibility report followed in 1996 recommending a 7,000 MW multireactor facility; with the discovery of the giant Natuna gas field in 1997, however, the plant was deferred indefinitely. Another study in 2001 on a plan to expand the national electricity system concluded that a nuclear plant could be linked to the Java/Bali grid by 2016, and that by 2025 the country could build 6–7 GWe of nuclear capacity using proven 1,000 megawatts electrical (MWe) reactor technology at a cost of about $2,000 per kilowatts electrical (kWe) (the Java/Bali grid meets more than 75 percent of the country's electricity demand).[48] In 2006 the National Electricity Planning Scheme 2006–26 and a decree by the president called for tenders for two 1,000 MWe reactors, with awards scheduled for 2010 and commercial operations to begin by 2016–17.[49] Fuel services were to be leased from abroad if such commercial terms were available. Spent fuel would be stored in a central repository. Additional tenders for two units would be awarded by 2016 and be in commercial operation by 2023.[50]

This schedule has clearly slipped, yet it remains official government policy to allocate $4.8 billion for 6 GWe of nuclear power that is supposed to be in operation by 2025. The government insists that by 2017 nuclear energy will meet 2 percent of power demand, rising to 4 percent by 2025.[51] In March 2010 Indonesia's House of Representatives approved the government's plan for nuclear power.[52] Jakarta identified three candidate sites and invited vendors, particularly from South Korea, to join in exploratory discussions.

Despite these plans, it is difficult to assess the government's commitment to nuclear power, especially in view of the environmental movement's strong opposition. Nonetheless, Indonesia has established a dynamic institutional and regulatory structure after studying best international practice, which suggests that at least some people in the government believe the country will eventually have a robust commercial nuclear energy program.

Indonesia has nuclear cooperation agreements with the United States, Australia, Russia, and South Korea. In 2007 officials signed an agreement with the Korea Electric Power Company and the Korea Hydro and Nuclear Power Company to conduct a feasibility study for two 1,000 MWs units at a cost of $3 billion.[53] In addition, BATAN has embarked on a prefeasibility study for a small Korean reactor for power and desalination on Madura Island. Also in 2007, Indonesia signed a nuclear cooperation agreement with Japan for the preparation, planning, and promotion of Indonesia's nuclear power program and for assistance to the government in its public relations efforts to garner support for the program. Unlike many other developing countries, Indonesia has a skilled work force for atomic power since it began training engineers and scientists in the 1980s in anticipation of a major nuclear power expansion.

Malaysia

Malaysia has a fledging nuclear program, which includes a 1 MW research reactor operating since 1982 under the Malaysian Nuclear Agency.[54] In August 2006 the Malaysian Nuclear Licensing Board announced that the country's dependence on fossil fuels had made it necessary to accelerate the nuclear program and to build at least two reactors. In July 2008 the government ordered the state-owned utility, TNB, to establish a task force to examine the feasibility of nuclear energy. This was followed in September by a proclamation stating the government saw no alternative to nuclear power and consequently was setting a target date of 2023 for the commissioning of the nation's first reactor.[55] Malaysia's electric power sector is heavily dependent on natural gas (64 percent) and coal (25 percent). Like other gas exporters, Malaysia lost export revenue when natural gas demand soared as a result of subsidized prices and export volumes declined.[56] Government interest in atomic energy stepped up in May 2010 when the Ministry of Energy, Green Technology, and Water was tasked with finding a site where the first plant could begin operating in 2021. The government announced it would retain a team of consultants to complete a feasibility study by late 2013, develop a legal and regulatory framework, and launch a public relations campaign to garner public support.

In January 2011 the government formed a new company, the Malaysian Nuclear Power Corporation, to spearhead planning for the development of nuclear power plants in the country.[57] Kuala Lumpur is currently preparing a comprehensive Atomic Energy Act in accordance with all IAEA standards, while the Atomic Energy Licensing Board, established in 1985 to enforce the provisions of the Atomic Energy Licensing Act of 1984, is in consultations with other governmental institutions about how to strengthen the nation's legal infrastructure to oversee nuclear activities. The new act is expected to address all requisite concerns including export controls and provide a list of offenses and full delineation of criminal and civil penalties for the breach of its provisions. The government is studying best international practice for the contents of a nuclear generation license. Finally, Malaysia is rationalizing all the acts pertaining to nuclear power development.

In response to these developments, many reactor vendors are showing an interest in Malaysia, although Korean suppliers appear to be moving ahead of their competitors, with a Korean consortium already conducting a prefeasibility study. The Malaysians also have a memorandum of understanding with Indonesia's Nuclear Energy Regulatory Agency about sharing regulatory experience and training.

The financing of Malaysia's plants is a controversial issue. Malaysia had originally intended to finance its first reactor with public funds ($7 billion) but is now seeking private financing. Although it had 40 billion ringgit (equivalent to US$13 billion) set aside for the first two reactors as part of a larger national economic transformation program, the assumption was that 400 billion ringgit would be forthcoming from the private sector for economic development.[58] Public acceptance for nuclear energy is still an unknown but to date has not been a factor in the country's nuclear plans.

The Middle East: Gulf Oil Suppliers

In the wake of rapid population growth and economic expansion, energy and electricity demand in the Gulf Cooperation Council countries is accelerating at a staggering rate.[59] Energy consumption has grown by 74 percent since 2000 and is projected to double again by 2020.[60] With nearly 37 percent of the world's proven oil reserves and 25 percent of global gas reserves, the GCC region would at first glance appear to be a poor candidate for a major nuclear power expansion. Oil and gas exports are the main drivers of the GCC economies, and hydrocarbon reserves have led to a rapid expansion of the industrial production of steel, aluminum, petrochemicals, plastics, and refineries. Aviation fuel growth rates are among the highest in the world.

Despite the GCC's incredible resources, soaring electricity demand, combined with highly subsidized prices, is cutting into export volumes of oil and natural gas and thus into government cash flows. At the same time, emerging concerns about energy and carbon intensity and uncertainty about the availability and future pricing of Qatari gas have led some GCC countries to look at other non-carbon-based alternatives (solar, wind, energy efficiency, and demand-side management). With Qatar, Bahrain, the United Arab Emirates, and Kuwait all in the top ranks of global emitters of greenhouse gas on a per capita basis, attention is turning to the possible role of nuclear power as a future GCC energy resource.

Many recognize that the region's scarce water resources (already supplied largely by desalination), decreasing arable land, accelerating air pollution, and projected increases in coastal flooding owing to climate change can no longer be ignored. Nuclear energy, some argue, could be vital for desalination and over the longer term for moving the region toward a hydrogen economy. Furthermore, with domestic demand for oil and gas skyrocketing, less oil and gas will be available for export and thus less revenue for other pressing social and economic priorities.

Against this backdrop, at a summit meeting in Riyadh in December 2006 the GCC decided to explore the idea of establishing a joint nuclear energy program by forming a group within the GCC Secretariat to conduct a prefeasibility study in concert with technical experts from the IAEA. This collaboration led to reports and workshops guiding the GCC states in designing the requisite legislation, infrastructure, and training in critical matters such as nuclear reactor efficiencies, nuclear safety, and nonproliferation.

Effecting a common approach to nuclear energy development in the GCC has been stymied by disagreements over which country should host the reactors. The GCC has been able to agree on the construction of a high-capacity power grid connecting plants fueled by oil and natural gas in Saudi Arabia, Kuwait, Qatar, and Bahrain with the United Arab Emirates. The interconnection is expected to be finished in 2011. For nuclear energy, however, countries seem to be embarking on separate national plans for atomic power development.

United Arab Emirates

Despite its vast energy resources the UAE faces a looming supply crunch in the power sector as burgeoning economic growth puts further pressure on its already strained electricity sector, which relies primarily on natural gas to meet energy demands. Although the country also has the seventh largest natural gas reserves in the world and produced 1.725 trillion cubic feet of natural gas in 2009, rising electricity demand has forced it to become a net importer of natural gas, with imports of around 2 billion cubic feet a day (bcf/d) from Qatar, entering through the Dolphin Pipeline. The UAE's chronic shortage of natural gas is bound to continue as the country's primary energy demand is expected to grow by 71 percent by 2019.[61] The country therefore has ample reason to diversify its sources of electricity generation in order to increase its energy security while preserving gas and liquids for its long-term future and international trade.

The UAE's interest in a nuclear power program began in 2008 with the findings of a national energy study by an interagency working group established by the Economic and Energy Affairs Unit of the country's Executive Affairs Authority that estimated electricity demand will increase 9 percent a year to 2020, precipitating a shortfall in power supply of 15,000 to 20,000 MW.[62] In its final report, titled "Policy of the United Arab Emirates on the Evaluation and Potential Development of Peaceful Nuclear Energy," the group identified the issues and steps the country will need to consider in developing a civil nuclear power program.

The report laid out legal and institutional issues that had to be addressed, international commitments that had to be negotiated or signed, and required technical and financial arrangements. It called for the creation of a Nuclear Energy Program Implementation Organization to lead an evaluation of nuclear power and the development of related human, technical, and security infrastructure; made provision for the creation of an independent regulator (the Federal Authority for Nuclear Regulation); and summarized this entity's responsibilities and mechanisms for the maintenance of its independence. The report also set out the requirements for the legal framework necessary to underpin a nuclear power sector, including domestic legislation on liability, spent-fuel management, and the decommissioning of plants. The necessary international commitments pertained to the country's evaluation of nuclear power and any decision to proceed with civil nuclear power development. Most notably, the report included a commitment to renounce "any intention to develop a domestic enrichment and reprocessing capability and undertaking to source fuel from reliable and responsible foreign suppliers.[63] Following negotiations with the United States in 2008, the UAE government signed a nuclear cooperation agreement on May 21, 2009, which entered into force on December 17, 2009.

The agreement provides for a "comprehensive framework for peaceful nuclear cooperation . . . based on a mutual commitment to nuclear nonproliferation" and covers a period of thirty years.[64] Under its terms, the United Arab Emirates agrees to forgo enrichment and reprocessing for thirty years and is permitted to receive "the transfer of technology, material, equipment (including reactors), and components for nuclear research and nuclear power production."[65] The agreement with the United States suggested that the UAE was willing to forgo its rights to enrich and reprocess nuclear fuel as the price for convincing the world of its program's peaceful intentions. The commercial arrangements outlined in the 2008 policy document reflect a clear preference for third-generation technology. Any partnerships with international companies would follow a build-own-and-operate model predicated on a joint venture agreement between the government and international investors. The business model suggested for the UAE's nuclear program would replicate the partnerships between the government and companies in the water and power sectors.

In a follow-up document, the government defined criteria to be met in construction of the plants: for example, the prime contractor must deliver according to the contract schedule, provide the entire scope of supply, and be willing to abide by the UAE's contractual terms. It also took a "technology-agnostic approach" in developing the program, examining a number of technologies before producing a short list of reactor technologies: AREVA's EPR, Westinghouse's AP1000, Korea Hydro and Nuclear Company's APR1400, and GE-Hitachi's ABWR. In its commercial negotiations for the contract, the UAE engaged in "competitive dialogue" with potential bidders that outlined technology-neutral requirements linked to a target cost. Contract incentives were focused on early delivery, reduced cost, and the maintenance of top-class quality and safety. Owing to its strong financial position, the UAE was able to determine the structure of the bid, demanding an integrated bid in which the prime contractor and subcontractors would be jointly and severally liable for the project instead of having separate responsibilities, as in a consortium. According to energy planners at the Executive Affairs Authority (EAA), a Korean consortium led by the Korea Electric Power Company (KEPCO) was the most accommodating in this regard as it already operated under a model similar to the one that the UAE was looking to implement. EAA officials found the established nuclear vendors in Japan and France less willing to adapt their bids to the new model, although at least one vendor told the authors that they were not informed on a timely basis of the requirement. South Korea also appealed to the UAE's schedule: in the view of UAE officials, Korean companies had proven themselves able to construct a nuclear fleet in a relatively short space of time and to a predictable schedule.[66] In December 2009 the UAE announced a contract award to KEPCO for the construction of four APR1400 reactors, including the associated maintenance, fuel supply, and training and education of UAE personnel.

The timetable for implementing the UAE program is ambitious and unprecedented: the first reactor is to be connected to the grid by 2017, and the remaining three reactors by 2020. The four-unit nuclear facility is to be built at Braka on the Arabian Gulf in the emirate of Abu Dhabi. In November 2010 the Emirates Nuclear Energy Corporation (ENEC) received two licenses from the Federal Authority for Nuclear Regulation permitting work to start on non-plant-related features at Braka, as well as on mechanical elements of the plants themselves. In December 2010 ENEC submitted a full application for a construction license, but at the time of writing it was still under review. In January 2011 the IAEA sent a delegation to conduct an integrated nuclear infrastructure review, an assessment of a country's progress toward the development of a civil nuclear program conducted at the request of a member state. The resulting mission in 2011 found the program "progressing well," with some "good practices for other countries starting nuclear power programs to consider."[67]

Aware of the need for a systematic approach to building indigenous technical capacity for its nuclear venture, the UAE has established several academic and vocational training programs to prepare both the engineers and operators to run and maintain its plants. To this end, it has also engaged with numerous international institutions to launch exchange and learning initiatives. A broad base of domestic knowledge will be critical to the success of the UAE's nuclear program; otherwise, it will have to rely more on imported expertise and will risk becoming unsustainable.

While the UAE has definitively stated its intention to forswear enrichment, some questions about other aspects of the fuel cycle remain unanswered. According to the government, the agreement with KEPCO provides for "nuclear fuel supply and operation and maintenance support." A regulatory filing stipulates that KEPCO will supply fuel for the program for the first three years of operations, but beyond that, no public policy is in place for fuel supply. In 2008 the UAE announced that it had pledged $10 million toward an international fuel bank initiative comprising a stockpile of low-enriched uranium fuel administered by the IAEA. The IAEA's governing body approved the multilateral facility in December 2010.[68] Whether arranged through bilateral agreements or a multilateral mechanism, the secure supply of fuel will be a high priority for the UAE nuclear program.

Saudi Arabia

As the world's second largest producer of oil and tenth largest producer of natural gas, the Kingdom of Saudi Arabia has long depended on hydrocarbons to supply domestic energy and drive economic growth. In 2008, 62 percent of the country's total primary energy consumption rested on oil, the remaining 38 percent on natural gas. In the same year, fully 57 percent of all electricity was generated from oil, the remaining 43 percent from gas-fired operations.[69]

Buoyed by rising oil prices and increasing industrial investment, the Saudi Arabian economy is expected to grow about 4.5 percent a year to 2015.[70] This growth, coupled with rapid population growth, is driving up energy, electricity, and water demand. In 2005 the International Energy Agency predicted that Saudi Arabia's electricity demand would increase by about 4 percent a year to 2030, doubling the kingdom's electricity demand by 2035.[71] The Saudi Electric Company, the major national electric utility, is more bullish in its projection, forecasting total load capacity in excess of 65,000 MW by 2018, and 75,000 MW by 2020, up from an estimated 44,000 MW in 2010.[72] A growing water shortage is also a major driver. With desalination already accounting for 70 percent of the kingdom's water utilization, nuclear energy is considered a vital long-term source of power both for electricity and for desalination.

Although Saudi Arabia is better endowed with oil and natural gas resources than many of its neighbors, its reliance on finite hydrocarbon resources to meet the burgeoning demand for electricity and water comes at an increasingly high economic and environmental cost. As Hashim Yamani, president of the King Abdullah Center for Atomic and Renewable Energy (KA-CARE), notes, "Oil exports and economic growth will be constrained if there is no mix of alternative energy. We won't be able to leverage prices of oil to build our institutions."[73]

With such considerations in mind, Riyadh recently expressed renewed interest in civil nuclear power as a means of diversifying the existing electricity demand mix and of freeing up oil and gas reserves currently used in power generation for export. Saudi Arabia's ambitions for civil nuclear power may also be based, at least in part, on a desire for both the industrial opportunities and the prestige that such a capability offers. Whatever the reason, its interest was clearly evident in December 2006 when, under Saudi leadership, the Gulf Cooperation Council launched a "joint program in nuclear technology for peaceful purposes according to international standards and arrangements."[74] In May 2008 Saudi Arabia and the United States signed a memorandum of understanding on civil nuclear energy cooperation.[75] Though not legally binding, the agreement committed the two governments to "establish a comprehensive framework for cooperation in the development of environmentally sustainable, safe, and secure civilian nuclear energy through a series of complementary agreements."[76] The United States indicated it would assist Saudi Arabia in the development of nuclear technology for medicine, industry, and power generation and in the development of "human and infrastructure resources." The text of the agreement made explicit reference to Saudi Arabia's intent to "rely on international markets for nuclear fuel and to not pursue sensitive nuclear technologies."

The kingdom's nuclear ambitions took several more steps forward in April 2010 when the government issued Royal Decree 35/A, stating "the development of atomic energy is essential to meet the Kingdom's growing requirements for energy to generate electricity, produce desalinated water and reduce reliance on depleting hydrocarbon resources."[77] The decree also included a plan to establish the Center for Atomic and Renewable Energy in Riyadh to serve as the competent agency for treaties on nuclear energy signed by the kingdom, supervise works related to nuclear energy and radioactive waste products, and act as the kingdom's representative to the IAEA. Two months later, Saudi Arabia commissioned Pöyry, a Finnish energy and engineering consultancy, to draft a "national vision and high-level strategy in the area of nuclear and renewable energy applications . . . and help define [the center's] strategy, operating model, key short and longer term priorities, and the immediate initiatives and action plan."[78]

As the largest economy and the largest consumer of electricity on the Arabian Peninsula, Saudi Arabia has attracted great interest among commercial nuclear vendors around the world, although the business model and operational details of a potential Saudi civil nuclear program have not been made public.[79] U.S. commercial support became evident in July 2010, when three leading nuclear companies—Shaw Group, Toshiba, and Exelon—agreed to jointly pursue contracts for the design, engineering, construction, and operation of new nuclear power plants in Saudi Arabia. Under the terms of the "teaming agreement," the group would jointly develop Toshiba's advanced boiling water reactor (ABWR).[80] During a December 2010 visit to the King Abdullah Center, U.S. deputy secretary of commerce Francisco Sanchez said the Saudis "seem to be very committed to having civil nuclear as part of what generates energy for them and to do it relatively quickly, like within the next 10 years," adding that U.S. suppliers would be appealing to Saudi officials.[81] On June 1, 2011, KA-CARE announced its intention to have 16 nuclear reactors in operation by 2030.[82]

By early 2011 Saudi Arabia was moving toward bilateral cooperation with a number of countries. Furthering a dialogue that started in 2007, in October 2010 the Saudi cabinet agreed to a draft cooperation agreement with Russia, and negotiations to a final agreement continued in December 2010.[83] In January 2011 Japan offered aid in technical capacity building and training and in developing the rules and regulations necessary for a nuclear energy program.[84] In February 2011 Saudi Arabia signed its first official nuclear cooperation agreement, in which the kingdom and France pledged to "enhance cooperation in the fields of production, use, and transfer of knowledge of peaceful uses of nuclear energy."[85] And in March 2011 the Saudi cabinet approved a draft agreement on nuclear energy cooperation with Argentina.[86] Although the 2008 memorandum of understanding with the United States indicated the kingdom intended to rely on international markets for nuclear fuel and not to pursue sensitive nuclear technologies, it left open the door to the possibility of developing other parts of the fuel cycle: indeed, the contract with Pöyry on drafting a future national nuclear strategy asked the company not to exclude fuel enrichment in the long term.[87] Some in the nuclear power industry believe that Saudi Arabia will build up to thirty-two nuclear units to meet its desalination and electricity needs.[88] For a variety of reasons, the kingdom may be more interested in buying turnkey plants in the near future while moving to develop its own technical and administrative capacity. The Saudis were very impressed by the way South Korea entered the nuclear technology market and believe that such an industry could be a future source of revenue for the day when the kingdom's oil and gas run out.[89]

Saudi Arabia has also embarked on a major mapping of its uranium potential, thought by some analysts to be extensive though its size and quality remain unproven at this time. If Saudi Arabia were found to have large-scale uranium reserves, it could make uranium enrichment viable and provide a credible motive for developing the front end of the fuel cycle. Long-standing rumors of Saudi Arabian financing of Pakistan's nuclear weapons program cast proliferation shadows on such an enterprise.[90]

Other Middle Eastern States

Several other countries in the Middle East have also expressed an interest in nuclear power, most notably Turkey, Jordan, and Egypt.

TURKEY

Turkey's primary energy sector relies heavily on hydrocarbon imports, which have been rising in parallel with the country's strong economic growth since 2000. In 2008 oil provided 37 percent of all energy consumption, followed by natural gas at 18 percent and coal at 17 percent. These were the three largest contributors to Turkey's energy mix. Fuel used in generating electricity was dominated by fossil fuels, with natural gas providing 49 percent of power, followed by coal at 28 percent, and oil adding a further 3 percent.[91]

Electricity use in Turkey has more than tripled in twenty years, from about 50 terrawatt hours (TWh) in 1990 to 162 TWh in 2008, and from 2001 to 2008 grew by 8.8 percent.[92] According to the Ministry of Energy and Natural Resources, Turkey will need to invest $70 billion in energy production and ancillary distribution networks by 2020 to meet its projected demand. The cost of net energy imports—which totaled $46 billion to $47 billion in 2008 alone—is expected to soar.[93]

In order to meet the growing demand and balance its grid, Turkey has become both an importer and exporter of electricity and carries out electricity trade with most of its neighbors (including Bulgaria, Azerbaijan, Iran, Georgia, Armenia, Syria, Iraq, and Greece).[94] Interconnection with Europe through the European Network of Transmission System Operators of Electricity is also being explored.[95]

The vast majority of Turkey's growing demand for electricity has been met with newly built gas-fired plants, which increased output by 48 to 94.4 TWh a year between 2000 and 2009, accounting for 72 percent of overall power growth.[96] Despite this prodigious growth, Turkey's domestic hydrocarbon resources do not come close to meeting its energy needs. In 2008 Turkey produced 42,000 barrels of oil a day and about 35 billion cubic feet of natural gas. Remaining recoverable reserves of natural gas are estimated at 210 billion cubic feet.[97] The country imports more than 98 percent of all the natural gas it consumes.[98] As is the case with other countries in the region, Turkey is considering nuclear power as a means of reducing its import dependence on fossil fuels to meet its rising energy demand.

Turkey has a long history of attempting to develop nuclear power, and the current revival is the sixth such venture. It was one of the first participants in President Dwight Eisenhower's Atoms for Peace Initiative and has had a nuclear regulatory body since its General Secretariat for Atomic Energy Commission was chartered in 1956. The secretariat was reorganized into the Turkish Atomic Energy Authority (TAEK) in 1982. Along with its subsidiary research institutions—Çekmece Nuclear Research and Training Center (ÇNAEM) and Sarayköy Nuclear Research and Training Center (SANAEM)—TAEK and its predecessor have therefore overseen Turkey's nuclear program for over fifty years.[99] In 2006 the IAEA announced that Turkey had "achieved IAEA Milestones related to establishing a regulatory framework and controlling occupational radiation exposure."[100]

The country launched its first feasibility study for nuclear power in the early 1960s and opened its first research center, ÇNAEM, in 1961.[101] Nuclear power first appeared in Turkish development plans in 1968. In 1983 a 600 MWe reactor, to be built at the Mediterranean site of Akkuyu Bay, made it to the planning stage. Akkuyu was revived and underwent several rounds of bidding in the 1990s before once again being shelved in 2000. These plans failed largely because of financing problems.[102] In 2004 the government commissioned a study to look into potential sites for a nuclear plant, and in 2006 it sent a draft bill for new nuclear projects to parliament. Following a dispute between the president and the parliament, the new bill was passed into law in November 2007. The political commitment to increasing nuclear penetration in the generation mix was reemphasized in a May 2009 policy statement titled "Electricity Energy Market and Supply Security Strategy" and issued by the prime minister's office. It set out a goal of 5 percent nuclear power by 2020.[103] In 2011 Undersecretary Metin Kilci of the Energy Ministry said the country's target was to have "a minimum 20 reactors in operation by 2030."[104]

TAEK officials favor having the Turkish government in charge of future nuclear power or putting it under a public-private partnership. Accordingly, recent nuclear deals have taken the form of intergovernmental agreements between the government and international partner consortiums, conditional on the approval of financing from the partner consortium's government.[105] This was the approach in the recent agreement between Turkey and Russia for the construction of up to four nuclear reactors on the old Akkuyu site. According to TAEK, the first nuclear power plant is "expected to be online after 2020."[106] Completed in May 2010 and ratified by the Turkish parliament in July 2010, the Turkish-Russian agreement calls for the formation of a joint stock company by the participating Russian entity, Atomstroyexport.[107] Initially, Atomstroyexport will be wholly funded by the state nuclear agency Rosatom, the Russian party to the agreement. Rosatom will serve as the contractor for the construction of a VVER 1200 nuclear reactor.[108] The Turkish government has significantly limited its financial risk by ensuring that Rosatom is responsible for all construction costs.

During the operations phase of the reactors, Rosatom will hand over increasing ownership stakes to the Turkish government.[109] Under the terms of the contract, Rosatom's ownership stake may never fall below 51 percent. The joint stock company is to remain the ownership entity for all nuclear plants built under the agreement. Once the four reactors are built, Turkey and the company will operate under a negotiated power purchase agreement. The Turkish state single-purchaser, Turkish Electricity Trading Company, is obligated to buy 70 percent of the electricity from reactors 1 and 2 and only 30 percent of the electricity from units 3 and 4. The term of the power purchase agreement is fifteen years.

In addition to the commercial arrangements, the Turkey-Russia agreement covers a range of fuel and decommissioning issues. Over the life of the project, the joint stock company is liable for decommissioning costs and spent fuel disposal costs. It is to pay 0.15¢/kWh, generated into separate funds for each contingency. Furthermore, the radioactive fuel for the reactors will be provided on long-term contracts between supplier entities and the company. The contracts allow for a separate agreement under which any fuel of Russian origin used in the reactors could be returned to Russia for spent fuel reprocessing. The agreement also includes provisions for local Turkish content and expertise to be used in the construction and operation of the plant "to the extent possible."[110] In light of the Fukushima accident in Japan, Turkey's minister of energy and natural resources Taner Yildiz has indicated that final approval for the Turkish-Russian project would likely be delayed by twelve to eighteen months.[111]

The Turkish government's preference for intergovernmental agreements and government-backed financing is also evident in the collapse in late 2010 of negotiations between Turkey and the Korea Electric Power Corporation for a second nuclear facility. The deal is said to have fallen apart over multiple issues, including Korea's failure to approve financial guarantees for the project and the distribution of ownership shares in the project company.[112] Turkey has since engaged Japan's Toshiba in talks to build a second nuclear reactor facility at Sinop on the Black Sea coast.[113] Toshiba has so far been successful in gaining the required support of government-tied entities for its bid, with the Japan Bank for International Cooperation signing on to help finance the project.[114] Yildiz has also said that he hopes to conclude negotiations with the Toshiba team (which includes the embattled Japanese electricity company TEPCO) before the end of 2011.[115]

Turkey currently has international nuclear cooperation agreements with Azerbaijan, Kazakhstan, Kyrgyzstan, Uzbekistan, Tajikistan, Canada, Argentina, South Korea, France, and the United States, among others. Turkey has uranium deposits and is in the early stages of developing uranium conversion and fuel fabrication capabilities. Energy Minister Guler has said that Turkey is interested in fuel fabrication but not enrichment.[116]

Turkey geopolitically straddles the Middle East and Europe, and this is reflected in its views about nonproliferation and nuclear energy. It is committed to the nonproliferation regime but would like to play a brokering role between the "haves" and "have-nots." Two examples illustrate its uneasy stance—its collaboration with Brazil to help broker a swap of highly enriched uranium for fuel for Iran's Tehran research reactor, and its efforts within the NSG to eliminate subjective criteria restricting enrichment and reprocessing transfers. Turkey reportedly does not wish to foreclose future enrichment or reprocessing for itself.

Jordan

Jordan faces serious challenges in its energy sector. Rising energy demand and a lack of domestic resources hinder economic development and growth and saddle the country with high energy costs. This situation worsened as oil prices escalated throughout the first decade of the twenty-first century, prompting the government to intensify its efforts to diversify the energy economy, especially through the development of domestic energy resources.

Jordan's current National Master Strategy of Energy (NMSE) estimates that primary energy demand will increase 4.5 to 6.2 percent a year between 2007 and 2020, depending on low- and high-growth assumptions, respectively.[117] Demand in the electricity sector is expected to increase 7.4 percent a year in the period 2007–20. Meeting this demand would require an additional 4,000 MW at a cost of $4.2 billion to $5.2 billion, excluding transmission.[118]

The country is highly dependent on imports, which accounted for 96 percent of all energy use in 2007. Moreover, fossil fuels dominate the energy sector, accounting for 98 percent of all energy consumption in 2009. The cost of imported fossil energy has risen dramatically, from $1.1 billion 2003 to $3.9 billion in 2008. This import bill is accounting for an increasingly larger share of GDP: rising from 11 percent to 20 percent over the same period.[119]

Water scarcity is also a major factor in Jordan's energy future: with rising energy demand and population growth, as well as limited indigenous water resources, demand for water is rapidly outstripping supply. In current estimates, water demand exceeds supply by 30 percent; if this trend continues, per capita water supply could decline to levels signifying an absolute water shortage.[120] To address this situation, one option being discussed on the supply side is to build desalination capacity, but such facilities also require large amounts of electricity.

Given its worsening energy security situation, Jordan is seriously considering nuclear power, as seems clear from the advanced program in place, with committed plans and efforts to develop a legal and regulatory infrastructure to support it.[121] In July 2004 King Abdullah II authorized a royal commission to review and update the NMSE to improve the "availability and openness of the energy market . . . and achieve energy supply security."[122] After examining the costs and benefits of various electricity sector scenarios, the commission concluded that Jordan should develop a mechanism to promote nuclear power as part of its overall program to expand electricity generation. On January 19, 2007, the king announced that Jordan was "looking at nuclear power for peaceful and energy purposes."[123] The decision to incorporate nuclear energy in Jordan's energy mix was formalized with the publication of the updated master strategy in December 2007, which called for 6 percent of the mix to be met by nuclear power by 2020.

In another important development for the nuclear program, the government announced in December 2010 that the central region of the country has 70,000 metric tons of uranium (tU), and that additional reserves totaling 140,000 tU could be extracted from phosphate countrywide. Uranium exploration in central Jordan is now at an advanced stage, with AREVA of France becoming a key partner in assessing resources there. With the signing of a nuclear cooperation agreement between Jordan and France in August 2008, the government and AREVA entered a mining agreement in February 2010 granting AREVA a twenty-five-year concession in central Jordan.[124] Uranium production in this area is expected to become operational in 2013 and to yield 2,000 tU annually.[125] Jordan's overall strategy is to "secure fuel for [its] plants," and to use the proceeds from uranium extraction to support the development and establishment of its first nuclear power plant.[126]

In July 2007 the government amended the existing legal and regulatory framework governing nuclear activities in Jordan and passed two new laws separating management and promotion of the nuclear program under the Jordan Atomic Energy Commission (JAEC) from regulatory activities under the Jordan Nuclear Regulatory Commission. Both organizations fall under the prime minister's portfolio and are governed by a board of directors with broad representation, including members from other relevant government agencies.

To aid in training local human resources, the JAEC has instituted two programs: to build a subcritical assembly and the Jordan Research and Training Reactor (JRTR), both to be housed at the Jordan University for Science and Technology (JUST). In November 2008 JAEC signed a contract with the China Institute of Atomic Energy for the construction of the subcritical assembly, which would allow students to "modify core configurations, work closely with the reactor core, and familiarize themselves with the basic features of the reactor."[127] In December 2009 JAEC awarded a consortium of the Korean Atomic Energy Research Institute and Daewoo Engineering and Construction a $173 million contract for construction of the 5 MW JRTR.[128] It is expected to be commissioned in 2015 and to produce radioisotopes for medicine, agriculture, and industry; provide training facilities; and serve as a nuclear science and technology center.[129] Jordan's objective is to have a 700–1200 MW Generation III or Generation III+ reactor operating by 2019.[130]

The total capacity of the country's power system is now 2,400 MW, which would not be sufficient to handle the addition of a large nuclear reactor. The JAEC has conducted grid capacity studies to assess how to accommodate the planned nuclear power plants. Total generation capacity is expected to grow through the addition of nonnuclear generation—such as natural gas—and through the possible establishment or expansion of interconnections and export agreements.[131]

To achieve its goals, the JAEC is implementing a two-track strategy for the selection of an engineering, procurement, and construction contractor who would provide the reactor technology and construction; and for the selection of a strategic partner for a joint utility that would operate the plant. In January 2010 the JAEC sent a questionnaire to nuclear vendors and received responses in March 2010.[132] Then in May 2010 it arrived at a short list of three firms and technologies for its nuclear program: AREVA and Mitsubishi Heavy Industries (ATMEA 1), AECL Canada (CANDU-6), and Atomstroyexport (AES-92 VVER-1000).[133] In January 2011 the JAEC requested bids from these three firms.[134] The final bids were due at the end of March 2011, with the winning bid to be announced later in 2011 and a contract expected to be signed in early 2012.

In addition, Jordan has been searching for a strategic partner for the utility operator. In February 2011 it called for bids from GDF Suez of France, Datang of China, Rosatom of Russia, and Kansai Electric Power of Japan.[135] Under the business model that JAEC has proposed, the strategic partner and the government will own 50 percent, and the remaining 50 percent will be open to other investors. The operator of the plant will sell electricity to Jordan's National Electric Power Company, the transmission asset provider and system operator in Jordan, under a power purchase agreement.[136] The project is to be financed under a typical limited recourse approach, with debt (70 percent) and equity (30 percent) provided from a variety of sources. The Jordanian government will also contribute financing, principally from uranium mining revenues.

As of February 2011, Jordan had signed nuclear cooperation agreements with France, China, South Korea, Canada, Russia, the United Kingdom, Argentina, Spain, Japan, Romania, and Turkey and is currently in negotiations with the United States, Italy, and Czech Republic.[137] Jordan also has memorandums of understanding for nuclear cooperation with the United States and Japan.[138]

A question that has arisen in its negotiations on a nuclear cooperation agreement with the United States is whether Jordan will pursue domestic uranium enrichment. The United States would prefer that states rely on the existing commercial market for fuel cycle services, whereas Jordan does "not agree on applying conditions and restrictions outside of the NPT on a regional basis or a country-by-country basis."[139] However, Jordanian officials have also indicated that in the near term it does not make economic sense to pursue enrichment; rather, Jordan will likely aim to process its uranium ore domestically and then ship it outside the country for enrichment and fuel fabrication (although JAEC has stated that the JRTR could house a fuel fabrication plant in the future). [140]

Egypt

Egypt has been highly dependent on oil and natural gas for energy and electricity consumption. However, growing demand for both oil and gas is constricting domestic supplies, which, particularly in the case of natural gas, are also exported in abundance. Nearly all of its energy comes from oil (46 percent of its primary energy consumption) and natural gas (49 percent).[141] Hydrocarbons also dominate the electricity sector. In 2008 Egypt's installed capacity totaled 23.4 GWe, of which 20.3 GWe was conventional thermal generation, 2.8 GWe hydropower, and 0.3 GWe wind power.[142] Natural gas is used to generate about 69 percent of the nation's electricity, with oil, hydropower, and wind accounting for the rest.[143] In addition, in a government-endorsed effort to reduce dependency on oil, compressed natural gas is increasingly used in the transportation sector. This is expected to reduce the amount of gas previously marked for export and thus require Egypt to accelerate its natural gas production.[144]

The rapid increases in domestic gas demand in the electricity and transportation sectors mean that Egypt finds itself facing a growing supply crunch. Moreover, the combination of an aging infrastructure, lack of maintenance, and rising consumption has led to blackouts.[145] In response, the Ministry of Energy and Electricity is adopting a multipronged strategy to diversify the nation's energy sector through wind and solar resources, stronger ties with its neighbors in Jordan, Syria, and Lebanon, efficiencies throughout the power sector, and civil nuclear generation.[146] Specifically, Egypt plans on having four nuclear power plants by 2025.[147]

While it has no operational power reactors, Egypt has a long history in pursuing a nuclear energy program. Its Atomic Energy Commission (now the Egypt Atomic Energy Authority, or AEA) dates back to 1955, and in 1957 it entered into a nuclear cooperation agreement with the Soviet Union.[148] As part of the agreement, the Soviet Union built ETRR-1, Egypt's first research reactor, a 2 MW unit that reached criticality in 1961.[149] In 1963 Egypt attempted—and failed—to purchase a French reactor for power generation.[150] The country issued international tenders for an electricity and desalination facility outside of Alexandria in 1964. West Germany's Siemens and Westinghouse of the United States competed, but the project did not come to fruition.

In the mid-1970s, Egyptian president Anwar Sadat sought nuclear power to help rebuild the country's economy.[151] In 1974 Egypt and the Soviet Union tentatively agreed on the construction of a 460 MW reactor. Cairo granted Westinghouse another contract for a plant outside of Alexandria. However, neither plant was built: the latter failed because Egypt and the United States could not agree on a spent fuel storage plan.[152] In 1976 the government established the Nuclear Power Plants Authority, and the following year the Nuclear Materials Authority. In 1978 it announced that 7200 MW of nuclear capacity would be installed by 1999 and the following year selected the coastal town of El-Dabaa for a new nuclear facility.[153]

In 1981, following the spike in international petroleum prices in 1979–80, President Hosni Mubarak established the Supreme Council on Nuclear Energy.[154] However, any momentum from this and the bidding for the El-Dabaa site dissolved in the wake of the 1986 Chernobyl accident.[155] In the 1990s, Egypt widened its search for international partners, with Argentina, Canada, and France competing to supply its second research reactor. Argentina won the bid and in March 1993 began construction on the Egyptian second research reactor (ETRR-2), also known as the multipurpose nuclear reactor. The reactor went into operation in 1998 at Inshas on the Nile Delta, northwest of Cairo.[156] According to a 1999 AEA document, the 22 MW pool-type reactor is supplied by enriched fuel (uranium hexafluoride enriched to 19.75 percent uranium by weight) produced by a fuel-manufacturing pilot plant.[157] The Inshas facility also houses a hot laboratory and waste management center, which, according to the Federation of American Scientists, "includes a small French-supplied hot cell complex for plutonium extraction research."[158] Despite full-scope safeguards, the IAEA found in 2004 that Egypt had engaged in several plutonium-related experiments and research activities but failed "to report [them] to the Agency in a timely manner."[159] The IAEA deemed that "failures by Egypt to report nuclear material and facilities to the Agency in a timely manner are a matter of concern," but they were not reported to the United Nations Security Council as safeguards violations.[160]

By 2006 Egypt resumed its interest in civil nuclear power, spurred to action by the country's deteriorating supply-demand balance in electric power, its desire to conserve domestic resources, and high international prices for oil and gas. With a presidential initiative in September 2006, the government relaunched its nuclear power program, articulating a new national energy strategy based on the following principles: guaranteeing the rights of future generations to Egypt's petroleum and natural gas resources, facilitating the utilization of renewable resources, and facilitating the peaceful uses of nuclear energy. [161]

That same year, the government announced international tenders for a 1,000 MW nuclear power plant at El-Dabaa, a cooperation agreement with China, and the creation of a state system of accounts for controlling nuclear materials.[162] Egypt also launched a policy in 2007 to start a reactor construction program, reform institutions and legislation related to nuclear energy, and build a more robust, independent regulator.[163] In 2008 Egypt signed a nuclear cooperation agreement with Russia, announced that it would select the winner of the contract for the construction of its first nuclear power plant, and awarded a contract to Bechtel, a U.S. engineering firm, for the selection of the reactor technology, the siting of the first plant, the training of operating personnel, and the provision of technical support services for twenty years. In May 2009 the agreement with Bechtel was transferred to WorleyParsons, an Australian engineering firm. At the time, the Ministry of Energy and Electricity announced that at least one nuclear generation facility would be constructed by 2017 and fully interconnected to the grid by 2019.[164]

In 2010 President Mubarak announced definitively that the country's first nuclear power plant would be built at El-Dabaa. According to Hassan Younis, the country's energy and electricity minister, the government was preparing to issue a tender for the construction of the new plant by the end of January 2011. On January 16 two of Egypt's leading infrastructure companies—Orascom Construction Industries and Arab Contractors—announced that they had formed a partnership and were in active negotiations with international nuclear vendors to bid on the project. Other interested bidders were said to include France, the United States, China, Russia, and Japan.[165]

The civil unrest and the ousting of President Mubarak in March 2011 rendered civil nuclear plans unclear. According to a statement from the Egyptian cabinet, the uprisings in Egypt "have not had much effect on the nuclear program," but no tenders have been issued.[166] In late March 2011 the government asked the IAEA to review the technical specifications of its proposed nuclear plant in the wake of the nuclear disaster at Japan's Fukushima plant following the catastrophic earthquake and tsunami.

At the time of writing, few details had been made available regarding the commercial arrangements for Egypt's civil nuclear program. According to the Nuclear Power Plants Authority, Egypt has opted for a "turnkey contract approach" for its first nuclear power plant project and is pursuing an open-fuel cycle. The authority has also emphasized that it prefers the civil nuclear program to be part of a national industrial strategy to modernize Egyptian industry and scientific research through local participation in every plant. As part of its requirements, WorleyParsons is required to assess this when devising a plan for procurement, component suppliers, and other services.[167] Egypt's legal framework has been revised to accommodate the most recent push toward nuclear power development. Its long-awaited nuclear law, produced with input from the IAEA and others in the international community and passed in early 2010, addresses all aspects of plant licensing, safety and security, civil liability, spent fuel management, and the creation of a new regulatory body.

Egypt has a long and active history in bilateral cooperation in the nuclear energy sphere and currently has bilateral agreements with more than ten countries. Egypt's refusal to sign an additional protocol to its safeguards agreement, however, may dampen enthusiasm of foreign vendors. Egyptian officials argue that the country will sign when Israel signs the NPT. Moreover, the Egyptian nuclear establishment insists on keeping open its options under Article IV of the NPT. In its general statement to the Second Preparatory Committee, the Egyptian delegation stated that Egypt "rejects any attempts to impose additional obligations on non–nuclear weapon states" in compliance with their commitments under the NPT, and reaffirmed that "Non–nuclear weapons States Party to the Treaty have a right to the full enjoyment of the benefits of peaceful uses of nuclear energy pursuant to Article IV of the NPT."[168] Egypt's decision on how far it exercises this right will have implications both for its domestic energy program and for regional security.

Other Emerging Nuclear States

Two other emerging nuclear states that merit attention are South Africa and Kazakhstan.

SOUTH AFRICA

South Africa's interest in nuclear energy began in the mid-1940s with the formation of the Atomic Energy Corporation (AEC). In 1959 the government announced plans to develop a domestic nuclear industry and in 1960 started the construction of a research reactor in collaboration with the U.S. Atoms for Peace Program. In 1961 Pretoria established a nuclear site at Pelindaba and built the 20 MW Safari research reactor, which reached criticality in 1965.

South Africa's interest intensified under the apartheid regime and the ever-tightening embargo isolating it from the international arena. Pretoria believed that with a complete fuel cycle it would gain greater energy independence and avoid a complete cut-off of imported petroleum. Therefore in 1970 it founded the Uranium Enrichment Corporation (UCOR) as it embarked upon an extensive fuel cycle and weapons development program.[169]

Throughout the 1970s and 1980s South Africa developed significant uranium enrichment capabilities at Valindaba and Pelindaba, the latter of which supplied the country's Koeburg plant. The Valindaba facility closed in 1990 under IAEA supervision, and Pelindaba closed in 1995 because it was not economically viable. South Africa also experimented with centrifuge and laser enrichment technology, the latter research done in association with Cogema in France until 1997.[170]

According to the IEA, in 2008 roughly 93 percent of South Africa's electricity was generated from coal, with another 5 percent coming from two 900 MW pressurized water reactors (Koeburg plant).[171] The first unit went critical in 1984.[172]

In the face of rising electricity demand, more than 3 million households still do not have access to electricity.[173] In 2008 South Africa's cabinet approved a nuclear energy policy calling for a more diversified fuel mix.[174] The strategy is to increase nuclear capacity to 14 percent of total generation by adding 9,600 MW of new nuclear generation from 2023 to 2030.[175] Nuclear infrastructure will be built through "skill development, legislation and regulation, industrialism and localization, fuel cycle security, procurement as well as communication and stakeholder engagement in South Africa."[176] Attention will be given to all aspects of the fuel cycle, including fuel conversion, fuel fabrication, and enrichment and reprocessing. In partnership with firms such as URENCO, TENEX, or AREVA, the government thus plans to build a new 5-10 million SWU centrifuge enrichment facility, the larger version of which could not only supply South Africa's nuclear plants but also help the country become a major player in the global market for enrichment services.[177]

Although greatly diminished following the end of apartheid, the nuclear infrastructure still possesses important resources such as the uranium slurries that are a by-product of its gold mines. AngloGold Ltd., the company in charge of uranium mining throughout South Africa, announced a plan in May 2009 to build a uranium recovery plant at the Kopanang mine, raising total production to 900 tons of uranium a year by 2012.[178]

In the aftermath of the cold war, South Africa seemed intent on joining the rest of the world in finding peaceful ways of using nuclear energy. In the words of its energy minister, Dipuo Peters, "When we took the decision to voluntarily give up our nuclear options we were joining the rest of the world in a new epoch: of using nuclear to generate electricity. . . . Nuclear energy is becoming a preferred solution [to] address matters related to energy security and energy independence and in efforts to mitigate the dangers posed by climate change."[179] Peters has also emphasized the need to educate the South African public as to the true nature of civilian nuclear power and its benefits. This public campaign is intended not only to sustain support and boost transparency for the program but also to retain much-needed nuclear industrial talent as the old cadre of nuclear scientists from the cold war years retires.

South African officials found the initial bids for new nuclear facilities submitted in 2008 by AREVA and Westinghouse prohibitively expensive, bringing the implementation phase of the new strategy to a halt. Although officials asserted that government support remained strong, talk of the "magnitude of the investment" indicated the financial means to begin constructing new reactors at that time were lacking.[180]

South African officials rightly point out in public statements that South Africa was the first country to voluntarily dismantle a nuclear weapons arsenal. Since joining the NPT as a non–nuclear weapon state in 1991, South Africa has supported the Treaty of Pelindaba creating an African nuclear weapons–free zone and signed the Additional Protocol in 2002. Nonetheless, South African officials are hesitant to support further enrichment and recycling restrictions within the Nuclear Suppliers Group.

Some South African officials have voiced support for Iran in asserting that under Article IV of the NPT it has the right to all components of the nuclear fuel cycle if designed for peaceful uses of nuclear energy. That sentiment was evident in a statement by Ebrahim Mohammad Sali, South Africa's ambassador to Tehran in 2010: "Any signatory to the NPT reserves the right to make use of [nuclear] technology for peaceful purposes. This is Iran's right and no one can deprive you from your right."[181]

KAZAKHSTAN

In 2009 Kazakhstan became the world's largest uranium producer (14,020 tons), accounting for 27 percent of global production.[182] It possesses 15 percent of the world's uranium and plans to expand its mining infrastructure to increase annual uranium production capacity to 30,000 tons a year by 2018.[183]

Despite its current commercial success, uranium has not always been a source of wealth for Kazakhstan. During the 1990s, the country was forced to sell many of the rights to its uranium mines to Western conglomerates owing to its poor mining infrastructure and concerns about its stability following the collapse of the Soviet Union and the breakdown of long-standing institutional arrangements and commercial networks. Despite these early problems, the Kazakhstan government is now reasserting control over these valuable deposits and establishing a civilian nuclear power program in addition to one for uranium extraction.

The catalyst for this political change was the global economic crisis, which severely damaged the Kazakh economy. In January 2010 Energy Minister Sauat Mynbayev notified foreign multinationals to expect to begin paying taxes and export duties on the resources they exploit, a policy sharply at odds with the previous approach of President Nursultan Nazarbayev. Some analysts believe that this radical redirection of policy reflected the government's attempt to regain popular support after domestic criticism of the earlier deals made with Western multinational energy companies and the government's handling of the economic crisis.[184]

All nuclear matters in Kazakhstan are headed by Kazatomprom, the country's state-owned nuclear energy company established in 1997. The goal is to establish "a vertically integrated company having all stages of the nuclear fuel cycle and producing the final product of high value added."[185] In 2008 Kazatomprom announced a joint venture with Russia's TENEX to expand a small uranium enrichment plant at Angarsk in southern Siberia—in which Kazakhstan has a 10 percent interest—into a world-class uranium operation capable of enriching all of Kazakhstan's uranium production. Also in 2008, Kazatomprom set specific goals to furnish 30 percent of the world's uranium supply by 2015 and, through collaboration with other organizations, 12 percent of the uranium conversion market, 6 percent of the global enrichment market, and 30 percent of the fuel fabrication market.[186] The company also plans to begin building two plants in 2011 that will produce sulfuric acid, a key input for in situ leaching of uranium.[187]

Kazakhstan's nuclear assets predate the fall of the Soviet Union. Until it was closed in mid-1999, the Russian BN-350 fast reactor at Aktau (formerly Shevchenko) on the Caspian Sea generated 155 MW of electricity and 80,000 cubic meters a day of potable water used for heat and desalination for twenty-seven years. Kazakhstan also operates another nuclear power reactor for desalination as well as four nuclear research reactors.

The country is planning a wider geographic distribution of smaller nuclear facilities, including light-water reactors throughout the south, 300 MWe units in the west, and "smaller cogeneration units" in metropolitan areas.[188] To date, bids have been submitted for a 600 MWe nuclear plant in or near each of Lake Balkhash, Aktau, Kustanai, and Kurchatov. The Japan Atomic Energy Agency has signed an agreement for the construction of a 600 MWe boiling water reactor in the eastern part of the country. Finally, the Kazakh National Nuclear Center is considering building at least twenty small 50 to 100 MWe reactors to produce power for isolated areas.[189]

In recent years, Kazatomprom has signed commercial agreements with a number of entities, including Canada's Cameco to build a 12,000 ton UF_6 conversion facility.[190] Kazatomprom also has a joint venture with AREVA to sell the 4,000 tons of uranium it produced to AREVA until 2039. AREVA provides Kazatomprom with fuel fabrication technology and will assist in building fuel fabrication lines at the Ulba metallurgical plant in eastern Kazakhstan expected to come into operation in 2014.[191]

Kazakhstan has also signed framework cooperation agreements with Japan, Russia, China, India, South Korea, EURATOM, and the United States. China and Russia are emerging as two key export markets and as critical energy allies. In July 2006 Kazatomprom signed a joint venture agreement with Russia's Atomstroyexport worth $10 billion to develop and market small and medium-size nuclear reactors and uranium enrichment services. Atomstroyexport is expected to build the OKBM VBER-300 as the first reactor model at the Aktau site.[192] Kazatomprom has established deals with China's Guangdong Nuclear Power

Group Holdings for uranium mining and fuel fabrication. Kazakhstan is China's main supplier of uranium, nuclear electricity generation equipment, and power plant construction. Kazakhstan signed an agreement with India's Nuclear Power Corporation in January 2009 to transfer 2,100 tons of uranium to India and to allow the construction of Indian pressurized heavy-water reactors in Kazakhstan.[193] The April 2010 agreement with South Korea contemplates the transfer of Korean SMART 100 MWe nuclear reactors to Kazakhstan and the establishment of joint uranium mining projects.

Since 1990 Kazakhstan has been taking steps to transfer, dismantle, and destroy the nuclear, biological, and chemical weapons it inherited from the time it was part of the Soviet Union. Kazakhstan is continuing these efforts particularly with respect to fissile material remaining in the country. For example, 3 metric tons of plutonium are currently contained at a shuttered breeder reactor in the western part of the country, while small amounts of highly enriched uranium (HEU) remain at two nuclear research institutes. As part of the Global Threat Reduction Initiative, efforts are under way to down-blend HEU fuel to commercial reactor fuel while converting the VVR-K reactor at the Institute of Nuclear Physics.[194] In November 2010 news reports revealed clandestine cooperation efforts with the United States to continue the transfer of nuclear materials away from unsecured or sensitive areas in Kazakhstan. The $219 million operation moved 11 tons of HEU and 3 tons of plutonium across the country to a new IAEA-licensed storage facility in northeastern Kazakhstan. The now secured material could have been used to make at least 770 bombs.[195]

Conclusions

Renewed enthusiasm for nuclear energy offers unique commercial opportunities for vendors of nuclear power plants, equipment suppliers, uranium producers, and providers of ancillary services throughout the nuclear fuel chain. As this enthusiasm spreads into emerging markets with small electricity grids, prospects open for new technological developments of small-scale modular reactors more appropriate for these economies than the traditional 900 or 1200 MW reactors found throughout the developed world. Small modular reactors may also find a growing market in advanced industrialized nations owing to their lower cost and quicker construction and licensing periods. Vendors will compete fiercely for these new customers, but any nuclear power hopefuls will have to develop considerable infrastructure before their nuclear commitment is realistic, and they may not be able to commit to more than a handful of reactors in the next two decades.

The United Arab Emirates intensified vendor competition by declaring it would commit to one technology for all its planned ten reactors, even though the initial tender was just for four plants. This raised the stakes considerably and, one could argue, provided incentives for bidders to sweeten the deal. It is unclear that other nuclear aspirant countries will be as politically astute as the UAE or will be able to commit credibly to building ten or more reactors in a decade. It is also unclear whether the UAE's atypical approach in choosing one technology to increase its negotiating leverage and to simplify training and maintenance will be followed by other countries. The mainstream model pursued by most countries to date is to diversify risk by having a mix of technologies supplied by a mix of vendors.

The UAE-KEPCO deal offers other lessons, including the competitive advantage that a state-owned vendor may have over private vendors. A question for further research is whether more government involvement could also help ensure that proliferation concerns are given high priority during the negotiation and implementation of cooperation agreements. The UAE model relies heavily on foreign supply of all fuel cycle services, including the back end.

While the proliferation of nuclear reactors around the world does not in and of itself represent an enhanced risk of nuclear proliferation, clearly the expansion of the sensitive parts of the fuel cycle (enrichment and recycling), especially into politically sensitive parts of the world, poses a major challenge to the nonproliferation regime. Other nuclear aspirant states could opt for a varied procurement approach that relies on domestic capabilities for some services and the international market for others. Furthermore, they may turn to one, two, or multiple international vendors for nuclear reactors, uranium fuel fabrication, or enrichment and back-end services such as recycling and long-term nuclear waste storage. Reliability of supply is likely to be a key concern, but this is most often a question of perceived rather than actual reliability. The provision of cradle-to-grave services may be attractive to some countries, but others may wish to diversify their suppliers for reasons of energy security.

A country may wish to acquire domestic fuel cycle capabilities for several reasons: to improve reliability of supply, to take advantage of an existing or perceived future commercial market in enrichment, to keep a nuclear weapons option open under the rubric of a civilian nuclear power program, to enhance national prestige associated with becoming a declared or undeclared nuclear weapons state, or to balance regional security if a powerful, hostile neighbor has a declared or undeclared nuclear weapons capability. States could be motivated by one or all of these factors.

With regard to energy and nuclear fuel supply security, the countries in our sample are pursuing diverse paths. As nuclear weapons states with large-scale plans for nuclear power expansion, both India and China will drive to have indigenous fuel cycles that they can also export. While India's plans call for a rapid expansion of its heavy-water CANDU reactor technology combined with new light-water technology imported from abroad, its vast thorium reserves are generating great interest in developing a heavy-water thorium breeder reactor both for domestic use and export. India's entry into the world reactor market selling heavy-water reactors or breeder reactors would raise proliferation concerns since they are more susceptible to plutonium diversion without detection than light-water reactors.

In the case of China, there is little doubt that it will emerge as a major domestic market and as a fierce competitor for reactor, enrichment, and recycling services in the international market. China has already approached AREVA for help in building a recycling facility, although AREVA is pondering how to protect intellectual property as well as ensure no transfer of such technology to a third party before making a final decision.

South Korea is also poised to become a leader in nuclear exports. Supported fully at all levels by the Korean government, the country's nuclear industry is a model of state capitalism. If successful, it could emerge a giant in international nuclear commerce. South Korea's nuclear diplomacy has already reaped rewards in the UAE, and it appears that South Korean nuclear companies are gaining the inside track in Indonesia and Malaysia. South Korea's fuel cycle ambitions are unlikely to be positively regarded by the major technology holders, however, most of all the United States. Despite perceived costs to the nonproliferation regime, a South Korean decision to develop commercial enrichment services cannot be ruled out.

For countries that are just starting out with nuclear power, a few may have fuel cycle capabilities in their sights, but most will want to keep the option open without actually going down that path. Vietnam, for example, most likely will focus on building nuclear power plants before fuel cycle capabilities, which may come in a few decades. Other states in Southeast Asia are less ambitious. Jordan will seek to capitalize on its uranium resources, reserving the right to pursue enrichment. Kazakhstan is likely to take a collaborative or multinational approach to fuel cycle capabilities, given its stake in the International Uranium Enrichment Center. Brazil may seek to export enriched uranium once its own domestic requirements are met. Turkey may turn out to be an ambitious emerging nuclear energy state, viewing itself as a leader at the crossroads of Central Asia and the Middle East, and serving as a commercial bridgehead to those regions. Turkey also sees nuclear energy as a vital step toward building a linked grid from Egypt to Istanbul and beyond.

One interesting dynamic in this evolving market is that commercial nuclear vendors are becoming involved in developing uranium resources as an adjunct to reactor deals. Two examples of this phenomenon raised in this volume's country profiles are Russia's consummation of a reactor sale to Turkey in which Turkey agreed to have the reactors fueled by a Russian-owned uranium company in Namibia; and AREVA's assistance to Jordan in the development of its uranium resources with a view to winning the solicitation for Jordan's first commercial reactor. In the first case, Turkey had little leverage since few vendors were interested in its initial bid; in the second, Jordan has had significant leverage in the buildup to its planned 2011 decision on a reactor technology. If the expansion of nuclear energy doubles or triples, one can expect even more of these kinds of commercial transactions as countries strive to meet increased uranium demand.

Table 4-2. *Summary of Nuclear Energy in Emerging Markets*

Country	Profile	Development targets	Selected key relationships
New potential suppliers			
China	*Status* Fourteen reactors currently operating[a] Domestic capacity for conversion, enrichment, and fabrication[c] Large uranium deposits[e] *Main drivers* Energy demand, environmental benefits, eventually will look to export expertise/ reactors	Twenty-seven additional plants under construction;[a] fifty-one reactors planned 2020: 5% of national electricity supply to be produced by nuclear power[d] (approximately 2% in 2009) 2030: Add fast breeder reactors to capabilities[b] 2040–50: 10% of national electricity supply to be produced by nuclear power	Russia is building two BN-800 units at Sanming in Fujian Province to reach initial operating capacity by 2020.[b] Contracts with AREVA, Westinghouse, which involve technology transfer.[b] Negotiating with AREVA to build reprocessing plant.[b] National uranium mining company, SinoU, is investigating mining production in Niger, Kazakhstan, Uzbekistan, Mongolia, Namibia, Algeria, and Zimbabwe.[b]
India	*Status* Twenty reactors currently operating[a] Domestic capacities for reprocessing[c] Medium uranium deposits[e] *Main drivers* Growing electricity demand, electricity diversification, dependence on imports, domestic technology capacity development, environmental benefits	Five reactors under construction;[a] twenty reactors planned[f] 2032: 63,000 MWe[f] 2050: Have nuclear power provide 25% of all electricity[f] Three-stage plan: (1) pressurized heavy-water reactors; (2) breeder reactors; (3) transition to a thorium-based fuel cycle	Russia has been building another two light-water reactors at Kudankulam for several years.[f] Russia also has a memorandum of understanding (MoU) with India to expand scientific and technical cooperation in nuclear energy.[g] MoU with AREVA for reactor construction, fuel supply assurances.[f] Agreement with the United States to reprocess U.S.-obligated nuclear fuel. Also has a civilian nuclear cooperation agreement with Canada.

(*continued*)

Table 4-2 (*continued*)

Country	Profile	Development targets	Selected key relationships
South Korea	*Status* Twenty-one reactors currently operating[a] *Main drivers* Growing electricity demand, dependence on imports, desire to become major reactor supplier	Five reactors under construction;[a] six reactors planned[h] Push for self-sufficiency in the nuclear cycle will be complete in next few years Plans to export eighty reactors valued at $800 billion by 2030[i]	International cooperation agreement with the United States set to expire in 2014. Building four 1400 MW APR 1400 reactors in UAE. Cooperation or MoU agreements with Jordan, Kazakhstan, Malaysia, Philippines, Turkey, among others. Has a 2.5% equity stake in the George Besse II enrichment plant in France.[h]

New nuclear energy markets

Country	Profile	Development targets	Selected key relationships
Egypt	*Status* Well-developed plans, but commitment pending;[j] Currently has two research reactors[j] *Main drivers* Electricity demand; freeing up fossil fuel reserves for export	None under construction 2019–25: Four plants to come online, the first to be commissioned in 2019[j] 2028: A total of seven plants to be online	Deal with WorleyParsons to construct first 1,000 MW site at el-Dabaa.[j] Consulted with AREVA and Westinghouse Electric as well.[k] Cooperation agreements with: Russia, Tunisia, Argentina, Canada, Germany, India, Italy, China, Unied States, and twenty-nine African countries; MoU with the European Union.
Indonesia	*Status* Well-developed plans, but commitment pending[j] Small uranium deposits[e] *Main drivers* Growing electricity demand, lack of electricity access, electricity diversification from fossil fuel sources	After a period of government opposition to nuclear power, the government has once again expressed interest in nuclear power Targeting nuclear power between 2015 and 2019	International cooperation agreement with the United States.[j] South Korean vendors in discussions to provide reactors.[j]

Country	Profile	Development targets	Selected key relationships
Jordan	**Status** Committed plans, legal and regulatory infrastructure developing[j] Medium uranium deposits[e] **Main drivers** Reduce dependence on energy imports	2015: JRTR 5 MW research reactor at Jordan University for Science and Technology[j] 2017: One reactor near Aqaba (1,000 MWe)[j]	Signed agreement with WorleyParsons for feasibility study of Aqaba site. Korean conglomerate will help build the research and training reactor site; AREVA granted access to uranium mines.[j] Cooperation agreements with Russia, South Korea, Argentina, Canada, China, France, Spain, United Kingdom (among others); MoUs with United States, Japan.
Malaysia	**Status** Developing plans[j] Currently has one research reactor[j] **Main drivers** Growing electricity demand	2013: Nuclear feasibility study[j] 2021: Commissioning of its first reactor[j]	Preliminary supply agreement between TNB (national utility) and Korea Electric Power Corporation (KEPCO).[j] Companies from China, France, Japan, Hungary, Romania, Russia, United Kingdom, and United States have expressed interest in Malaysia's nuclear program.
Turkey	**Status** Contracts signed, legal and regulatory infrastructure well developed;[j] Currently has two research reactors[j] Small uranium deposits[e] **Main drivers** Growing electricity demand; domestic technology capacity development	2018: First 1,200 MWe reactor to be commissioned[j] 2019–21: Commissioning of three more 1,200 MWe reactors[j] Future fuel conversion and fabrication capacity (no timeline)[j]	Agreement with Rosatom to build, own, operate new Akkuyu plant.[j] Agreement with KEPCO to prepare proposal for second site at Sinop.[j] International cooperation agreements with Azerbaijan, Kazakhstan, Kyrgyzstan, Uzbekistan, Tajikistan, Canada, Argentina, South Korea, France, United States.

(continued)

Table 4-2 (*continued*)

Country	Profile	Development targets	Selected key relationships
Vietnam	*Status* Committed plans, legal and regulatory infrastructure developing[j] One research reactor currently operating *Main drivers* Electricity demand, electricity shortages	2025: Eight reactors, 8 GWe[m] 2030: Fourteen reactors, 15 GWe[n]	International cooperation agreements with China, India, Argentina, Japan, and Russia; preliminary agreement with United States (not a civilian nuclear cooperation agreement). Agreement between CEA (France) and Vinatom.

Nuclear capacity for oil suppliers: Persian Gulf

Country	Profile	Development targets	Selected key relationships
Saudi Arabia	*Status* Developing plans[j] *Main drivers* Growing electricity demand, electricity diversification, desalination	2030: Sixteen reactors[o]	International cooperation agreements with France and Russia; MoU with United States.
United Arab Emirates	*Status* Contracts signed, legal and regulatory infrastructure well-developed[j] *Main drivers* Growing electricity demand, electricity diversification, desalination	2017: First 1,400 MWe reactor to be commissioned[j] 2018–20: Commissioning of three more 1,400 MWe reactors[j]	Contract awarded to South Korean consortium. International cooperation agreements with United States, South Korea, and France; MoU with United Kingdom and Japan.

New potential fuel cycle suppliers

Country	Profile	Development targets	Selected key relationships
Brazil	*Status* Two reactors currently operating[a] Domestic capacities for enrichment, fabrication[c] Large uranium deposits[c] *Main drivers* Electricity diversification	One reactor under construction;[a] four reactors planned 2025: Four new reactors[p] 2050: 50 GWe	Main cooperation agreements with China, France, Germany, and United States. Areva building the reactor under construction.[p] Agreement with Areva for conversion services.[p]

Country	Profile	Development targets	Selected key relationships
Kazakhstan	*Status* No reactors currently operating; only operating reactor was shut down in 1999 Well-developed plans but commitment pending[j] Large uranium deposits[e] *Main drivers* Economic benefits through expanded energy-related exports (wants to take advantage of growing uranium demand)	Reactors, expanded mining operations, and full fuel cycle production capabilities[q] 2017: 300 MWe unit;[j] a series of twenty small reactors distributed throughout isolated areas[q] Increase annual uranium production to 30,000 tons/yr by 2018; supply 12% of the world's uranium conversion market, 6% of the enrichment market, and 30% of fuel fabrication market by 2015[r]	Kazatomprom has joint venture agreements with Russia's Atomstroyexport, Canada's Cameco, France's AREVA.[q] Range of deals with China's Guandong Nuclear Power Group on uranium mining, fuel fabrication, export of uranium to China, nuclear electricity generation, power plant construction.[q] Agreement with Japan's Atomic Energy Agency to build a 600 MWe plant.[q] Agreement to export uranium to India, and possible construction of reactors in Kazakhstan.[q] Cooperation agreements with Japan, Russia, China, India, South Korea, Euratom, United States.[q]
South Africa	*Status* Two reactors currently operating[a] Large uranium deposits[e] *Main drivers* Growing electricity demand	2030: 9.6 MWe of nuclear generation capacity[s] Looking to export nuclear components[t]	Construction bids submitted by AREVA and Westinghouse in 2008 put on hold because of financial constraints.[s]

a. International Atomic Energy Agency (IAEA), Power Reactor Information System (www.iaea.org/programmes/a2/).

b. World Nuclear Association (WNA), paper on China (http://world-nuclear.org/info/inf63.html).

c. OECD Nuclear Energy Agency (NEA), "Market Competition in the Nuclear Industry" (Issy-les Moulineaux, France, 2008).

(continued)

Table 4-2 (*continued*)

d. Zhu Xuhui, China National Nuclear Corporation, remarks at American Academy of Arts and Sciences (AAAS) conference "Emerging Nuclear Power in Regional Contexts: Southeast Asia," Singapore, November 3, 2010.

e. Assessment of uranium resources refers to reasonably assured resources (RAR) at less than $130 Kg/U, as detailed in the 2009 OECD NEA Uranium "Red Book." Large resource base = RAR > 150,000 tons U; medium resource base = RAR 50,000–149,999 tons U; small resource base = RAR < 49,999 tons U.

f. WNA, paper on India (www.world-nuclear.org/info/inf53.html).

g. "Russia and India Strengthen Cooperation," *World Nuclear News,* December 21, 2010 (www.world-nuclear-news.org/newsarticle.aspx?id=29001&terms=India).

h. WNA, paper on South Korea (www.world-nuclear.org/info/inf81.html).

i. "South Korea Seeks to Boost Reactor Exports," *World Nuclear News,* January, 13, 2010.

j. WNA, *Emerging Nuclear Energy Countries* (http://world-nuclear.org/info/inf102.html).

k. "International World News," *Power Engineering International,* September 2010.

l. "Egypt's Nuclear Ambition Reignites," *The National,* December 7, 2010 (www.thenational.ae/business/energy/egypts-nuclear-ambition-reignites).

m. Ta Minh Tuan, Diplomatic Academy of Vietnam, remarks at AAAS conference "Emerging Nuclear Power in Regional Contexts: Southeast Asia," Singapore, November 3, 2010.

n. "Vietnam Plans Ambitious Nuclear Energy Program," *World Nuclear News,* June 24, 2010 (http://world-nuclear-news.org/newsarticle.aspx?id=27932&terms=vietnam 2020).

o. "Saudi Plans to Build 16 Nuclear Reactors by 2030," *Reuters,* June 1, 2011 (http://af.reuters.com/article/energyOilNews/idAFLDE75004Q20110601).

p. WNA, paper on Brazil (http://world-nuclear.org/info/inf95.html).

q. WNA, "Uranium and Nuclear Power in Kazakhstan," November 18, 2010 (www.world-nuclear.org/info/inf89.html).

r. "Progress in Kazakh Ambitions," *World Nuclear News,* August 12, 2009 (www.world-nuclear-news.org/newsarticle.aspx?id=25806).

s. WNA, paper on South Africa (www.world-nuclear.org/info/default.aspx?id=372&terms=south%20africa).

t. "Nuclear Industry Set to Gain from Increase in Capacity," *Financial Times,* December 1, 2010.

Notes

1. We define "emerging nuclear energy markets" as non-OECD countries that are projecting significant development or expansion in one or more of the following: construction of commercial nuclear reactors, reactor sales, uranium production, new enriched uranium producers, new entrants into recycling, or waste storage facilities either for themselves or others.

2. International Atomic Energy Agency (IAEA), "International Status and Prospects of Nuclear Power" (Vienna, September 2010), p. 10.

3. IAEA, *Energy, Electricity, and Nuclear Power: Developments and Projections—25 Years Past and Future* (Vienna, 2007), p. 57.

4. See World Nuclear Association (WNA), "Emerging Nuclear Energy Countries," February 2011 (www.world-nuclear.org/info/inf102.html).

5. Jose Goldemberg, "Nuclear Energy in Developing Countries," *Daedalus* 138 (Fall 2009): 72.

6. International Energy Agency (IEA), *World Energy Outlook 2010* (Paris, 2010), pp. 88–89. These projections reflect the "new policies scenario," which "assumes introduction of new measures (but on a relatively cautious basis) to implement the broad policy commitments that have already been announced, including national pledges to reduce GHG emissions and, in certain countries, plans to phase out fossil energy subsidies."

7. Ibid., pp. 64–65.

8. Ibid., p. 56.

9. "Emerging Focus: Rising Middle Class in Emerging Markets," *Euromonitor Global Market Research,* March 29, 2010 (http://blog.euromonitor.com/2010/03/emerging-focus-rising-middle-class-in-emerging-markets.html).

10. Anthony Deutsch, "Indonesia's Middle Class Comes of Age," *Financial Times,* November 18, 2010.

11. Kamal J. Araj, "Jordan's Nuclear Programme," paper presented at the First Arab Conference on the Prospects of Nuclear Power for Electricity Generation and Seawater Desalination, Hammamet, Tunisia, June 23–26, 2010.

12. Institute for International Strategic Studies (IISS), "Nuclear Programs in the Middle East: In the Shadow of Iran" (London, 2008), p. 65.

13. "Prison Sentence for Former Kazatomprom Head," *World Nuclear News,* March 15, 2010 (www.world-nuclear-news.org/IT-Prison_sentence_for_former_KazAtomProm_head-1503104.html).

14. "The Rise and Fall of Kang Rixin," *Uranium Intelligence Weekly,* December 13, 2010, p. 3.

15. IAEA, "Milestones in the Development of a National Infrastructure for Nuclear Power" (Vienna, 2007), p. 6, table 1.

16. Ibid., p. 2.

17. In 2004 President George W. Bush called for a moratorium on enrichment and reprocessing transfers to states that did not already have the technology. The G-8 decided to implement that moratorium until 2008, when the restriction was lifted under the conditions specified in the following statement: "We welcome the significant progress made

by the Nuclear Suppliers Group (NSG) in moving toward consensus on a criteria-based approach to strengthen controls on transfers of enrichment and reprocessing equipment, facilities and technology. We support the NSG effort to reach consensus on this important issue. Additionally, we agree that transfers of enrichment equipment, facilities and technology to any additional state in the next year will be subject to conditions that, at a minimum, do not permit or enable replication of the facilities; and where technically feasible reprocessing transfers to any additional state will be subject to those same conditions." See G8 Declaration, Hokkaido Toyako Summit, 2008 (www.mofa.go.jp/policy/economy/summit/2008/doc/doc080714__en.html). Beginning in 2004, the NSG considered strengthening criteria for such transfers, including requirements that states at least have an additional protocol in place and are NPT members. The criteria have not yet been agreed upon, but earlier, more stringent criteria have been rejected.

18. IEA, *World Energy Outlook 2010*, p. 77.

19. WNA, "Nuclear Power in the United Arab Emirates," March 2011 (www.world-nuclear.org/info/UAE_nuclear_power_inf123.html). In the United States, 5600 MW of Greenfield nuclear capacity would cost about $48 billion, assuming a price of roughly $8 billion per 1,000 MW.

20. "South Korea Seeks to Boost Reactor Exports," *World Nuclear News*, January 13, 2010 (www.world-nuclear-news.org/NP-South_Korea_seeks_to_boost_reactor_exports-1301104.html).

21. Data from the Power Reactor Information System (PRIS), International Atomic Energy Agency (www.iaea.org/programmes/a2/).

22. Zhu Xuhui, China National Nuclear Corporation, remarks at a conference sponsored by the American Academy of Arts and Sciences on Emerging Nuclear Power in Regional Contexts: Southeast Asia, Singapore, November 3, 2010.

23. Zhu Xuhui estimated 90 GWe by 2020 (see n. 24). For other figures compiled by the World Nuclear Association, see www.world-nuclear.org/info/inf63.html.

24. For China's attempts to reduce coal consumption, see Pei Yee Woo, "China's Electric Power Market: The Rise and Fall of IPPs," Working Paper 45 (Stanford University, Program on Energy and Sustainable Development, August 16, 2005); for projections on China's coal consumption, see IAE, *World Energy Outlook 2010*, pp. 202–03, 232.

25. "China Nuclear Power Poised for Export in 'Self-Reliance' Bid," *Bloomberg*, November 29, 2007 (www.bloomberg.com/apps/news?pid=newsarchive&sid=aSpqDJ5SWe28).

26. Ibid.

27. IAEA, Power Reactor Information System.

28. WNA, "Nuclear Power in South Korea," January 5, 2011 (www.world-nuclear.org/info/inf81.html).

29. Lee Soon-Hyuk, "S. Korea Found to Loan $10B for UAE Power Plant," *The Hankyoreh* (Seoul), February 1, 2011 (http://english.hani.co.kr/arti/english_edition/e_national/461703.html).

30. WNA, "Nuclear Power in South Korea."

31. WNA, "Nuclear Power in India," January 20, 2011 (www.world-nuclear.org/info/inf53.html).

32. IEA, *World Energy Outlook 2010,* p. 228.

33. Author's meeting with Indian Atomic Energy Commission, November 1, 2010.

34. See "Nuclear Power in Brazil," January 20, 2011 (www.world-nuclear.org/info/inf95.html).

35. "Funding for Angra-3, Plans for Four New Sites," *Nuclear News,* February 2011.

36. Joao Montenegro, "Customers beyond the Borders," *Brazil Energy,* May 8, 2010 (www.energiahoje.com/brasilenergy/2010/08/05/415219/customers-beyond-the-borders.html).

37. IEA, "Electricity/Heat in Vietnam in 2008" (http://iea.org/stats/electricitydata.asp?COUNTRY_CODE=VN).

38. WNA, "Emerging Nuclear Energy Countries."

39. "Vietnam Likely to Face Serious Power Shortage This Month," *Vietnam Business News,* October 8, 2010 (http://vietnambusiness.asia/vietnam-likely-to-face-serious-power-shortage-this-month).

40. According to the World Nuclear Association, in 1980 Vietnam established the 500 kW Da Lat research reactor in collaboration with the Soviet Union. The United States helped convert the facility to use low-enriched uranium in 2007.

41. "Vietnam Plans Ambitious Nuclear Program," *World Nuclear News,* June 25, 2010 (www.world-nuclear-news.org/NN-Vietnam_plans_ambitious_nuclear_program-2406104.html). See also WNA, "Emerging Nuclear Energy Countries."

42. Vivian Wai-yin Kwok, "Japan, Vietnam Warming to Nuclear Power Deal," *Forbes,* March 20, 2009.

43. "Russia Gets Vietnam's First Nuclear Power Deal," *AsiaOne,* February 9, 2010 (ww.asiaone.com/News/AsiaOne+News/World/Story/A1Story20100209-197685.html).

44. Partly in response to the loss in the UAE, the Japanese government brought together thirteen Japanese companies—nine Japanese electric utilities, along with Toshiba, Hitachi, Mitsubishi Heavy Industries, and the joint public-private sector fund, Innovation Network Corporation of Japan—to create a new entity, the International Nuclear Energy Development of Japan Company (JINED). JINED has $2.46 million in capital to develop proposals for countries planning new nuclear power plants. JINED shareholding is as follows: Tokyo Electric Power, 20 percent; Kansai Electric Power, 15 percent; Chubu Electric Power, 10 percent; INCJ, 10 percent; and the remaining companies 5 percent each.

45. Yuziro Takano, "Japan Bags Vietnam Nuclear Deal," *Asahi Shimbun* (Japan), November 1, 2010.

46. "Vietnam, France to Cooperate on Nuclear Energy," *Vietnam Business News,* March 15, 2011.

47. "Indonesia Wrestles with Its Chronic Electricity Crisis," *Power Engineering International,* October 2010, pp. 18–22.

48. IEA, "Energy Policy Review of Indonesia" (Paris, 2008).

49. Achmad S. Sastratenaya and Ariyanto Sudi, "Nuclear Energy Development in Indonesia," Center for Nuclear Energy Development, paper presented at International Atomic Energy Agency Workshop on Long-Range Planning, Vienna, June 14–17, 2010.

50. WNA, "Emerging Nuclear Energy Countries."

51. Ibid.

52. "Nuclear Power a Possibility for Indonesia," United Press International, March 17, 2010 (ww.upi.com/Science_News/Resource-Wars/2010/03/17/Nuclear-power-a-possibility-for-Indonesia/UPI-27851268854191/).

53. WNA, "Emerging Nuclear Energy Countries."

54. Until 2007 this was called the Malaysia Institute for Nuclear Technology Research, or MINT.

55. WNA, "Emerging Nuclear Energy Countries."

56. U.S. Department of Energy, Energy Information Administration, Malaysia Country Data (www.eia.doe.gov/countries/country-data.cfm?fips=MY#undefined).

57. "Malaysia's Nuclear Company," *World Nuclear News,* January 13, 2011.

58. Noramly bin Muslim, Malaysian Atomic Energy Licensing Board, paper presented to an American Academy of Arts and Sciences conference, "Emerging Nuclear Power in Regional Contexts: Southeast Asia," Singapore, November 3, 2010.

59. The sections on Jordan, Egypt, Saudi Arabia, Turkey, and the United Arab Emirates are drawn from Charles K. Ebinger and others, "Models for Nuclear Power Development in the Middle East," Policy Brief 11-02 (Brookings, July 2011).

60. J. Kinninmont, "The GCC in 2020: Resources for the Future," *Economic Intelligence Unit,* 2010, p. 7.

61. Ibid.

62. UAE Ministry of Foreign Affairs, "Policy of the United Arab Emirates on the Evaluation and Potential Development of Peaceful Nuclear Energy," April 2008.

63. Ibid.

64. White House press release, May 21, 2009 (www.whitehouse.gov/the_press_office/Message-from-the-President-on-the-US-UAE-Peaceful-Uses-of-Nuclear-Energy-Agreement/).

65. Ibid.

66. From one of the author's interviews with UAE Executive Affairs Authority, Abu Dhabi, October 3–8, 2010.

67. IAEA, "IAEA Reviews Progress of UAE Nuclear Power Programme," Staff Report, January 24, 2011 (www.iaea.org/newscenter/news/2011/npprogramme.html).

68. IAEA, "Assurance of Nuclear Fuel Supply: Resolution Adopted by the Board of Governors on 3 December 2010," International Atomic Energy Agency Board of Governors, GOV/2010/70 (December 3, 2010).

69. See IEA (www.iea.org).

70. According to the International Monetary Fund, World Economic Outlook Database, October 2010 (www.imf.org).

71. IEA, *World Energy Outlook 2005: Middle East and North Africa Insights* (Paris, 2005).

72. Saudi Electric Company, "Annual Report 2009" (Riyadh, 2009).

73. Abeer Allam, "Saudi to Develop Solar and Nuclear Power," *Financial Times,* January 24, 2011.

74. Ibid. See also William J. Broad and David E. Sanger, "With an Eye on Iran, Rivals Also Want Nuclear Power," *New York Times,* April 15, 2007.

75. U.S. Department of State, "U.S.-Saudi Arabia Memorandum of Understanding on Nuclear Energy Cooperation," May 16, 2008.

76. Ibid.

77. Stimson Center, "Nuclear Dangers Nuclear Realities Workshop Report" (Riyadh, Saudi Arabia, April 11–12, 2010), pp. 8–9.

78. "Pöyry Awarded Nuclear and Renewable Energy Strategy Project in Saudi Arabia," Pöyry PLC press release, June 10, 2010 (www.poyry.com/Press_and_Stock_releases/1422909.html).

79. AREVA, GE-Hitachi, Toshiba, Exelon, the Shaw Group, and the Japanese government are among the groups interested in Saudi Arabia's nuclear energy program. See Allam, "Saudi to Develop Solar and Nuclear Power"; "GE-Hitachi Venture to Pursue Nuclear Contracts in Saudi Arabia," *Bloomberg Business Week,* December 15, 2010; or "Japan to Help Saudi Arabia Build Nuclear Power Plants," *RIA Novosti,* January 8, 2010.

80. "Shaw, Toshiba, and Exelon Sign Teaming Agreement for Nuclear Projects in Saudi Arabia," Shaw Group press release, July 12, 2010 (http://ir.shawgrp.com/phoenix.zhtml?c=61066&p=irol-newsArticle_print&ID=1446255&highlight).

81. "Saudi Arabia Expected to Be Generating N-power in 10 Years," *Saudi Economic Survey,* December 19, 2010.

82. "Saudi Plans to Build 16 Nuclear Reactors by 2030," Reuters, June 1, 2011 (http://af.reuters.com/article/energyOilNews/idAFLDE75004Q20110601).

83. "Saudi and Russia in Talks to Sign Nuke Deal: Report," *Al-Arabiya,* December 28, 2010.

84. "Japan Offers Help for Saudi Arabian Nuclear Power Project," *BBC Monitoring Asia Pacific,* January 8, 2011.

85. "Saudi Arabia, France Sign Nuclear Agreement," *Saudi Economic Survey,* March 4, 2011.

86. "Saudi Cabinet Discusses Arab Developments, Approves Appointments," *BBC Monitoring Middle East,* March 29, 2011.

87. "Saudi Arabia May Turn to Uranium Enrichment," June 17, 2010 (www.utilities-me.com/article-601-saudi-arabia-may-turn-to-uranium-enrichment/).

88. IEA, "Emerging Nuclear Energy Countries."

89. Jean-François Seznec, Center for Contemporary Arab Studies, Georgetown University, interview with the authors.

90. Mark Hibbs, "Saudi Arabia's Nuclear Ambitions" (Washington: Carnegie Endowment for International Peace, July 20, 2010) (www.carnegieendowment.org/publications/index.cfm?fa=view&id=41243#4).

91. IEA, "Energy Policies of IEA Countries: Turkey 2009 Review" (Paris, 2009).

92. Ibid.

93. "Turkey Moves One Step Closer to Nuclear Plant," *Today's Zaman,* September 24, 2008 (www.todayszaman.com/newsDetail_getNewsById.action;jsessionid=865D2E1D9 03BDEEA491E840D87683AF4?load=detay&link=154129&newsId=153926).

94. IEA, "Energy Policies of IEA Countries: Turkey 2005 Review" (Paris, 2005).

95. European Network of Transmission System Operators of Electricity, *Annual Report 2009* (Brussels, 2009).

96. IEA, "Energy Policies of IEA Countries: Turkey 2009 Review."

97. Ibid.

98. Ibid.

99. Turkish Atomic Energy Authority website (www.taek.gov.tr/eng/about-us/history.html).

100. Mohamed ElBaradei, "Nuclear Power: A Changing Landscape by Director General," address to the Turkish Atomic Energy Authority, July 7, 2006.

101. Mustafa Kibaroglu, "Turkey's Quest for Peaceful Nuclear Power," *Nonproliferation Review,* Spring-Summer 1997.

102. IISS, "Nuclear Programs in the Middle East: In the Shadow of Iran."

103. Turkish Prime Ministry, Secretariat of the Higher Board of Planning, Undersecretariat of State Planning Organization, "Electricity Energy Market and Supply Security Strategy" (Ankara, May 21, 2009).

104. "Turkey Targets 20 Nuclear Reactors by 2030—Official," Reuters, January 31, 2011.

105. Sehat Köse, "Recent Status of Nuclear Program in Turkey," paper presented to IAEA workshop "The Introduction of Nuclear Power Programmes: Management and Evaluation of a National Nuclear Infrastructure," Vienna, February 8–11, 2011.

106. Ibid.

107. "Turkish Parliament Ratifies Russian-Turkish NPP Agreement," *RIA Novosti,* July 15, 2010 (http://en.rian.ru/business/20100715/159820318.html).

108. "Building of Turkey's First Nuclear Plant, Sited on a Fault Line, Facing Fresh Questions," *Sabah,* March 26, 2011 (http://english.sabah.com.tr/Economy/2011/03/26/building_of_turkeys_first_nuclear_plant_sited_on_a_fault_line_facing_fresh_questions).

109. Vladimir Sotnikov, "Russia to Build Nuclear Power Plant in Turkey," *RIA Novosti,* June 8, 2010 (http://en.rian.ru/international_affairs/20100608/159347024.html).

110. Köse, "Recent Status of Nuclear Program in Turkey."

111. "Turkey May OK Nuclear 18 months after Japan Crisis," Reuters, March 24, 2011.

112. "Disagreements Snag Turkey–S. Korea Talks on Nuclear Plant," *Hürriyet,* April 8, 2010.

113. Jonathan Soble, "Toshiba Upbeat on Turkey Nuclear Deal," *Financial Times,* February 6, 2011.

114. "Japan Bank to Support Toshiba in Turkish Nuclear Plant Bid," *Hürriyet,* March 3, 2011.

115. "Turkey May OK Nuclear 18 Months after Japan Crisis."

116. Ibid.

117. Hashemite Kingdom of Jordan, "Summary: Update Master Strategy of the Energy Sector in Jordan for the Period 2007–2020" (Amman, December 2007).

118. Ibid.

119. Ibid.

120. Khaled Toukan, Jordan Atomic Energy Commission, "Jordan's Nuclear Energy Program," paper presented to Brookings research team, February 2011; and Mousa S. Mohsen, "Water Strategies and Potential of Desalination in Jordan," *Desalination* 203 (February 2007).

121. As categorized by the World Nuclear Association (www.world-nuclear.org/info/inf102.html).

122. Jordan, "Summary: Update Master Strategy of the Energy Sector in Jordan for the Period 2007–2020."

123. "King Abdullah to Haaretz: Jordan Aims to Develop Nuclear Power," *El Haaretz,* January 19, 2007.

124. Toukan, "Jordan's Nuclear Energy Program."

125. "Jordan: Uranium Hotspot," *Industrial Fuels and Power,* January 14, 2010 (www. ifandp.com/article/00560.html).

126. Jordan Atomic Energy Commission officials, interview with the authors, February 2011.

127. Ned Xoubi, "Project Overview of Jordan's First Nuclear Facility," paper presented to the Commissariat à l'énergie atomique (France) Mission on the SR of Subcritical Assemblies, Amman, Jordan, December 5, 2010.

128. "Korean Consortium for Jordan's First Reactor," *World Nuclear News,* December 7, 2009.

129. Toukan, "Jordan's Nuclear Energy Program."

130. Kamal J. Araj, Jordan Atomic Energy Commission, "Jordan's Nuclear Power Program," paper presented to the First Arab Conference on the Prospects of Nuclear Power for Electricity Generation and Seawater Desalination, Hammamet, Tunisia, June 23–26, 2010; and IAEA, "Country Report: Jordan," July 2010 (www-pub.iaea.org/ MTCD/publications/PDF/CNPP2010_CD/countryprofiles/Jordan/CNPP2010 Jordan.htm).

131. Ibid.

132. Araj, "Jordan's Nuclear Power Program."

133. "Financing to Influence Choice of Nuclear Technology," *Jordan Times,* July 29, 2010.

134. "Nuclear Commission to Bring International Company on Board," *Jordan Times,* February 7, 2011.

135. "Jordan Reaches Out to Nuclear Plant Operators," *Jordan Times,* February 22, 2011.

136. Ibid.; and Toukan, "Jordan's Nuclear Energy Program." NEPCO functions as the single buyer in Jordan.

137. From Toukan, "Jordan's Nuclear Energy Program."

138. Ibid.

139. Jay Solomon, "Jordan's Nuclear Ambitions Pose Quandary for U.S.," *Wall Street Journal,* June 12, 2010. Quotation is from Khaled Toukan, former chairman of JAEC and current minister of energy and mineral resources.

140. JAEC officials, interview with the authors, February 2011. See also "All Systems Go for Jordan's First Nuclear Reactor," *Jordan Times,* July 27, 2010.

141. On 2008 data, see IEA (www.iea.org).

142. U.S. Energy Information Administration, "Country Analysis Brief: Egypt," February 2011 (www.eia.doe.gov/countries/cab.cfm?fips=EG).

143. According to the International Energy Agency.

144. U.S. Energy Information Administration, "Country Analysis: Egypt" (Washington: Department of Energy, 2006).

145. Ibid.

146. Shaher Anis Mahmoud, Egyptian Electricity Holding Company, "Electricity Sector in Egypt," paper presented to the DSM & EE Workshop, Tripoli, Libya, February 9–11, 2009.

147. IEA, "Emerging Nuclear Energy Countries."

148. Yair Evron, "The Arab Position in the Nuclear Field: A Study of Policies up to 1967," *Cooperation and Conflict* 8 (March 1973): 19–31; and IISS, "Nuclear Programs in the Middle East: In the Shadow of Iran."

149. According to the IAEA Research Reactor Database (http://nucleus.iaea.org/ RRDB/RR/ReactorSearch.aspx?rf=1).

150. UX Consulting Company, "Nuclear Energy Prospects in Three Middle East Countries," Special Report (Roswell, Ga., May 2009).

151. Ibid.

152. Ibid.

153. IEA, "Emerging Nuclear Energy Countries."

154. Y. M. Ibrahim, chairman, Nuclear Power Parts Authority, "Status of the Egyptian Project of First Nuclear Power Plant," paper presented to the First Arab Conference on the Prospects of Nuclear Power for Electricity Generation and Seawater Desalination, Hammamet, Tunisia, June 23–26, 2010.

155. IAEA, "Country Report: Arab Republic of Egypt" (Vienna, July 2010) (www-pub.iaea.org/MTCD/publications/PDF/CNPP2010_CD/countryprofiles/Egypt/ CNPP2010Egypt.htm).

156. Ibid.

157. W. I. Zidan, "LEU Fuel Element Produced by the Egyptian Fuel Manufacturing Plant," in *Advanced Methods of Process/Quality Control in Nuclear Reactor Fuel Manufacture* (Vienna: IAEA, 2000).

158. Etel Solingen, *Nuclear Logics: Contrasting Paths in East Asia and the Middle East* (Princeton University Press, 2007).

159. "Implementation of the NPT Safeguards Agreement in the Arab Republic of Egypt: Report by the Director General," GOV/2005/9 (Vienna: IAEA Board of Governors, February 14, 2005) (www.globalsecurity.org/wmd/library/report/2005/egypt_iaea_ gov-2005-9_14feb2005.pdf).

160. Mohamed ElBaradei, "Introductory Statement to the Board of Governors," IAEA Board of Governors Meeting, February 28, 2005 (www.iaea.org/newscenter/ statements/2005/ebsp2005n002.html).

161. Ibrahim, "Status of the Egyptian Project of First Nuclear Power Plant."

162. IEA, "Emerging Nuclear Energy Countries."

163. IAEA, "Country Report: Arab Republic of Egypt."

164. IEA, "Emerging Nuclear Energy Countries."

165. "Egyptian Joint Venture Eyes Nuclear Contracts," *World Nuclear News,* January 17, 2011 (www.world-nuclear-news.org/C-Egyptian_joint_venture_eyes_nuclear_ contracts-1701114.html).

166. "Egypt Says to Press Ahead with Nuclear Tender," Reuters, March 9, 2011.

167. Ibid.

168. Egypt, General Statement to the Second Preparatory Committee of the NPT Review Conference, April 28, 2008.

169. In 1985 UCOR became part of the Atomic Energy Commission, which, in 1999, became the South African Nuclear Energy Corporation.

170. See WNA, "Nuclear Power in South Africa," November 2010 (www.world-nuclear.org/info/default.aspx?id=372&terms=south%20africa).

171. Information from Eskom Holdings Limited, "Annual Report 2009," p. 226.

172. "South Africa's Nuclear Strategy in Motion," *World Nuclear News,* October 8, 2010 (www.world-nuclear-news.org/NP_South_Africas_nuclear_strategy_in_motion_0810101.html).

173. Government of the Republic of South Africa, "Integrated National Electrification Programme: Briefing by Department of Energy," March 10, 2011.

174. "South Africa Goes Ahead with Nuclear Energy Plan," *Xinhua,* December 3, 2010.

175. "South African Power and Energy," *Financial Times,* December 2, 2010.

176. "South Africa Goes Ahead with Nuclear Energy Plan."

177. See WNA, "Nuclear Power in South Africa."

178. "Anglo Gold Ashanti Plans New Uranium Mine as Income from Energy Minerals Lifts 225%," *Creamer's Mining Weekly,* February 17, 2011.

179. "South Africa Goes Ahead with Nuclear Energy Plan."

180. WNA, "Nuclear Power in South Africa."

181. "South Africa Backs Iran Nuclear Rights," PressTV, October 5, 2010 (www.presstv.ir/detail/145245.html).

182. WNA, "World Uranium Mining," May 2010 (www.world-nuclear.org.info/inf23.html).

183. WNA, "Uranium and Nuclear Power in Kazakhstan," February 11, 2011 (www.world-nuclear.org/info/inf89.html).

184. Stefan Nicola, "Kazakhstan Eager to Win Back Energy Assets," United Press International, January 29, 2010 (www.upi.com/Science_News/Resource-Wars/2010/01/29/Kazakhstan-eager-to-win-back-energy-assets/UPI-23561264802200).

185. WNA, "Uranium and Nuclear Power in Kazakhstan."

186. "Progress in Kazakh Ambitions," *World Nuclear News,* August 12, 2009 (www.world-nuclear-news.org/newsarticle.aspx?id=25806).

187. Ibid.

188. Ibid.

189. Ibid.

190. "Progress in Kazakh Ambitions."

191. Ibid.

192. WNA, "Uranium and Nuclear Power in Kazakhstan."

193. Ibid.

194. See "Kazakhstan Profile," Nuclear Threat Initiative, May 2010 (www.nti.org/e_research/profiles/Kazakhstan/index.html).

195. Jonathan S. Landay, "U.S., Kazakhstan Complete Secret Transfer of Nuclear Materials," *Miami Herald,* November 16, 2010 (www.miamiherald.com/2010/11/16/1929048/us-kazakhstan-complete-secret.html).

PART II

Industry's Views

5

Nuclear Risks:
The Views of Industry, Governments,
and Nongovernmental Organizations

SHARON SQUASSONI

Nuclear commerce is one of the most heavily regulated areas of global trade. In traditional supplier countries, exports often are preceded by government agreements setting a framework for bilateral nuclear cooperation, usually handled as important diplomatic events. Major reactor sales generally require such agreements, although there is no international standard for them. Typically such agreements lay out the scope of cooperation, kinds of research and development, and restrictions on the use of equipment and technology. Actual exports must be approved (licensed) and in some cases subjected to multiple regulations for equipment, technology, and know-how. On an international level, the governments of nuclear suppliers coordinate and harmonize their export control regulations under the auspices of the Nuclear Suppliers Group (NSG), sharing sensitive information about attempted proliferation.

In such circumstances, it would be easy to assume that governments play the most important role in nonproliferation and in the formulation, implementation, and enforcement of export policy. Actually, this is not far from the mark. One of the common assumptions underlying industry responses to the Brookings survey is that the nuclear power industry has limited responsibility for the proliferation of nuclear weapons. This attitude permeates not only industry's understanding of proliferation but also the way it assesses ideas, suggestions, and recommendations for bolstering its role as a partner in the fight against nuclear power's misuse. If anything, it gives industry little motivation to become more involved in either assessing the risks or finding solutions.

Even so, a potential expansion of nuclear commerce raises some questions that industry cannot afford to ignore:

—Are views from industry already incorporated in government policies and regulations, and if so, to what extent?

—What is the role of industry in helping prevent the spread of nuclear weapons?

—Do industry representatives view proliferation risks, challenges, and solutions in the same way that their governments and nongovernmental organizations (NGOs) do?

As the U.S.-Indian nuclear cooperation deal and NSG's subsequent exception for nuclear trade with India demonstrated so clearly a few years ago, nuclear firms and entities can be significantly affected by governmental decisions related to nonproliferation. Yet they may not engage directly in political discussions affecting them. One clear result of the Brookings survey of industry, government, and expert observers is that the level of interaction between government and industry varies from country to country. Where nuclear vendors are government owned either in full or in part, collaboration tends to be close. This does not mean, necessarily, that industry and government share the same objectives.

The survey posed two sets of questions. The first set focused on respondents' opinions of the current challenges to the nonproliferation regime:

1. What does your company/organization consider to be the biggest nuclear proliferation risks?

2. Which elements of the fuel cycle pose the greatest proliferation risk?

3. Does the projected expansion of nuclear energy present proliferation risks?

4. What are the weaknesses and institutional gaps of the current regime? What mistakes can we learn from and what have been the successes to date?

5. To what extent do new technologies increase/decrease risk?

The second set elicited views on potential solutions to proliferation challenges:

1. How should the Nuclear Nonproliferation Treaty (NPT) be modified, if at all, to better address risks?

2. What is your view of multilateral approaches to fuel cycle assurances?

3. How could the International Atomic Energy Agency (IAEA) better address twenty-first-century challenges?

4. How should we prioritize technical versus institutional solutions?

5. Does industry need to partner with government? What should be the relationship?

Specific responses to questions about proliferation challenges can be seen in table 5-1 (p. 131), and those about potential solutions for strengthening the nonproliferation regime in table 5-2 (p. 136).

Industry Views on Challenges

Industry respondents overwhelmingly share the view that the expansion of the nuclear energy sector per se is not a proliferation risk. In their view, the regime is "robust" as it applies to industry. The current system of "close and efficient" monitoring and regulation of industry by government and international organizations, they argue, has worked for more than three decades.

Some observed, however, that governments are increasingly concerned about the spread of enrichment and reprocessing capabilities and suggested a "growing consensus" to limit those capabilities, at least among countries that already have mastered the technology. These respondents made no comment on the divisive debate over limiting enrichment and reprocessing in the Nuclear Suppliers Group, or the assertion that the NPT affords an "inalienable right" to such capabilities. Although industry respondents judged most multilateral nuclear approaches (MNAs) to enrichment and reprocessing to be infeasible (see further discussion in the next section and in chapter 6), they did not find supply-led restrictions on enrichment and reprocessing unworkable.

About half of the industry respondents saw fuel cycle risks only at the front end of the cycle—that is, in relation to the spread of uranium enrichment technology. One respondent identified dual-use technologies as a risk at both the front and back end of the fuel cycle. Another perceived the leakage of information as a significant risk.

One respondent remarked that the growth in civilian nuclear activities and facilities is likely to increase the verification responsibilities of the IAEA. And if that were to happen without a commensurate expansion in IAEA human and financial resources, the risk of proliferation could grow.

This insight resonates in the context of what the vast majority of respondents saw as the major proliferation challenge: "rogue" or "isolated" nations or governments engaged in illicit, hidden, or illegal activities in violation of their NPT obligations. The problem, in their view, is not that nuclear materials or technology will be diverted from safeguarded civilian nuclear facilities (although one respondent did indicate that this risk might grow). Rather, it is one of "cheating" by countries involved in smuggling sensitive nuclear material and technology or operating undisclosed, covert facilities. About half of the responses identified Iran's and Pakistan's current and past actions as a significant risk. There was also a nod to illegal smuggling and "hidden activities" by groups or individuals.

About a third of the industry respondents deferred to government expertise in identifying the weaknesses of the current nonproliferation regime; another third said that the export-licensing regime was functioning well, and that the problem of proliferation has been generally one of rogue regimes. The remaining third suggested that the regime was outdated and lacked enforcement mechanisms.

In general, industry respondents were optimistic about the contributions technology could make to reducing proliferation, primarily in the application of new techniques for international safeguards and in enhancing the proliferation resistance of recycling techniques for spent fuel. One noted, for example, that recycling technologies that avoid separating plutonium in an isolated stream could make vital contributions to nuclear nonproliferation. However, there was strong acknowledgement that technology could not solve proliferation on its own.

Government and NGO Views on Challenges

Government and NGO respondents echoed industry's view that enforcement of the regime and the spread of sensitive nuclear technologies were major challenges. However, their responses also identified additional risks: nuclear weapon stockpiles and large stockpiles of HEU and plutonium are targets of interest for terrorists to steal or sabotage; double standards can inflict damage on consensus within the nonproliferation regime; and emerging nuclear power countries might not have an adequate regulatory infrastructure to support nonproliferation. Government and NGO respondents also were less confident about import and export controls than industry. A few believed, like their industry counterparts, that competition arising from more interest in nuclear power could pose some proliferation risks. The fact that new nuclear power plants could be constructed in countries in which there is little or no real industrial culture could mean a lack of basic infrastructure to manage security, safety, and nonproliferation matters. In the words of one respondent, "This prospective market is already attracting competition among technology suppliers, which should not be done at the expense of security and nonproliferation standards."

A common theme among these respondents was that the commercialization of laser enrichment technology posed another proliferation risk. Although some believed that centrifuge technology risks could be managed with appropriate safeguards and physical protection, laser enrichment was believed to be more sensitive. One respondent noted that a critical factor today is greater access to information about the technology (this respondent did not mention the role that Pakistani scientist A. Q. Khan played in sharing centrifuge technology).

At the back end of the fuel cycle, responses were similar to those of industry in identifying new recycling methods as a potential way to reduce proliferation risks. Both mentioned the threat that fast breeder reactors could pose.

Responses were slightly more nuanced regarding alternatives to recycling. One suggested that "as long as reprocessing is involved, the advantages of an advanced fuel cycle are minor. The best way is to shift away from reprocessing and the plutonium fuel cycle."

Overall, government and NGO respondents appeared to see more potential risks in nuclear energy expansion than their industry counterparts. At the same time, many believed that the risks could be mitigated by taking appropriate actions, which ranged from improving IAEA resources to universalizing the Additional Protocol, getting all countries to sign the NPT, and implementing fuel bank and fuel assurance proposals. Several acknowledged that fast breeders, HEU-fueled research reactors, more widespread enrichment capabilities, and vastly expanded quantities of material could overwhelm the system.

Industry Views on Solutions

Not surprisingly, the nuclear industry's view of critical actions to strengthen the nonproliferation regime corresponds with what they perceive to be its essential problems. Although one respondent described the NPT as an "outdated cold war relic" that needs more teeth, the majority of respondents were unwilling to comment on how the NPT specifically might be modified to address nuclear proliferation threats more effectively. In their view, that is a task best left to government.

Moreover, as described in more detail in chapter 6, half of the respondents were reluctant to comment on measures about multilateral approaches to the fuel cycle, although those that did were generally positive, if cautious. One respondent suggested that every model had feasibility problems; another, that the potential to gain more control over nuclear material would have to be balanced against the risk of increasing the international flow of nuclear material. Still another supported the concept of MNAs, with the caveat that the market currently functioned well and reliably.

More generally, however, industry respondents tended to argue that the major problem—the risk of illicit action by rogue states—is exacerbated by the nonproliferation regime's inability to enforce commitments made by nations under the NPT. As one respondent put it, clear misconduct requires a "collective answer from the international community." Industry respondents overwhelmingly supported the need to enhance the IAEA's capabilities in safeguards, safety, security, and enforcement. Several suggested the IAEA should allocate more resources to verification; one added that the IAEA should simultaneously seek to implement integrated safeguards in more states. Another felt the IAEA could best respond to the challenges of nonproliferation by fostering discussions between existing nuclear power states and states that are seeking to acquire nuclear power, and by assisting newcomer states.

Respondents strongly supported a close industry partnership with government. A "key incentive for industry," one said, "is to preserve its reputation and to be recognized as a responsible nuclear stakeholder and actor." Whether this attitude translates into industry willingness to do significantly more in the nonproliferation arena is unclear, however. Some think a close partnership and strict regulatory control already exist. In other words, industry is willing to work closely with government but not get out ahead of government in developing innovative approaches to reduce proliferation risks. In the words of one respondent, "Proliferation is a political problem that needs political solutions."

One area in which they agreed industry could and should partner with government relates to technology. With a reservoir of key design knowledge that can be used to foster technical improvements to strengthen safeguards, for example, industry can and must work closely with governments. Although new technology can help make civilian nuclear activities more "proliferation resistant," one respondent usefully cautioned that technology will never achieve perfect proliferation resistance, so it can never solve the proliferation problem on its own. Indeed, the majority believe that technological advances must go hand-in-hand with institutional improvements in order to bolster the nonproliferation system. Some respondents suggested, however, that while both institutional and technological advances are essential, they may not always be of equal weight, with technical solutions somewhat outweighing institutional ones.

Government and NGO Views on Solutions

Whereas industry respondents were reluctant to comment on how the NPT might be modified to better address the threats of nuclear proliferation, government and NGO respondents were not shy: they emphatically rejected any modification to the treaty. As one respondent noted, "It would be impossible to amend the NPT and disastrous to try." That said, respondents suggested alternative approaches like developing shared interpretations of obligations and linking mechanisms. Countries should agree on the terms for peaceful uses of nuclear energy, for example. While acknowledging the problems inherent in the NPT's withdrawal clause (Article X) and the lack of penalties for noncompliance, respondents did not believe that modifying the NPT was the appropriate route for addressing these issues.

Respondents found multilateral arrangements appropriate and useful for strengthening transparency and trust, although not always attractive to the targeted supply recipients and possibly prone to information leaks. They emphasized the need for black-box provision of technology, yet also recognized that new recipients might view any new arrangements as further restrictions on their rights.

Suggestions for strengthening the IAEA were quite specific, as detailed in table 5-2. One idea was that the IAEA begin a "systematic dialogue with suppliers and customers, by exchanging information on what both sides are doing and by giving advice to each other. The same approach should occur between the Nuclear Suppliers Group and industry." Others focused on what the IAEA was not doing—namely, prioritizing its programs; coordinating its safety, security, and safeguards programs; integrating technical cooperation and safeguards responsibilities; and beefing up staffing resources.

Like industry, the government and NGO respondents suggested a partnership between industry and government was vital, but differed on how to get there or whether it was an automatic partnership or an informal one that needed coaxing. Some respondents believe that strong sanctions would provide a deterrent to misbehavior and favor stronger government enforcement through prosecution of individuals and seizure of assets, among other measures. Others suggested industry needs incentives to deepen its partnership with government in managing proliferation risks.

The risks, said one, lie not with the mainstream nuclear industry but with the component manufacturers. This suggests that countries should pay more attention to end-user certification in their export control regulations. It is not clear how widespread such certifications are, but even where they are required, they are often performed perfunctorily or not at all.

On balance, this group's views on technical and institutional approaches to mitigating proliferation risks were very much aligned with industry responses: both approaches are needed, and neither can fully compensate for deficiencies in the other.

Conclusions

The rise of nongovernmental organizations in the nonproliferation field has contributed new thinking about proliferation challenges and solutions in the past two decades. Industry is a relative newcomer in this area but over time could also help spur new thinking about responding to challenges. Industry should recognize that it is on the front line of defense against this threat and help shape its role. Industry's role as a partner in managing proliferation risks is likely to become even more important in light of the potentially significant expansion of civilian nuclear power across the globe. It is therefore critical to assess where gaps exist between government, international organizations, and industry perceptions of challenges and solutions.

The survey conducted is by no means comprehensive, but some conclusions from the data suggest consensus-building and education are in order. The common industry view that proliferation is essentially a political challenge shaped by demand rather than supply is only half the picture: governments and NGOs acknowledge the political challenges, but also see a continuing need to shut down targets of opportunity for rogue states and terrorists. All agree that enforcement of NPT compliance is a problem, but there is no unanimity about risks emanating from lax export control implementation or information security. These are two areas where industry should have keen interests.

All groups agree that the further spread of sensitive nuclear fuel cycle technologies poses the greatest proliferation risk. Some industry responses revealed a somewhat naive view about the ability to mitigate this risk. For example, "As long as there is control over the use of enrichment services, there should not be a concern for proliferation," and "Activities in the nuclear energy sector are closely and efficiently monitored by states and international organizations who collectively take commitments to prevent proliferation from occurring in the civilian nuclear industry. This system has been effective for the last thirty years."

With respect to enrichment, all agree that laser enrichment poses a serious risk, but only one company (GE-Hitachi) is involved in commercializing this technology. This suggests that the governments of Japan and the United States should take a more active role in monitoring this commercialization. Industry is largely concerned about buying and selling current technology, which suggests that the target audience for perhaps restraining or directing research and development into fast breeders and recycling is the governments themselves. They should focus on how their international collaboration in nuclear fuel cycle research and development is going to mitigate potential risks. On the back end of the fuel cycle, all responses seem to be optimistic about the potential for new technology to improve the proliferation resistance of recycling, but those in the government and NGO sector were wary of the risks of expanded recycling.

In nonproliferation, industry's preference to be a junior partner to government shapes its outlook. In a number of other security-related areas, however, government is increasingly looking to industry (for example, for countermeasures for cyber attacks) for innovation. Government working with industry in the chemical arena represents an important precedent for the kind of partnership that can be promoted in managing proliferation risks (this is explored in greater detail in chapter 6).

For the nuclear industry, is it possible to spur innovation in an area that is not generally perceived to be a threat to industry's "bottom line?" Although industry widely acknowledges that one major nuclear accident can affect the future of the nuclear energy industry around the globe, it is not clear that the same holds true for proliferation. In fact, a persuasive argument could be made that few vendors have suffered loss of business from documented proliferation cases. This could change in the future, particularly if governments tighten restrictions and improve enforcement. For its part, industry could also adopt a corporate citizen approach, choosing to be a partner with government in managing proliferation risks. This would require a recognition that industry is a stakeholder in the fight against proliferation for more than commercial reasons.

Table 5-1. *Responses and Selected Comments on Current Challenges to the Nonproliferation Regime*

Challenges	Industry	Nonindustry
1. What does your company/organization consider to be the biggest current nuclear proliferation risks?	Rogue states (especially outside the NPT) and countries violating their nonproliferation commitments Illegal smuggling Acquisition of dual-use technology from the front and back end of the fuel cycle (that is, enrichment, reprocessing) Highly enriched uranium stored in countries without effective oversight *Major themes* "Our experience shows that nuclear proliferation originates from illegal smuggling and hidden activities by groups or groups of individuals or States in violation of their own commitments and in breach of international conventions." *Minor themes* "The lack of code of conduct charter." "Increasing competition in the nuclear projects market." "Leakage of company's technical information. The most important thing is information management/security."	Wide range of views, including: Ensuring that emerging nuclear power countries have effective regulatory infrastructure Existence of large stockpiles of HEU and plutonium Inadequately secured fissile material in all forms Existing stockpiles of nuclear weapons Spread of sensitive nuclear technologies Lack of support/understanding of nonproliferation by developing countries (politicization of nonproliferation) Lack of will to enforce treaty compliance Lack of effective import/export control *Major themes* "Measures taken to prevent theft are quite effective [but] highly enriched uranium is to be considered as more sensitive than plutonium" "The rapid spread of national nuclear programs including countries with no (or little) nuclear infrastructure. " "Nuclear proliferation risks are increasing as a result of: existing geopolitical tensions in regions like Asia and Middle East . . . loss of credibility of the NPT system . . . ; competition among suppliers due to a 'nuclear renaissance' . . . new technology developments for enrichment increase the risk of clandestine activities (the characteristics of centrifuge technology allow for rapid breakout and make it easy to hide). . . . The possibility of terrorists obtaining a nuclear weapon, nuclear material or radioactive material remains a very important threat. . . . The absence of effective sanctions to stop proliferation activities by a NPT state signatory remains a crucial problem for the credibility of the non proliferation regime."

(*continued*)

Table 5-1 (*continued*)

Challenges	Industry	Nonindustry
2. Which elements of the fuel cycle pose the greatest nonproliferation challenge?	Front and back end of the fuel cycle *Major themes* "The civil nuclear fuel cycle poses a very, very low risk of proliferation—the risk of proliferation arises from clandestine weapons programs with no connection to the civil nuclear power industry." "Enrichment services, especially if laser separation is commercialized." "Enrichment is currently the weakest link. Wider adoption of 'black box' would help. Need to strengthen export controls and vigilance against illicit trafficking. Reprocessing is less of a threat but may become a greater risk if recycle is pursued more widely, or if spent fuel disposal is delayed." *Minor themes* "Political influence in development of nuclear technology. Self control versus incentive must be beneficial to both parties." "Confidential information control" is broken.	Front and back end of the fuel cycle, including enrichment, reprocessing, MOX fuel fabrication, and transportation *Major themes* "The greatest proliferation challenge arises in advances in technology that make information about sensitive fuel cycle processes easier to access. Current enrichment and reprocessing technologies have been available for over sixty years; the ability of certain actors to access that information has increased, however. In addition, all countries treat information differently (e.g., what is deemed commercial/proprietary information might be restricted weapons-usable data in another), which complicates efforts to protect information flow. There also needs to be continued effort to find reprocessing methods that are less risky. A leader needs to emerge that has used the new technology—either the United States or another advanced nuclear country. There is a downside to taking a point of view that reprocessing is bad, and there are advantages to support less risky reprocessing as that would be more in line with reality and possibly encourage the next user to use something that is less risky." "Potentially, fast breeder reactors with high-fissile blanket assemblies (need to avoid conventional fast breeder reactors with blankets)—having weapons-grade Pu in commercial circulation is both a proliferation and a terrorism risk." "The present nonproliferation and physical protection regimes are working quite well to prevent the large spread of nuclear weapons. There are unfortunately a few countries that work outside these regimes or try to circumvent them by developing their own technologies (either on their own, or by obtaining the necessary items in a crooked way, by trying to mislead some countries)." *Minor themes* "Small reactors (e.g., research reactors)." "Uranium mining poses one of the greatest nonproliferation challenges because it is not easy to follow up on production and also uranium can be extracted from other ore-like phosphates. . . . In the near future, laser separation will be also a very important challenge."

| 3. | To what extent does the projected expansion of the nuclear energy sector (in new and existing countries) represent a threat to the current nonproliferation regime? | Most respondents noted the expansion of the energy sector was not a threat per se, but that the actions of rogue nations posed the biggest threat, not the energy side. Several responded that an escalation of IAEA verification requirements without a corresponding increase in IAEA resources could pose risks. | Views ranged from: No threat if IAEA resources keep pace and all countries sign the NPT and Additional Protocol to Some threat Threat if it leads to the spread of fuel cycle technologies or the installation/maintenance of HEU-using research reactors or the introduction of fast reactors without adequate management of the Pu breeding potential |

Major themes

"Activities in the nuclear energy sector are closely and efficiently monitored by states and international organizations who collectively take commitments to prevent proliferation from occurring in the civilian nuclear industry. This system has been effective for the last thirty years. There is a growing consensus among the countries that have mastered the sensitive technologies at an industrial level that the export of enrichment and reprocessing facilities should be limited to a restricted number of countries to avoid any risk of proliferation."

"The expansion of the nuclear energy sector itself will not be a threat. If a country that is isolated from the international society projects the nuclear activities, it could be a threat."

"As long as there is control over the use of enrichment services, there should not be a concern for proliferation."

"A minor threat—important to make sure that important institutional arrangements are in place and that full-scope IAEA safeguards are applied."

Major themes

"Expansion of nuclear power reactors with once-through fuel cycle does not pose too much proliferation risk. But growing interests in sensitive fuel cycle technologies (enrichment and reprocessing) may represent a major threat to nonproliferation regime. The double standards in dealing with developing nuclear countries may also pose significant threat. In this context, U.S.-India nuclear cooperation was a major setback for global nonproliferation regime."

"The use of high enriched uranium would constitute a greater challenge to the current nonproliferation regime. Even for reactors that don't use high enriched uranium, there needs to be work done by industry, the International Atomic Energy Agency and national Ministries of Energy to identify which reactor technologies pose less or more of a proliferation risk, and strategies to promote or discourage their use need to be developed. For example, newer technologies for fast breeders have a significant risk, where smaller reactors with light water are less risky. An overall strategy to identify and encourage less risky technologies would be useful."

Minor themes

"The greatly expanded quantity of materials of concern and the active development of many national programs threaten to overwhelm the capacity of the regulatory system. Also, the current system spends a huge amount of effort controlling materials of no proliferation significance (e.g., sub-kg quantities of depleted uranium in university and small research labs), reducing the effort available to address facilities of real concern."

"A considerable number of new nuclear power plants are likely to be constructed around the world in countries in which there is no real industrial culture and consequently characterized by an absence of basic infrastructures to manage security, safety, and nonproliferation matters. This prospective market is already attracting competition among technology suppliers, which should not be done at the expense of security and nonproliferation standards."

(continued)

Table 5-1 (*continued*)

Challenges	Industry	Nonindustry
4. What are the weaknesses and institutional gaps of the current nonproliferation regime? What mistakes can we learn from? In what ways has the nonproliferation regime been successfully strengthened to date?	The current regime is "robust and efficient" but needs to universalize implementation of the Additional Protocol and enforce sanctions. *Major themes* "To reinforce the existing regime, the focus should be put on the collective answer the international community could take when confronted with a clear misconduct from one of the signatories of the relevant conventions." "Strengthened through coordinated political pressure and sanctions." *Minor themes* "The problem is there is no direct means for deterrence . . . to nonsensible states." "The current system is an outdated cold war system and does not enforce the commitments or treaties that it has." "Weaknesses: the possibility to ignore treaties, mistakes: underestimate determination to develop enrichment."	Major weaknesses include: Lack of universality of the NPT The discriminatory nature of the treaty Double standards for countries Import/export controls Disconnect between safeguards and security Imprecision in NPT on Article IV "rights" Unwillingness of nuclear suppliers to make Additional Protocol a condition of supply Inadequate resourcing of IAEA safeguards *Major themes* "Safeguards/physical protection measures have shown tremendous improvements (technically). Still, we cannot rely solely on technical measures (failure in Iraq, North Korea, and now with Iran). Improvements in safeguards (Additional Protocol) and UNSC 1540 are . . . successes to strengthen non-proliferation and nuclear security." *Minor themes* "The declared nuclear weapons states need to engage in a more constructive dialogue with the non–nuclear weapons states equally on all aspects of the NPT." "The safeguards regime is tailored to be effective in countries with open democratic regime because the safeguards system is founded on states' voluntary declarations regarding all its nuclear materials and nuclear activities. North Korea and Iran are good illustrations [of] inspectorate difficulties [in verification]."

5. To what extent do new technologies increase/decrease proliferation risk?	Generally, technologies were viewed as helping decrease risks (with an implicit assumption that they would not be deployed if they increased risks), except for laser enrichment.	Those technologies that make it more difficult for proliferators to conceal their activities decrease the risk; some technologies, like laser enrichment, increase the risk. New recycling technologies could increase or decrease the risks.

Major themes

Technologies can incorporate design features that aid in the implementation of safeguards ("safeguardability"), but none can solve proliferation by themselves.

"If the technical capability (of safeguards) in real time with a higher precision and less manpower could be developed, it could help reduce nuclear proliferation risks. And when dry reprocessing is industrialized enough, it could improve proliferation-resistance in the future."

"Generation IV reactors reduce the risk and new laser-based enrichment technologies may increase the risk. However, these risks are trivial compared with clandestine programs disconnected from the nuclear fuel cycle."

"More effective/efficient enrichment is a threat as could be FBR [fast breeder reactor] developments."

"Proliferation resistance can be designed in. Burning of plutonium stocks in fast reactors should be encouraged. Co-processing should replace reprocessing."

Major themes

"New technologies are critical to the safe and secure operation of nuclear facilities. In addition, some technologies—e.g., remote-sensing devices— make it more difficult for proliferators to conceal their activities. The information security practices, not the technology itself, proves to be the proliferation risk."

"Small- and medium-reactor technologies with lifetime cores could be a big step forward in limiting fuel cycle risks."

"As long as reprocessing is involved, the advantages of an advanced fuel cycle are minor. Best way is to shift away from reprocessing/plutonium fuel cycle. Uranium from seawater and chemical enrichment process can provide long-term fuel cycle solution without relying on plutonium (and potential HEU capability)."

Minor themes

"Proliferation risk depends mainly on political factors, and hardly on technological factors. . . . The availability of an enrichment or reprocessing technique that is technologically very easy to develop and very cheap would probably increase the proliferation risk, but still the decision is a political one. So new technologies will not influence to a large extent the proliferation risk."

"Centrifuge enrichment is more sensitive to proliferation than diffusion enrichment, but it can be well managed with the appropriate safeguards and physical protection measures. Laser enrichment is even more sensitive, allows you to reach any enrichment you want and could be used to enrich plutonium also (contrary to the present commercially available enrichment technologies). With respect to reprocessing: (a) using the PUREX-process to separate uranium and plutonium and with further development of this process, neptunium, americium and curium, has a certain proliferation risk, although this can be well managed by appropriate safeguards measures. (b) COEX reduces the risk. Quickly transforming the Pu into MOX-fuel would be a further advantage. (c) Rrecycling so that plutonium is separated from uranium, but remains with the minor actinides would be a further improvement, making it more difficult to use the materials for nuclear weapons."

Table 5-2. *Responses and Selected Comments on Solutions for Strengthening the Nonproliferation Regime*

Solutions	Industry	Nonindustry
1. How could the current Nonproliferation Treaty (NPT) be modified to better address the threats of nuclear proliferation? Which articles?	Only nine of twenty-two respondents answered, with the others deferring to governments or declining to comment. *Comments* "The NPT needs more teeth and is outdated." "The NPT needs to be updated to account for countries that have developed nuclear weapons. Industry should be engaged to inform government discussions." *Minor themes* "Need international agreement on terms for peaceful use."	The treaty should be left alone. Alternative approaches include developing shared interpretations and other, linked mechanisms. *Major themes* "Need to change 'withdrawal' clause. May need stronger clause on penalties on noncompliance." "Impossible to amend NPT, disastrous to try." "Renegotiation of NPT is politically impossible and nobody wants to open the 'Pandora's Box.'"
2. What are your views on the proposed multinational agreements (MNAs) for the management of the fuel cycle? Would fuel-cycle related MNAs strengthen/weaken the current nonproliferation regime? Which fuel-cycle MNA model do you think would work best?	Concerned that multilateral nuclear approaches (MNAs) will negatively influence competition in the industry. *Major themes* "There is potential to gain more control of the nuclear material, at the risk of increasing the international flow of nuclear material. These two aspects need to be addressed simultaneously." "The role of any MNA mechanism should be to ensure the capacity of delivery in case of fuel shortages or default of a provider on the market, except when the suspension of delivery has been decided in the appropriate international context or level. Today the market is performing very well in meeting demand and addressing nonproliferation."	Multinational arrangements for the fuel cycle were largely viewed as appropriate and useful, provided that they do not leak information and are welcomed by recipients. *Major themes* "Will need a broad menu of MNA approaches to meet varied needs of current and newcomer users. Front-end-only approaches are a good starting point to help develop the concept, but approaches (like fuel leasing or regional repositories) that address the back end will be most effective because solving the back-end problem has the best chance to be seen as valuable enough that it's worth accepting limitations on indigenous fuel cycle facilities." "Internationalization (multinational ownership) of the nuclear fuel cycle is the most practical and effective way to go. URENCO is a good model, although technology leak was a bad example. Spent fuel take-back is a good idea but on-site spent fuel storage might be a better, quicker, and more economical way to minimize reprocessing activities." "MNAs are essential, provided they do not result in proliferation of technology know-how. The ideal model is a fuel cycle center operated on a black-box

"The impact of the proposed MNAs on the commercial actors in the nuclear fuel cycle must be very carefully examined before implementation. The industry must be substantively engaged in the process to design these MNAs to ensure that they do not result in unexpected perverse outcomes."

basis, with involvement of technology holder, and with carefully selected site [low-risk country]. Could be established on regional basis, with some participation by staff from regional countries, and equity interest [profit-sharing] by the members of the region."

"MNAs could strengthen the transparency and trust in a certain region, but will not prevent proliferation if a state really has taken the political decision to develop nuclear weapons. In the ideal case MNAs should incorporate all sensitive technologies (enrichment, reprocessing and possibly MOX fabrication), but from a pragmatic point of view starting with a nuclear fuel bank would already be an achievement."

"The fuel banks could work well, but they should not be situated in a large powerful country (which could misuse its power in case one should be obliged to call on the materials in the bank). The bank should be situated in a small country, which has, however, sufficient nuclear capacity and expertise to operate a fuel bank. Ideally the fuel bank should be situated on the same site as other nuclear fuel cycle facilities, in order to reduce the costs. Furthermore, the bank should best be situated in several countries, to reduce the impossibility not to be able to use it completely (this would however increase the operating cost). I am convinced that the multinational approaches as proposed by the IAEA will strengthen the current nonproliferation regime. Fewer countries will be inclined to try to obtain sensitive nuclear technology, which is certainly a positive development."

"MNAs would be attractive to governments and operators as an alternative to the costs, complexities, and burdens of sensitive fuel cycle facilities. But MNAs could be considered by some countries as a new restriction regarding nuclear energy access and could be a factor to increase the confrontation North-South and a possible emergence of new suppliers like Brazil. As a first stage, leasing for fuel can be a good solution regarding proliferation risk in front-end and for back-end fuel cycle by returning the spent fuel to the lessor."

(continued)

Table 5-2 (*continued*)

Solutions	Industry	Nonindustry
3. What could the IAEA do to better address the challenges of nonproliferation in the twenty-first century?	Resources were a major theme, including improving expertise, human resources, and the IAEA's capability to detect clandestine weapons programs. *Major themes* "Every effort should be made to technically restrict proliferation through maintaining plutonium and uranium in mixed oxides and limit the ability to separate the two." "IAEA is heading in the right direction. It should look for more resources, global outreach, stricter enforcement, universal adoption of the additional protocol." *Minor themes* "The current role of IAEA is limited to monitoring the technical aspect without considering political environment. It means the international monitoring program and/or institute on political aspects must be added or supplemented."	Responses were quite specific, from the need for the IAEA to prioritize its programs and safeguards objectives, and to cross-train between safety, security, and safeguards. *Major themes* "The IAEA needs to more clearly articulate funding needs and how they relate to programs. . . . The expert panel's 20/20 report on the future of the IAEA did not prioritize IAEA's activities, as it was asked to do; it simply added more to the wish list. Staffing practices also need to be addressed (e.g., mandatory retirement at sixty-two is detrimental to ongoing activities and knowledge management)." "Cross-train safeguards inspectors to observe security at sites they visit and report back to nuclear security staff at IAEA to help prioritize and focus outreach/IPPAS [International Physical Protection Advisory Service] missions; increase nuclear security budget/staff/IPPAS missions/assistance; implement MNA mechanisms." *Minor themes* "1. Better integrate technical cooperation [TC] with safeguards—TC has contributed to proliferation problems. 2. Promote MNAs—which means less emphasis on building national programs and capabilities. 3. Better promotion of the national interest of all states in an effective nonproliferation system. 4. Stronger attitude toward safeguards violations. 5. Campaign to reduce the politicization of the agency has damaged the IAEA." "The IAEA could . . . [organize] a systematic dialogue with the companies involved (suppliers and customers), by exchanging information in what both sides are doing and by giving advice to each other. The same should happen between the Nuclear Supplier's Group and the industry."

"The IAEA could take on a stronger role in helping newcomers to build their nuclear infrastructure. In the field of nuclear verification, the ability of the agency to detect possible clandestine nuclear material and activities depends on the necessary legal authority, technology, and resources given to the Safeguards Department. It is essential for IAEA to address the challenges of nonproliferation in the future."

"Develop a more technical, less political board of governors."

4. In making nuclear power more safe, secure, and proliferation-resistant, how would you prioritize technical vs. institutional approaches?

Equal importance. Institutional measures will always be needed, and technical measures can help make them more cost-effective.

Major themes

"Both strong institutional capability and advanced technological tools can assist with preventing and detecting proliferation and strengthening security. Technology can greatly improve safety as well as sound design, operation, and maintenance of facilities. Neither one should be prioritized over the other. Both are equally important and complementary. Proliferation is a political problem that needs political solutions."

"Both are necessary"

"Techniques and institutions work together to make [nuclear power] safe, secure, and proliferation-resistant. Progressing of techniques and creating institutions must be in parallel."

Minor themes

"Technical and institutional approaches should be pursued in parallel as one informs the other."

"Institutional (mandatory/sanctions) prevail."

The best technology cannot compensate for institutional deficiencies, while institutional strengths cannot fully compensate for technical shortcomings.

Major themes

"Needs a tailored balance. No technology will ever be perfectly proliferation-resistant, but different technologies will require different institutional approaches."

"Technical approaches can always be defeated by a determined proliferator. Proliferation risks associated with, for example, disposed fuel or nuclear materials, persist on a time scale of centuries or longer. We cannot envisage how technology will develop on this time scale so we have to have robust institutional controls to ensure nonproliferation. The institutional framework is therefore vital."

"Institutional approaches by international and national bodies should have the upper hand over technical approaches."

Minor themes

"We should try to obtain a kind of intrinsic proliferation-resistant fuel cycle, just like we strive for intrinsic safe nuclear power plants. On the other hand, [regardless of] the technical solution, institutional measures will always be necessary. Safeguards (surveillance, accountability, installation verification, etc.) will always have to be applied on the nuclear materials. . . . An appropriate equilibrium should be found in technical solutions which increase on the one hand proliferation resistance, while, on the other hand, allowing the appropriate application of the necessary safeguards measures. This is a difficult equilibrium exercise."

"Highest priority is to reduce inventory (stockpile) of HEU and plutonium and minimize further separation of plutonium. International arrangement may be possible and effective to "dispose" civilian plutonium stockpile."

(continued)

Table 5-2 (*continued*)

Solutions	Industry	Nonindustry
5. What is your view of the need for industry to be a partner with government in managing proliferation risks? How strong is the incentive for engagement? Beyond regulation, what should be the relationship between government and industry in such a partnership?	In some countries, nuclear industry is already in close partnership. Among many, common view that the government should take the lead. *Major themes* "There is no export of material, equipment, or facility without the prior written approval of the government. A key incentive for industry is to preserve its reputation and to be recognized as a responsible nuclear stakeholder and actor. Regular exchanges between the government and the nuclear energy industry providers already exist in most of the major providers' countries." *Minor themes* "The incentive for engagement is currently not very strong because the nonproliferation regime has been driven by governments and the IAEA (which is appropriate) with relatively little opportunity for input from industry. Industry should have greater opportunity to engage with IAEA and governments on nonproliferation regulation in order to continually review the effectiveness of the regime and to develop efficient improvements." "Industry does not need to be a "partner" (inter)national law should regulate the behavior." "Self-control by industry must be incentivized in participation of government-sponsored program."	Most respondents held that the role of industry is critical in minimizing proliferation risks, but that stronger incentives or a fundamental recognition that nonproliferation is essential in expanding civilian nuclear energy, just like safety, was needed. Some held that industry was already an integral partner, others that better cooperation was needed. *Major themes* "They are automatically partners, with serious advantages through collaboration. The best incentive is the possibility for sanctions by the government." "Mainstream nuclear industry is not a major problem . . . [but rather] the component manufacturers, where too many companies are prepared to turn a blind eye to make a sale. Need for strong enforcement by governments, including prosecution of individuals and seizure of assets." "Government [should] understand the needs and constraints of industry and . . . not impose unnecessary and unreasonable requirements for little gain, and industry [should] understand the government's needs and the international picture. This would allow effort to be appropriately targeted without unnecessarily restricting competitiveness." *Minor themes* "An informal partnership approach is essential. Industry and government have the same objectives but different roles. Increased dialogue, voluntary codes of practice, etc. should be encouraged." "Beyond regulation, effective implementation is the most important concern regarding export control, and it is the basis of effective cooperation between industry and governmental bodies."

6

Multilateral Approaches to the Nuclear Fuel Cycle

LAWRENCE SCHEINMAN AND GOVINDA AVASARALA

States may seek independence in fuel cycle development for many reasons, including national prestige, regional political prominence, technological independence, assurance of nuclear fuel supply, or even a determination to acquire nuclear weapons or to be in a position to do so.[1] Whatever the motivation, the link between national enrichment and reprocessing programs and nuclear proliferation suggests that the forthcoming expansion of the civil nuclear industry could bring a commensurate increase in the risk of proliferation if each state develops indigenous fuel cycle capabilities.

However, while the nonproliferation case for limiting facilities capable of producing weapons-usable material is clear, the means by which to do so in a system of sovereign states is not. For over fifty years attempts have been made to organize the nuclear fuel cycle on the basis of global or regionalized multilateral fuel cycle centers. Most of these have come to naught. Article IV of the Nuclear Nonproliferation Treaty (NPT) asserts an "inalienable right of all the Parties to the Treaty to develop research, production and use of nuclear energy for peaceful purposes without discrimination and in conformity with Article I and II of this Treaty," which most NPT signatories regard as including all fuel cycle activities carried out for peaceful purposes under international safeguards. Any attempt to infringe on the Article IV rights of states is seen as discriminatory and as an attempt to create a divide between nuclear "haves" and "have-nots."

While the disputes over nuclear sovereignty rumble on, the threats to the nuclear nonproliferation regime are increasing. Even without the projected increase in the number of states in the global nuclear sector, the regime is burdened by long-running weaknesses, not to mention new challenges arising from a changing commercial and geopolitical landscape (see chapter 1). If the global nuclear sector is indeed on the verge of a nuclear renaissance, the need for a secure, controlled approach to the fuel cycle is greater than ever before.

In the past such approaches have faltered on the inability of states to reach agreements. The commercial nuclear industry had been by and large absent from the discussion. However, in the globalized, nuclear sector of the twenty-first century, commercial industry has an increasingly important role. With this consideration in mind, the Brookings study sought to elicit the views of both the public and private sectors on a range of multilateral nuclear approaches (MNAs) to the fuel cycle.[2] After tracing the history of MNAs, this chapter outlines the responses of industry and nonindustry participants when asked to rank the effectiveness and feasibility of a series of MNA proposals. The conclusions drawn from their responses point to a prospective MNA mechanism for addressing the needs of states and companies while simultaneously strengthening the nonproliferation regime.

Historical Context of MNAs

When the United Nations Atomic Energy Commission held its first meeting in 1946, it was presented with a U.S.-backed proposal, known as the Baruch Plan, for the international control of atomic energy.[3] Based on the findings of the State Department's Acheson-Lilienthal report of the same year, the Baruch Plan proposed the creation of an international agency that would manage, oversee, and have the authority to control, inspect, and license all atomic energy activities. Though the proposal was ambitious at the time—and quixotic by today's standards—it represents the first effort to multilateralize nuclear energy. However, whatever chance there might have been for acceptance was foreclosed by the cold war tensions that dominated post–World War II relations.

Well before the Baruch Plan was finally abandoned, the United States, in its Atomic Energy Act of 1946, established a policy of secrecy and denial, prohibiting any peaceful nuclear cooperation until Congress was satisfied that effective international safeguards were in place. The limitations of this approach—demonstrated by the entry of the Soviet Union and the United Kingdom into the "nuclear club," concern about security implications of a nuclear arms race, and the emergence of unrestricted national nuclear programs in an increasing number of countries—led to a shift in policy to nuclear cooperation and assistance, spelled out in President Dwight Eisenhower's December 1953 "Atoms for Peace" speech at the United Nations.

The president's initiative called for, among other things, the establishment of an international agency as a focal point for promoting civil nuclear cooperation as well as for verifying peaceful use through a system of safeguards—a proposal that led to the creation of the International Atomic Energy Agency (IAEA). Although earlier judged by the Acheson-Lilienthal report to be inadequate for preventing nuclear proliferation, an international safeguards system was deemed to be the biggest possible step nations were willing to take in balancing the infringement upon national sovereignty and the prospect for access to nuclear equipment, material, and technology. Little has changed in this regard over the past sixty years—sovereign sensitivities and aversion to discrimination are still critical factors when states consider the acceptability of limitations on their activities and restraints that are selective rather than universal.

Several events in the 1970s generated renewed U.S. interest in multilateral institutional arrangements to limit the proliferation of sensitive nuclear technologies and materials. The most significant was India's May 1974 "peaceful nuclear explosion" using a reactor supplied by Canada and a heavy-water moderator from the United States, both of which were provided for exclusively peaceful purposes and which led the United States and Canada to suspend nuclear cooperation with India. The second set of events was France's offer to transfer reprocessing technology to Pakistan, and Germany's agreement to provide Brazil with advanced enrichment technology, both of which were strongly resisted by Washington. France then withdrew the offer to Pakistan, and Germany provided a less advanced enrichment technology to Brazil. With the oil price shocks of the mid- to late 1970s, interest in nuclear energy increased more generally as nations began seeking alternate ways to meet rising energy demand. However, this trend also enhanced the prospect of sensitive technology transfers.

The challenge of sensitive technology proliferation was raised at the 1974 IAEA general conference with attention given to the possibility of establishing internationally approved facilities to handle all spent fuel arising from power reactors as an alternative to individual countries developing their own technologies for this purpose. The final declaration of the ensuing 1975 NPT review conference included the finding that "regional or multinational nuclear fuel cycle centers may be an advantageous way to satisfy, safely and economically, the needs of many states, while at the same time facilitating protection and the application of IAEA safeguards and contributing to the goals of the Treaty."[4]

A number of proposals ensued, often, but not necessarily always, with U.S. leadership and strong encouragement. One was the establishment of the Nuclear Suppliers Group (NSG), initiated by the United States, which included only the key nuclear suppliers at the time and resulted in an agreed set of conditions and rules for nuclear cooperation. Other proposals focused on specific structural initiatives, including a recommendation for the establishment of regional nuclear fuel cycle centers (1975), and for international plutonium storage (1978–82). Others were more in the nature of studies intended to lead to specific institutional proposals: these include the International Nuclear Fuel Cycle Evaluation (1977–79), the IAEA Committee on Assurances of Supply (1980–87), and the Conference for the Promotion of International Cooperation on the Peaceful Uses of Nuclear Energy (1987). With the exception of the NSG initiative, none of the aforementioned approaches gained enough momentum to be implemented owing to a variety of political, economic, and technical reasons, although some lessons and ideas were utilized over time. The decline of civilian nuclear programs in the 1980s led to a decreased level of interest in such efforts.

Since the turn of the century, interest in MNAs has been renewed, starting with former IAEA director general Mohamed ElBaradei's call in September 2003 for a multilateral system for enrichment, reprocessing, and disposal.[5] ElBaradei followed up his proposal with a stark assessment of the necessity of a new approach to management of the fuel cycle in 2006. Writing about nuclear proliferation and arms control in the *Washington Post,* he concluded that "the fundamental problem is clear: either we begin finding creative, outside-the-box solutions or the international nuclear safeguards regime will become obsolete."[6]

ElBaradei's judgment reflects the new dynamics that have emerged in the past decade or so (summarized in chapter 1). It is critical to view a potential nuclear expansion through the lens of these changes in order to meet the challenges they pose for the current nonproliferation regime and for the global nuclear order. In particular, securing all aspects of the fuel cycle and ensuring that the nonproliferation regime has the means to exercise effective control over proliferation-sensitive technologies will require the "outside-the-box" thinking referred to by ElBaradei. International safeguards have been quite effective in deterring diversion of *declared* nuclear material but face a challenge in detecting *undeclared* nuclear activities, in particular enrichment facilities based on centrifuge technology. As indicated in chapter 2, even in the case of declared facilities that are under safeguards, there is the latent risk of a state withdrawing from the NPT and retaining control over facilities capable of producing weapons-usable material—a prospect already realized through North Korea's withdrawal from the NPT with all of its facilities intact, independent of safeguards, and under its national control.

Today's Proposals and the Growing Schism between the "Haves" and the "Have Nots"

In recent years a range of initiatives have been introduced in an effort to reconcile the development of nuclear energy for peaceful purposes with measures to prevent states from using their nuclear capacity to acquire nuclear weapons.[7]

Many multilateral organizations and some "supplier" states promote MNAs to transfer sensitive nuclear fuel cycle technologies from the jurisdiction of national governments to multilateral institutions. In engaging this "denationalization" of the nuclear fuel cycle, nations, the IAEA, and nongovernmental organizations such as the Nuclear Threat Initiative (NTI) and the World Nuclear Association (WNA) have proposed various mechanisms: international fuel banks, international enrichment facilities, multinationalization of enrichment and reprocessing facilities, lease and take-back offers, spent fuel repositories, fuel-supply guarantees (in exchange for commitments), and financing mechanisms (that is, subsidies) to guarantee supply.

Virtually all proposals seek to limit the further spread of enrichment and reprocessing technology and include provisions for assurance of nuclear fuel supply for civilian power reactors. More specifically, these initiatives include proposals by the United States (Global Nuclear Energy Partnership, GNEP), Russia (Global Nuclear Power Infrastructure, GNPI), the United Kingdom (enrichment bonds), a six-country proposal on reliable access to nuclear fuel (RANF), and an IAEA multilateral alternative to national nuclear fuel cycle proposals. Beyond these is Germany's more ambitious Multilateral Enrichment Sanctuary Project (MESP), a proposal that goes beyond assurances of nuclear supply by third parties to the establishment of a commercially run enrichment facility in an extraterritorial location administered by the IAEA. Such a facility would be owned and managed by an international commercial company with participating states as co-owners, and would provide the technology on a "black-box" basis, through which states would have access to the product but not the technology used to make it.

In a speech at the National Defense University in February 2004, President George W. Bush took matters a step further, calling upon NSG members to agree not to transfer sensitive nuclear technology to any country that did not already have a fully operational enrichment or reprocessing capability, and to ensure that those who forgo national enrichment and reprocessing would have a reliable supply of nuclear fuel for civil purposes. The aforementioned GNEP, a much broader enterprise with more emphasis on opportunity than on constraint and denial, sought to do the same thing: it would expand domestic and international use of nuclear energy, pursue proliferation-resistant recycling of spent fuel, develop advanced reactors, and establish reliable global fuel services by a consortium of suppliers for states that forgo national development of sensitive fuel cycle activities. It went further in calling for a "cradle-to-grave" concept of supply assurance, in which suppliers take responsibility for dealing with spent fuel. Without explicitly challenging the right of NPT parties to pursue fuel cycle development for peaceful purposes, the GNEP sought to offer a better alternative to states that chose to forgo domestic enrichment and reprocessing capabilities—which are high in costs and often less reliable than the international supply market—in exchange for reliable supply of nuclear fuel. States accepting that offer would qualify for nuclear fuel assurance.

ElBaradei took a more ecumenical and inclusive approach to the problem. He started from the premise that, under the NPT, sensitive nuclear technology development and use for civil purposes are not proscribed, and having that capability is not inconsistent with the NPT's rights and obligations. Nevertheless, in pursuing the capacity to do so for peaceful purposes, a state also acquires the ability to produce sensitive nuclear material for military use. To this end, he endorsed pursuing strategies that, while dependent upon international safeguards, reach beyond them. The objective of this approach was to achieve better control over sensitive nuclear fuel cycle activity, and to do so by institutional means through some form of multilateral control that would be effective as well as politically equitable.

In pursuit of this objective, ElBaradei appointed an international committee of experts to examine ways and means to manage the fuel cycle, with particular attention to how to bring about multilateral oversight for sensitive activities, including assurance of nuclear supply and options for dealing with spent fuel storage. On the assumption that countries would enter into multilateral arrangements according to the economic and political incentives and disincentives on offer, the committee argued that "a new binding international norm stipulating that sensitive fuel cycle activities are to be conducted exclusively in the context of MNAs and no longer as a national undertaking would amount to a change in the scope of Article IV of the NPT."[8]

However, while skepticism about multilateralism was not absent among those participating, it was included in a sequence of measures that were regarded as appropriate to the objective of facilitating increased use of nuclear energy for peaceful purposes while averting a proliferation of sensitive fuel cycle facilities. The committee concluded its report by stating that nonproliferation and security of fuel supply and services could be achieved through a set of "gradually introduced multilateral nuclear approaches." These included

> —Reinforcing existing commercial market mechanisms on a case-by-case basis through long-term contracts and transparent suppliers' arrangements with government backing. Examples would be fuel leasing and fuel take-back, commercial offers to store and dispose of spent fuel, and commercial fuel banks.
>
> —Developing and implementing international supply guarantees with IAEA participation. Different models should be investigated, notably with the IAEA as a guarantor of service supplies, e.g., as administrator of a fuel bank.

—Promoting voluntary conversion of existing facilities to MNAs, and pursuing them as confidence-building measures, with the participation of NPT non–nuclear weapon states and nuclear weapon states, and non-NPT states.

—Creating, through voluntary arrangements and contracts, multinational, and in particular regional, MNAs for new facilities based on joint ownership, drawing rights or co-management for front-end and back-end nuclear facilities, such as uranium enrichment, fuel reprocessing, disposal and storage of spent fuel (and combinations thereof). Integrated nuclear power parks would also serve this objective.

—The scenario for a further expansion of nuclear energy around the world might call for the development of a nuclear fuel cycle with stronger multilateral arrangements—by region or by continent—and broader cooperation involving the IAEA and the international community.[9]

The fundamental difference between President Bush's national approach to the fuel cycle and ElBaradei's multilateral approach is that the former was a *restrictive* strategy and the latter is more of a *cooperative* strategy. The restrictive approach requires non–nuclear weapons states (NNWS) to renounce development of the technology related to sensitive nuclear fuel cycle activity. The cooperative approach focuses on institutional alternatives to strictly national operation of such activities as enrichment or reprocessing by engaging in the development of regional or multilateral centers. Both strategies are reinforced by a reliable assurance-of-supply mechanism. A restrictive approach, as noted earlier, raises a basic issue regarding the provisions in Article IV of the NPT concerning the "inalienable right" of a non–nuclear weapon state party to the treaty to develop nuclear energy for peaceful purposes, and the obligation of all states party to the treaty to facilitate and cooperate in "the fullest possible exchange of equipment, materials, and scientific and technological information for the peaceful uses of nuclear energy." This is a highly contentious issue. Any attempt to redefine the conditions for "peaceful use" must take into account the consideration that any arrangement deemed not to be fair and universal could put the nonproliferation regime at risk of unraveling. Moreover, to be acceptable, any approach that places limits on the right to technological development will have to be applied universally, with no exceptions.

Herein lies the growing schism in international nuclear negotiations. As with proposals brought forth during the 1970s, a disconnect between two groups is impeding progress. Four decades ago, the disagreement was between nations intent on reprocessing spent fuel and those opposed to the process.[10] Today the schism is between states with and without nuclear weapons. Those without weapons refuse to give up sovereignty over national nuclear programs when nations having them fail to take concrete measures toward disarmament. The fact that all MNAs thus far have originated from "supplier states"—nations that currently supply more than 90 percent of total global enriched uranium— merely adds to the notion that nuclear weapons states are seeking to impose constraints on the pursuit of national nuclear independence.[11]

Nations with nascent nuclear capacity have publicly expressed displeasure with the proposals extended so far, contending that such multilateral mechanisms infringe on their "inalienable right" to civilian nuclear power as extended to them through Article IV of the NPT. Many emerging nuclear nations argue that an MNA creates a suppliers' cartel, as the NSG was perceived to be upon its inception in the mid-1970s. In hedging against this fear, current nonsupplier states such as Argentina, Australia, Brazil, Canada, South Africa, South Korea, and Ukraine have all shown interest in and, in some cases, taken steps to develop sensitive nuclear technologies, for the most part focusing on domestic uranium enrichment.[12]

As a result of this widening dispute, two concerns require consideration: whether to establish national nuclear fuel cycles or to depend on an international market dominated by a small number of states and cooperative enterprises; and whether the existing market structure can integrate newcomers successfully while averting a proliferation of independent facilities. Of particular importance in this regard is the perspective of those who dominate the international market for nuclear fuel, and within that framework the perspective of the nuclear industry.

The Brookings Survey

The prospect that non–nuclear weapons states will willingly forgo or limit a right that is regarded as inherent in Article IV while nuclear weapons states continue to retain, and in some cases enhance, their arsenals, is remote. Consequently, the world is no closer today to the point where an Acheson-Lilienthal initiative for international ownership and control of the fuel cycle would be acceptable than it was sixty-five years ago. However, with the proliferation of nuclear know-how, technology, material, and equipment, and a world rife with tensions and instabilities that go beyond the nation-state to include substate transnational terrorism, there is no option but to persevere in pursuing means by which to keep the nuclear risk under control.

Given that background, the Brookings survey included ten distinct proposals for the multinationalization of the nuclear fuel cycle through nuclear fuel banks, centralized facilities, lease and take-back programs, international storage or depositories, fuel guarantees, or market intervention mechanisms. The survey asked industry and government and international institutions to rank each proposal on its effectiveness (ability to strengthen the nonproliferation regime) and feasibility (ability to implement the proposal given logistical and political constraints). The responses and illustrative comments are summarized in table 6-1 (p. 162).

Nuclear Fuel Bank

Various plans for fuel banks have been discussed for decades, but past proposals were never viewed seriously owing to a lack of significant political support. This may be changing, as highlighted by President Barack Obama's explicit endorsement of the mechanism during a speech in Prague in April 2009.[13] Today more than a dozen fuel-assurance proposals have been put forward, including ones for the Russian-backed International Uranium Enrichment Center (IUEC) and the NTI-proposed IAEA-NTI Nuclear Fuel Bank, both of which have been approved.[14] Established in 2009, the IUEC will stock low-enriched uranium (LEU) at an enrichment facility at Angarsk, Siberia; the facility "is chiefly oriented to states not developing uranium enrichment capabilities on their territory."[15] The IUEC incorporates two principal components. First, as a production facility, it will provide enriched uranium to stakeholder countries. It has already signed supply agreements with Armenia, Kazakhstan, and Ukraine, all of which have an equity stake in the facility; there is a prospect that other nations will join in the future. Second, in coordination with the IAEA, the IUEC has established an "assurance arrangement"—a fuel bank—to provide fuel to nations that have no access to nuclear fuel but are in good financial and nonproliferation standing. The most distinctive feature of the IUEC is that it will ensure supply to nations that have been denied access to fuel for reasons unrelated to nonproliferation or commercial considerations; it is not intended to *replace* or *compete with* the existing system.

Proponents of the fuel bank system contend that by offering assurance of LEU supply, it will make nations interested in developing domestic nuclear power capacity less inclined to invest in domestic enrichment facilities. By limiting the number of enrichment facilities and consequently the diffusion of sensitive technologies and knowledge, the fuel bank proposal aims to prevent future abuse of Article X of the NPT, which gives a signatory nation the option to withdraw from the treaty should it ever "jeopardize the supreme interests of the country". (North Korea infamously invoked Article X and used the technologies and materials it acquired as a signatory state to develop its nuclear weapons program once it withdrew from the treaty.)

Concerns over the implementation of a fuel bank mirror the concerns regarding MNAs in general: most emerging nuclear states worry about exacerbating the growing divide between "supplier" and "importer" states, as well as the development of a nuclear cartel, particularly if fuel banks are located in nuclear weapons states, which the non-weapons states fear will increase the existing technological asymmetry between the two groups. Commercial vendors are also concerned about the impact of a multilateral fuel bank on the current market system, which to date has had no significant supply disruption issues.

SURVEY RESULTS

Though a number of variations of the fuel bank framework exist, the Brookings survey focused on two fundamental proposals:

—**Proposal 1.** An IAEA-administered international enriched uranium fuel bank accessible to all countries.

—**Proposal 2.** An IAEA-administered international enriched uranium fuel bank accessible to all countries in compliance with NPT regulations.

Most industry respondents ranked proposal 1 as *ineffective* and *unfeasible,* because of its indiscriminate inclusiveness; that is, it provides access to all nations regardless of compliance with NPT obligations. As one respondent commented, "Free availability of EUP [enriched uranium product] without strings attached to 'all countries' will not reduce the risk of proliferation, if these do not abide by safeguards verification provisions." The universality of this approach also presents difficulties in the political feasibility of implementation, with one respondent suggesting that "noncompliance [to the NPT] should be a show-stopper."

Most industry respondents ranked proposal 2 as the most effective of all the MNA proposals, in that it solves the problem of universal availability of LEU, but there was no consensus on its feasibility. A common theme among industry respondents was that even this approach will not deter non-NPT signatories or aspirant nuclear weapons states from pursuing enrichment programs. As one respondent noted, "A fuel bank has little value, since those states with good nonproliferation credentials have no problem in getting fuel supplies from the world market; whereas those states with poor nonproliferation credentials would not be eligible for supply from a fuel bank." Another industry participant went a step further, calling upon the IAEA to increase its enforcement capacity because some "countries will refuse to sign the NPT [or] comply with its regulations." Proposal 2 would "require the IAEA to become a stronger enforcement agency."

In the view of industry respondents, proposals 1 and 2 could become commercially disruptive, since a fuel bank could serve to replace the current market mechanism. However, this criticism seems irrelevant to most fuel-bank proposals currently under consideration, which merely provide supply assurances to the market in the event of a supply disruption for reasons other than proliferation or financial disputes, rather than replacing the existing market (but it may apply to centralized facilities, discussed in the next section).

Nonindustry respondents found proposals 1 and 2 much less effective than did industry respondents. Regarding feasibility, the majority of industry respondents judged proposal 1 to be infeasible but did not reach a consensus on the feasibility of proposal 2; nonindustry respondents did not reach a consensus on the feasibility of either proposal.

Both fuel bank proposals also elicited industry and nonindustry concerns about a variety of financial and technical issues that still need to be addressed in more detail to translate into a fully workable concept. These include

—Financing ("Who will cover the costs of the bank?")

—Fuel fabrication ("Fuel assembly supply must be addressed"; that is, how can states ensure the LEU in the bank is assembled [and where this will take place] for the reactor in which it will be used?)

—Stocks ("replenishment of the bank once it [LEU] has been used")

—Institutional ("How would the IAEA administer the use of fuel from such a fuel bank?")

—Location ("How to decide where the facility will be sited?")

Centralized Facilities

Centralized enrichment facilities differ from international fuel banks in one important respect: whereas a fuel bank acts merely as an insurance policy in allocating LEU in the case of a market disruption, a centralized facility shifts existing national nuclear facilities from domestic control to administration under a multilateral system (as in the case of proposal 3). Proposals of this nature tend to be far more contentious because in some circumstances they are in conflict with Article IV of the NPT.

There are existing examples of successful centralized facilities in URENCO, a multilateral consortium of Germany, the Netherlands, and the United Kingdom with enrichment facilities in each of those nations, and EURODIF, a consortium that includes France, Belgium, Spain, and, indirectly, Iran, which all own a stake in uranium enrichment at the Georges Besse I plant in France.[16]

Survey Results

The Brookings survey asked industry to assess the following concepts:

—**Proposal 3.** An IAEA-administered international enrichment facility.

—**Proposal 4.** Conversion of all existing nuclear enrichment and reprocessing facilities currently under national control and IAEA safeguards into multinational facilities.

Overall, the responses reflect substantial industry skepticism toward centralization. Industry responses to both proposals were lukewarm: they showed no consensus on their effectiveness, while an overwhelming majority ranked both approaches as *unfeasible* or *very unfeasible*. As with the fuel bank proposals, industry expressed concerns about the commercial impact and the technical and financial mechanics of making these proposals work. One industry respondent stated flatly that for proposal 3, "commercial acceptance would be difficult."

Industry participants were particularly critical of proposal 4. One respondent asserted that "private ownership of enrichment and reprocessing facilities has not been a weakness in the current nonproliferation regime," and felt "there may also be a conflict between the proposal and NPT Article IV (1)." Another respondent questioned why major enrichment firms such as AREVA and URENCO should be "punished," and highlighted the difficulty in "internationalizing" USEC and TENEX, for example. Proposal 4 was the only MNA concept ranked *unfeasible* or *very unfeasible* by *all* industry respondents.

A majority of nonindustry respondents ranked proposal 3 as either having *no impact* or being *ineffective* or *very ineffective*, indicating even more skepticism than among industry respondents toward the potential ability of this approach to strengthen the regime. Nonindustry respondents deemed the concept of an IAEA-administered international enrichment facility by and large *unfeasible* or *very unfeasible*, virtually mirroring industry's view that the challenges of coordinating with existing commercial entities were too great to make it work. One nonindustry respondent noted that such an arrangement should only be adopted in strict cooperation with "different market players (private and public companies) . . . respecting the competition among different players. It would have to be designed with the IAEA only playing a supervising role."

Nonindustry participants considered proposal 4 more effective than industry did, but a comparable large majority ranked it *unfeasible* or *very unfeasible*. Nonindustry respondents also highlighted the political obstacles to such an approach, expecting "national resistance," particularly from the countries owning the facilities. Of particular note, one nonindustry respondent observed that such an arrangement would be opposed by countries owning existing enrichment facilities, but it would be popular among "have-nots."

Lease and Take-Back Programs

One of the few multilateral proposals that also addresses the back end of the fuel cycle is the lease and take-back program, which provides nuclear energy nations with a disposal option for spent fuel. Currently, spent fuel is the responsibility of the nation that produced it, with most stored on site (the exception is Europe, where much of the spent fuel is sent to reprocessing facilities at Sellafield in the United Kingdom or at La Hague in France).[17] In fact, most spent nuclear fuel is stored aboveground, which, while safe, "clearly does not maximize security," in the words of several leading nuclear experts.[18]

Under a lease and take-back system, a leasing state would provide nuclear fuel through domestic vendors and, within the same agreement, manage the resulting spent fuel as well. The returned spent fuel could be stored in the lessor state or passed to an IAEA-approved or -administered third-party state, a multilateral storage facility, or both.

Aside from Russia's agreement to take back any Russian-supplied fuel and the U.S.-UAE deal under which spent fuel from UAE reactors can be transferred to France or the United Kingdom for reprocessing, there are at present no other existing bilateral or multilateral arrangements for spent fuel take-back. Early versions of the Bush administration's GNEP and Putin's GNPI proposals accounted for fuel take-back; however, public and political opposition to the ideas halted each one's progress.[19]

Although a lease and take-back program would decrease the proliferation risk of spent fuel—every ton of spent fuel contains approximately 10 kilograms of weapons-grade plutonium—its implementation is obstructed by a negative public perception and minimal political support.[20] The challenge has been to persuade citizens and politicians to store nuclear waste that has not been used domestically.

Survey Results

Brookings asked participants to assess the following proposal:

—**Proposal 5.** Commercial fuel leasing and take-back offers of spent fuel by internationally owned and operated bodies.

Industry was divided on the effectiveness of this proposal, with just over half ranking it *effective* and the remainder ranking it as *no impact, ineffective,* or *very ineffective.* However, a large majority regarded it as *unfeasible* or *very unfeasible.* Industry respondents expressed concerns about the commercial implications of fuel-leasing arrangements and the political pitfalls of spent fuel management. As one company noted, "Commercial enrichers and fabricators are unlikely to agree to take a share in spent fuel management costs. Should these costs be included in the leasing price, it would make leased fuel exorbitantly expensive." Another industry respondent pointed out this proposal would "increase global movement of civilian plutonium" and thus have serious implications for security. Nevertheless, some in industry cautiously cited positive aspects of this proposal, considering it "attractive for spent fuel, [but] very difficult [for] waste management," or "possibly effective if agreements are enforceable."

Some of industry's skepticism reflects varying interpretations of lease and take-back programs, particularly when it comes to spent fuel management. In one interpretation, commercial suppliers agree to take back the spent fuel, with vendors managing it rather than governments or a multilateral organization. Alternatively, some might define lease and take-back initiatives as a government nationalization of commercial vendors. According to one respondent, an arrangement such as this "would create monopolies for fuel supply and destroy the market."

By contrast, nonindustry respondents deemed this proposal *effective* or *very effective* in both respects, with more respondents viewing it as *feasible* (even though responses reflected a lack of consensus among the nonindustry participants). For example, one labeled it the "best solution," while another stated that

"Russia, the United States, and other major nuclear fuel suppliers should agree on these arrangements." Despite the general support for the mechanism, several nonindustry respondents noted the necessity of sound institutions in host countries, in that the effectiveness and feasibility of the proposal "depends on the sustainability of the commitments." This kind of proposal, remarked another respondent, might be feasible in a "country with a mature legal system, but there are many concerns where the state can illegally override commercial entities, and there are no effective responses."

International Storage and Depositories

Arguably one of the most contentious issues with respect to the fuel cycle, whether in domestic or international policy circles, is nuclear waste storage and disposal. However, while such facilities elicit a great deal of "not in my backyard" sentiment and receive little political support, there are examples of both domestic and international opportunities for storage and disposal. In the United States, the Waste Isolation Pilot Plant in New Mexico currently serves as a deep long-term geological repository for transuranic military waste. The 16-square-mile area has enough room, as well as ideal geological conditions, to provide long-term disposal for large amounts of nuclear waste. Elsewhere, France and Sweden have advanced national repository programs, and Finland is in the process of developing one.

The current global expansion of nuclear energy is creating a new impetus for multilateral solutions to short-term storage of spent fuel and long-term disposal of waste. States with new nuclear programs or programs that are still in early stages of development have small inventories of spent fuel, rendering back-end fuel cycle solutions uneconomic.[21] A multilateral facility provides an economically viable solution to such a problem. Moreover, there are existing regional opportunities for such a system: for example, several countries in the Middle East and Asia have nascent nuclear programs or have expressed serious interest in nuclear power but are without geological storage possibilities.[22]

Critics argue that a centralized storage or repository facility(ies) would actually increase the risk of proliferation as it would increase the amount of spent nuclear fuel that is transported. This is a concern in Germany, where the government currently encourages long-term interim storage at power plants, as opposed to the domestic centralized facilities at Ahaus and Gorleben.

SURVEY RESULTS

To ascertain stakeholder views on the concept of multilateral approaches to spent-fuel storage, Brookings suggested two proposals:

—**Proposal 6.** Commercial interim storage and disposal of spent fuel by internationally owned or operated bodies.

—**Proposal 7.** A long-term spent fuel repository under regional, multinational supervision.

Industry participants showed no consensus on the effectiveness of these proposals: in each case, most ranked them either *effective* or as having *no impact.* On the other hand, the majority ranked both proposals as *unfeasible* or *very unfeasible.* The common theme underlying industry's responses is that both are politically and logistically difficult to implement. As one respondent pointed out, "location" issues are critical. Despite the potential economic benefits of hosting a long-term repository, many nations have shown no interest in accepting foreign-generated spent fuel. Though an interesting concept, said another respondent, the political obstacles make it "impractical until countries permit the receipt and long-term storage of other countries' spent fuel." A clear example of this sentiment can be seen in the reaction to the PANGEA proposal, a research program in the 1990s that identified Australia, Argentina, southern Africa, and western China as ideal geological locations for an international repository. For political and economic reasons, Australia was chosen as the preferred location for the project. In response, the Australian government made clear that Australia does not import nuclear waste, and that any such project would be subject to a host of environmental regulations and have to obtain a number of government licenses and permits.

Another industry respondent thought that long-term political stability would also be an obstacle to centralized storage facilities, making it "impossible to get traction. . . . There would need to be considerations for generations of control/stability." Obviously, long-term political stability must be given consideration. Two industry respondents also questioned whether proposal 7 did anything to enhance proliferation prevention: "The recycling of spent fuel in facilities under safeguards of reliable countries is more efficient to prevent any risk of proliferation than long-term storage."

By contrast, more nonindustry respondents ranked proposals 6 and 7 as *effective* or *very effective.* At the same time, many found them *unfeasible,* although a majority ranked proposal 7 as *neutral.* Nonindustry respondents echoed industry's concerns about the political obstacles to implementing a centralized storage or disposal facility; one remarked that there should be "great confidence in the long-term institutional controls of the state in which the facility [is] located." Another pointed out that "technical and environmental concerns remain," which is one reason why political opposition to importing high-level waste is so strong. Still another respondent suggested that centralized or regional waste facilities are more likely to work "in a region where there is sufficient trust among neighbors" and regional political relations are cordial, such as Southeast Asia. This may even be a very important consideration in regions with existing or emerging tensions such as South Asia and the Middle East.

Fuel Guarantees

Fuel guarantees, similar to those promised by a nuclear fuel bank, provide a fuel supply arrangement that would supplement the existing world market for enriched uranium products. Rather than centralize enriched fuel at one location, however, fuel guarantees would issue directly from existing fuel providers "under terms specified by the IAEA and the enriched uranium service providers."[23]

Fuel guarantees consist of two principal categories: those provided to states that forswear enrichment and reprocessing, and those provided to states that do not forswear enrichment and reprocessing (on the assumption that fuel guarantees will serve as an incentive to prevent nations from investing in domestic enrichment, reprocessing services, or both).[24]

The former concept was most recently proposed by four major commercial suppliers of enriched uranium services—AREVA of France, Tekhsnabeksport (TENEX) of Russia, URENCO, and USEC of the United States—through the World Nuclear Association (WNA). The proposal stemmed from industry's concern that a multilateral system created by multilateral parties would intrude on the current market system for enrichment services. Consequently, these companies sought a complementary framework rather than an obstructive one. Under the proposal, "collective guarantees [would be made] by enriched uranium services providers supported by governmental and IAEA commitments" in the event that nuclear fuel supply is interrupted for political reasons (and not because of nonproliferation or financing concerns).[25] To support this network, the MNA has a third "tier," under which the supply of enriched uranium stocks is guaranteed by national governments in the event that the aforementioned nuclear network fails.

The WNA asserts that an essential criterion for the system is that "[the] customer State must have made a commitment to forgo the development of, or the building or operation of, enrichment facilities."[26] Three obstacles impede the implementation of such a framework at present: (1) a complex network of supply agreements would need to be crafted between governments and corporations and would be difficult to enforce; (2) political will for such an agreement may be difficult to secure; and (3) the proposition would require a funding source (for enrichment firms that would be required to supply fuel in the initial event of a supply disruption), which would prove expensive.

The second proposal, for a system that guarantees fuel to states that do *not* forswear enrichment and reprocessing, is based on the Nuclear Fuel Assurance Proposal (formerly the Enrichment Bonds Proposal) suggested by the United Kingdom in September 2006. That proposal calls for an agreement—or "bond"—between supplier and customer countries that may come into effect if certain criteria are met. The supplier governments must transfer the right to withhold exports of enriched uranium to the IAEA, which would make the decision exclusively on the basis of nonproliferation considerations. The consumer must not be able to secure enrichment services for reasons other than nonproliferation or financial delinquency in relation to existing commercial contracts, must be in full compliance with its IAEA safeguards agreements, and have an Additional Protocol for safeguards in force. In addition, the IAEA must deem it a peaceful nuclear state, the supplied material must be used for peaceful purposes and not for retransfer, and the physical protection levels of supplied material must meet internationally agreed standards.[27]

Survey Results

Brookings asked study participants to evaluate the following fuel guarantee proposals:

—**Proposal 8.** Internationally supervised guarantees of supplies of nuclear fuel to states that forswear enrichment and reprocessing outside of a formal "fuel bank" system.

—**Proposal 9.** Guarantees of internationally supervised supplies of nuclear fuel to states that do not forswear enrichment and reprocessing capabilities.

Industry respondents showed no consensus on either the effectiveness or feasibility of proposal 8. In general, proposal 8 was considered more effective than proposal 9 in strengthening the nonproliferation regime, given the requirement to forswear enrichment and reprocessing. Most felt that proposal 9 "would not strengthen the nuclear nonproliferation regime." Nevertheless, industry respondents failed to indicate a consensus on proposal 8's effectiveness.

At the same time, industry tended to rank proposal 8 as *unfeasible* since it conflicted with Article IV, as reflected in this response: "It is not clear that states are prepared to abandon their rights under NPT article IV(1)." This respondent also asked a question that probes the nuances of state interpretation of rights and responsibilities: "Would a state forswear reprocessing if it was guaranteed a supply only of fuel but not reprocessing or spent fuel disposal?"

As noted, there was no industry consensus on the effectiveness of proposal 9, but the majority here ranked it *unfeasible* or *very unfeasible.* The following two responses reflect these differences of opinion: "This proposal has real merit . . . more feasible than [proposal] 8 . . . requires no up-front costs." And "Makes no sense? [There is] no incentive to reduce enrichment and reprocessing capabilities."

A majority of nonindustry respondents found proposal 8 *effective* or *very effective* but failed to agree on feasibility, or on the effectiveness or feasibility of proposal 9. Nonindustry respondents also thought that proposal 8 infringes on national sovereignty and that the "Non-Aligned Movement will have problems with this proposal." Another nonindustry participant noted that states would have to "concede a great deal of autonomy, and many would find it difficult to accept, especially if a near neighbor retained an independent fuel cycle capability." This respondent then questioned the proposal from Saudi Arabia's vantage point in the face of a nuclear self-sufficient Iran.

Like industry respondents, nonindustry contributors suggested that proposal 9 would do little—if anything—to strengthen the nonproliferation regime. As one respondent put it, the proposal does "not really add value for nonproliferation," although the Non-Alignment Movement would likely support it. Another found the proposal more "plausible" than the previous one but wondered "how . . . this prevents clandestine proliferation." Yet another nonindustry respondent felt such a proposal would create an even greater divide between nuclear suppliers and customers, something that budding nuclear nations want to avoid.

Market Intervention Mechanisms

The last MNA proposal is for a market mechanism that keeps prices for enrichment services at relatively low levels in order to dissuade new entrants. This could be achieved by an international group of producers if they were to increase the supply of nuclear fuel to a level where it became uneconomic for countries to engage in enrichment activities, by some form of international regulatory action, or a tax and subsidy scheme.[28]

Brookings asked study participants to evaluate the following market intervention proposal:

—**Proposal 10.** An internationally subsidized mechanism to increase supply of nuclear fuel to a level at which it becomes uneconomic for countries to engage in enrichment activities.

This proposal was dismissed by a number of both industry and nonindustry respondents; very few ranked it as *effective* or *very effective,* and a large majority in each group viewed it as *unfeasible* or *very unfeasible.* Industry expressed overwhelming commercial concerns with this approach, as illustrated by the following remarks:

—"The market price will always be cheaper than any attempt by a single country to acquire national capacities of enrichment at an industrial level."

—"Subsidies kill innovation and competition."

—"This is an irresponsible proposition. It would undermine the functioning of a market efficiently allocating fuel supply resources . . . and . . . there is evidence of NNWSs' [non–nuclear weapons states] embarking on, say, a small enrichment program, even though it is clear that the unit cost of production is far higher than the world market price. Even if the subsidized price were zero, some countries may still embark on, say, an enrichment program."

Nonindustry contributors also expressed this concern: "Currently there's [not] much of a business case for a newcomer to get into the enrichment business. So weakening the business case by forcing down the price of the product would not seem to make much difference."

Conclusions and Recommendations

The responses to the survey indicate that industry, as represented in this study, is cautious about most MNAs and does not find them particularly effective. Industry's overall view of the MNAs is neatly summarized by the following remarks:[29]

> Generally, the MNAs will somewhat strengthen the existing NPT regime. However, they will not address the real proliferation risk—clandestine programs unrelated to civil nuclear power. The impact of the proposed MNAs on the commercial actors in the nuclear fuel cycle must be very carefully examined before implementation. The industry must be substantively engaged in the process to design these MNAs to ensure that they do not result in unexpected perverse outcomes.

The majority of industry respondents ranked all proposals as *unfeasible* or *very unfeasible,* with the exception of proposal 2 (an IAEA-administered international enriched uranium fuel bank accessible to all countries in compliance with NPT regulations), and proposal 8 (internationally supervised guarantees of supplies of nuclear fuel to states that forswear enrichment and reprocessing outside of a formal "fuel bank" system). Proposal 2 was ranked by far the most effective and had the lowest number of *unfeasible* or *very unfeasible* responses.

For those proposals considered potentially effective, industry views them as unlikely to be feasible in terms of acceptability or political viability. This view is more pronounced with respect to the back end of the fuel cycle, where lease and take-back and commercial storage are seen negatively in terms of feasibility or effectiveness—a judgment confirmed to date by the failure of efforts to identify acceptable locations where spent nuclear fuel could be stored for extended periods of time and finally disposed of.

The MNA approach to receive the most favorable grade from nonindustry respondents was proposal 5 (commercial interim storage and disposal of spent fuel by internationally owned/operated bodies): it had the most *effective* or *very effective* rankings and, along with proposal 2, was considered the most feasible, although there was no consensus on feasibility.

Industry and nonindustry responses differed in several other respects. In general, nonindustry respondents viewed proposals 1, 2, and 3, dealing with the front-end of the fuel cycle, as much *less effective* than industry did (but were just as skeptical about their feasibility); and they considered proposals 4 through 7 (concerning the back end) to be more effective and somewhat more feasible.

This likely reflects the opinion of governments and institutions that the political obstacles to the back end of the fuel cycle are not insurmountable. By contrast, industry, which has an explicit interest in finding a solution to the back end of the fuel cycle (much of the public opposition to nuclear energy stems from concern about nuclear waste), remains unconvinced that the political barriers can be overcome. These impediments lead industry to be more optimistic about a front-end-only solution, as put forth in proposal 2.

The results of the survey make clear that any MNA proposal will need to overcome significant challenges if it is to garner support from industry and non-industry stakeholders. It must respect states' rights under the NPT and ensure security of supply, while preserving an economic incentive for fuel cycle services. Such a proposal would also have to receive support from both and nuclear and non–nuclear weapons states.

Needless to say, the vision of an international fuel cycle including all states is ambitious (and very likely unattainable in the foreseeable future). Yet this concept can form the basis of more tangible, practical proposals that complement the benefits of the market efficiencies of enrichment supply, while limiting the number of facilities. Furthermore, a number of encouraging precedents are available to draw upon. The United States is currently constructing two new enrichment facilities on the basis of black-boxed technology: URENCO of Europe is constructing a national enrichment facility in New Mexico and AREVA of France is constructing one in Idaho. Both facilities are being constructed without the transfer of technology and are to be operated by foreign companies.

These cases can serve as a template for others interested in becoming actively involved in nuclear energy for civil purposes and wishing to be part of the fuel cycle process. At the very least, they help to "legitimize" the concept of an internationalized nuclear fuel cycle whereby all states—advanced and emerging, nuclear and non–nuclear weapons states—participate with a limited number of sensitive fuel cycle facilities. In turn, this helps to reduce the risk associated with proliferation of nationally owned and operated sensitive fuel cycle facilities. A broader model based on such international participation between public and private entities in a multilateral enterprise could ensure fuel supply while avoiding the spread of sensitive technologies. This means a private uranium-enrichment provider would be able to establish a facility with investment from foreign governments and (possibly) private utilities.

Such multilateralization of the sensitive aspects of the nuclear fuel cycle can result in a "win-win" situation for all concerned. The technology holder would find that multinationalization of an enrichment enterprise has several advantages: reduces and offsets the capital cost outlay necessary to construct and the operational costs necessary to run a facility; helps to rationalize the market; and, insofar as the technology holder seeks to reinforce nonproliferation objectives, contributes to that purpose as well. Insofar as the broad cross section of states (advanced industrial states, emerging and developing states) participates in such an approach, it serves to reinforce a global nonproliferation norm. By establishing the principle of having a limited number of multilateral enterprises dealing with the sensitive proliferation-relevant aspects of the nuclear fuel cycle (which also satisfies the economic objectives of the supplier), it helps to assuage the public's proliferation concerns. From the vantage point of the nonproliferation regime, the opportunity for states to partner, on an equitable basis, in a multilateral enterprise using state-of-the-art technology delegitimizes insistence on "going it alone," especially if multilateralism becomes the norm for sensitive nuclear fuel cycle activity.

This approach does not prohibit nations from pursuing indigenous enrichment programs, and states that are determined to go it alone cannot be forced to join in. Even so, it has the dual advantage of giving participating states access to advanced and economic technology and at the same time serving the nonproliferation goal by reducing the number of facilities capable of producing weapons usable material. This approach avoids some of the pitfalls of other concepts reflected in the Brookings survey. The examples of AREVA, URENCO, and the IUEC show that it can be done. And the U.S. acceptance of a black-box method for building new enrichment facilities is an important example of a leading weapons state accepting that kind of arrangement: this shows it is not something that some states are pushed to do (as in the case of a small newcomer to nuclear power) but an arrangement that even the most advanced states accept.

Table 6-1. *Industry and Nonindustry Responses to MNA Proposals and Selected Comments*[a]

Proposal	Industry	Nonindustry
1. An IAEA-administered international enriched uranium fuel bank accessible to all countries	Majority ranked it *ineffective/very ineffective* and *unfeasible/very unfeasible* *Major themes* Not workable without compliance requirements. Financial and technical implementation concerns. *Selected comments* "No access should be [granted] without NPT compliance and [adherence to] the Additional Protocol." "Does not provide the diversity of supply or commercial transparency that utilities desire." "There are countries that will refuse to have their nuclear programs controlled by a managed supply of enriched uranium."	Majority ranked it *ineffective/very ineffective;* no consensus on feasibility. *Major themes* Financial and technical implementation concerns. Not workable without compliance requirements. *Selected comments* "Aim of MNA is to provide nuclear fuel to those countries that comply with the NPT." "All this would mean is the open development of civil nuclear with a secure supply of fuel."
2. An IAEA-administered international enriched uranium fuel bank accessible to all countries in compliance with NPT regulations	Large majority ranked it *effective;* no consensus on feasibility. *Major themes* Ranked as most effective and feasible of all MNAs by industry (most positive responses). Would still not stop determined proliferators. Financial and technical implementation concerns. Commercial impact concerns. *Selected comments* "Countries that are not in compliance with NPT pose the greatest risk—this option does nothing to mitigate that risk." "An IAEA-administered facility would interfere with the allocative efficiencies of the enrichment market. The provision of enriched uranium to safeguards-compliant NPT signatory states is working well."	Majority ranked it as *no impact;* no consensus on feasibility. *Major themes* Would still not stop determined proliferators. Financial and technical implementation concerns. *Selected Comments* "There's a risk that a committed proliferator will simply not engage with the NPT process." "Fuel fabrication has to be provided elsewhere."

| 3. An IAEA-administered international enrichment facility | No consensus on effectiveness; large majority ranked it *unfeasible/very unfeasible.*

Major themes
Financial and technical implementation concerns.
Commercial impact concerns.

Selected comments
"Would eliminate the current efficiencies of a free market for enrichment."
"Competencies could be a challenge."
"The trick would be to sell to countries at market prices and manage the spent fuel."
"Location of facility . . . is critical. Several facilities needed?"<br>"Where does the capital come from?" | No consensus on effectiveness; large majority ranked it *unfeasible/very unfeasible.*

Major themes
Financial and technical implementation concerns.
Commercial impact concerns.

Selected comments
"Fuel conversion and fabrication have still to be provided elsewhere."
"It is doubtful if such a facility, with a large number of diverging views in the IAEA, can work properly. It should be left to the market."
"Such a facility, alone, will not prevent national enrichment programs and the associated proliferation risk."
"How to manage it with the commercial sector." |
| 4. Conversion of all existing nuclear enrichment and reprocessing facilities currently under national control and IAEA safeguards into multinational facilities | No consensus on effectiveness, and unanimously ranked *unfeasible/very unfeasible.*

Major themes
The only proposal unanimously ranked *unfeasible/very unfeasible* by industry.
Financial and technical implementation concerns.
Commercial impact concerns.

Selected comments
"Nationalization of all enrichment facilities is essentially impossible."
"Likelihood of governments agreeing? Does nothing to manage risk from rogue states."
"Private ownership of enrichment and reprocessing facilities has not been a weakness in the current nuclear nonproliferation regime."
"Would expect national resistance." | Majority ranked it *effective/very effective* and *unfeasible/very unfeasible.*

Major themes
Financial and technical implementation concerns.
Commercial and political concerns.

Selected comments
"This is a much better idea than [Proposal 3]."
"Could be very effective but feasibility is unknown."
"Commercial and political considerations make this unlikely." |

(*continued*)

Table 6-1 (*continued*)

Proposal	Industry	Nonindustry
5. Commercial fuel leasing and take-back offers of spent fuel by internationally owned or operated bodies	Majority ranked it *effective;* large majority ranked it *unfeasible/ very unfeasible.* *Major themes* About half ranked it *effective.* Commercial concerns over leasing arrangements. Political pitfalls of spent fuel management. "Would create monopolies for fuel supply and destroy the market." *Selected Comments* "Taking [other] countries' spent fuel/HLW [high-level waste] is politically very difficult." "Nuclear fuel can be leased on the commercial market, and such a service can be beneficial both to suppliers and to utilities. There are issues concerning liabilities for spent fuel here." "Increases global movement of civilian plutonium."	Large majority ranked it *effective/ very effective,* no consensus on feasibility. *Major themes* More nonindustry respondents ranked it feasible than did industry. Commercial concerns. Political and legal hurdles. *Selected comments* "Assuming the take-back is permanent . . . many newcomers would take advantage of the opportunity . . . [but] take-back will need more visionary and effective leadership than seems likely to emerge soon." "On the one hand . . . could be rather effective. On the other hand, one could fear the situation that only very few countries are in possession of the required facilities, which could create monopoly or oligopoly situations." "Depends on sustainability of commitments (of former USSR toward its former allies). What about guarantees for safe reprocessing/disposal? Is this reconcilable with commercial operation?"
6. Commercial interim storage and disposal of spent fuel by internationally owned or operated bodies	No consensus on effectiveness; majority ranked it *unfeasible/ very unfeasible.* *Major themes* Most ranked it *effective* or *no impact.* Political and logistical difficulty of implementation, that is, "location" issues. *Selected comments* "Where and by whom?" "Who would be the host country?" "Difficulty gaining approval to take other countries' waste."	Majority ranked it *effective/ very effective;* majority ranked it *unfeasible/ very unfeasible.* *Major themes* Political and legal concerns. *Selected comments* "Is this reconcilable with commercial operation?" "Most countries have totally forbidden the disposal of foreign spent fuel and waste on their territory." "Spent fuel storage might be feasible, but disposal is unlikely."

7. A long-term spent fuel repository under regional, multinational supervision	No consensus on effectiveness; large majority ranked it *unfeasible/very unfeasible.* *Major themes* Most ranked it *effective* or *no impact.* Political and logistical difficulty of implementation. Limitations in preventing proliferation. *Selected comments* "Who would be the host country? Need a mechanism to avoid 'free ride.'" "Good idea for managing spent fuel—politically difficult. Does not reduce proliferation risk." "Perceived to discourage national repository efforts."	Large majority ranked it *effective/very effective;* no consensus on feasibility (half ranked it neutral). *Major themes* Political and logistical difficulty of implementation. *Selected comments* "Technical and environmental concerns remain." "The legal and regulatory aspects of long-term spent fuel repository and a disposal facility are very different." "Problems will be encountered with the public."
8. Internationally supervised guarantees of supplies of nuclear fuel to states that forswear enrichment and reprocessing outside of formal "fuel bank" system	No consensus on effectiveness or feasibility. *Major themes* Political acceptability. Commercial concerns. *Selected comments* "Would have low credence by recipients." "Guarantee of supplies is a real challenge in uranium markets; with volatility of price." "A good idea that needs development." "Commercial transparency?"	Majority ranked it as *effective/very effective;* no consensus on feasibility. *Major themes* Political acceptability. *Selected comments* "An explicit forswearing requirement would lose votes in the IAEA Board. Guaranteeing fuel is also much harder than guaranteeing LEU." "Present fuel cycle facilities are already close to the multinational approach." "Would require states to concede a great deal of autonomy and many would find it difficult to accept."

(continued)

Table 6-1 (*continued*)

Proposal	Industry	Nonindustry
9. Guarantees of internationally supervised supplies of nuclear fuel to states that do not forswear enrichment and reprocessing capabilities	No consensus on effectiveness; majority ranked it *unfeasible/very unfeasible.* *Major themes* More feasible, but not as effective in proliferation prevention. "No deterrence effect." *Selected comments* "How do you police these arrangements? Do sanctions against countries that did not comply really work?" "This proposal has real merit . . . more feasible than [Proposal] 8 . . . requires no up-front costs" "Would not strengthen the regime."	No consensus on effectiveness (half ranked it *no impact*) or feasibility. *Major themes* Political difficulties. Weak on proliferation prevention. *Selected comments* "For Non-Aligned Movement OK, but not really added value for nonproliferation." "This gives the country concerned a kind of independence." "More plausible than [Proposal 8], but how does this prevent clandestine proliferation?" "Might divide 'haves' and 'have-nots.'"
10. An internationally subsidized mechanism to increase supply of nuclear fuel to a level at which it becomes uneconomic for countries to engage in enrichment activities	No consensus on effectiveness; and large majority ranked it *unfeasible/very unfeasible.* *Major themes* Significant commercial concerns. *Selected comments* "Subsidizes one sector of the reactor market (those using enriched fuel)." "Economic considerations will not prevent clandestine nuclear weapons programs." "Who provides the materials? Who manages the facility and inventory? Are these multinational facilities and companies?" "Too costly. Enrichment is uneconomic for small to medium programs already." "Can't imagine states agreeing to pay for this in current financial climate."	Majority ranked it *ineffective/very ineffective,* and *unfeasible/very unfeasible.* *Major themes* Significant commercial concerns. *Selected comments* "This system would not stimulate technological developments and would not stop those countries that want to develop sensitive technologies regardless the costs." "Unlikely to limit proliferation because proliferation is not an economically driven decision." "Subsidies are not good."

a. "No consensus" means no majority in ranking a proposal either favorably (effective/very effective or feasible/very feasible) or unfavorably (ineffective/very ineffective, or infeasible/very infeasible).

Notes

1. This statement refers to all countries interested in nuclear power, not just those discussed in chapter 4.

2. This study accepts IAEA definitions: "A distinction should be made between the words 'multilateral' (the broadest and most flexible term, referring simply to the participation of more than two actors), 'multinational' (implying several actors from different States), 'regional' (several actors from neighboring States) and 'international' (actors from different States and/or international organizations, such as the IAEA)." In order to address the broadest possible approaches, we refer to "multilateral" options, which encompass multinational, regional, and international approaches (and are abbreviated as MNA for "multilateral nuclear approaches"). See International Atomic Energy Agency (IAEA), *Multilateral Approaches to the Nuclear Fuel Cycle: Expert Group Report to the Director General of the IAEA*" (Vienna, 2005), par. 13.

3. Some of the information early in this chapter is drawn from Lawrence Scheinman, "Equal Opportunity: Historical Challenges and Future Prospects of the Nuclear Fuel Cycle," *Arms Control Today* 37 (May 2007).

4. "Final Declaration of the First Review Conference by the Parties to the Treaty on the Non-Proliferation of Nuclear Weapons, 1975: Review of Article IV (Para. 7)," reprinted in *PPNN Briefing Book*, vol. 2: *Treaties Agreements and Other Relevant Documents*, 8th ed,, compiled and edited by Emily Bailey and others (Southampton, U.K.: Mountbatten Centre for International Studies, 2000).

5. Mohamed ElBaradei, "Towards a Safer World," *The Economist*, October 16, 2003.

6. Mohamed ElBaradei, "Rethinking Nuclear Safeguards," *Washington Post*, June 14, 2006.

7. For further information on multilateral approaches to the nuclear fuel cycle, see Chaim Braun, "Technical Review of Fuel Assurance Proposals," IAEA Special Event, September 2006; Oliver Meier, "The Growing Nuclear Fuel Cycle Debate," *Arms Control Today*, November 2006; and Yuri Yudin, "Multilateralization of the Nuclear Fuel Cycle: Assessing the Existing Proposals" (Geneva: United Nations Institute for Disarmament Research [UNIDR], June 2009).

8. IAEA, *Multilateral Approaches*, par. 324.

9. Ibid., par. 342.

10. Ibid., par. 33.

11. The nations are France, Germany, Japan, the Netherlands, Russia, the United Kingdom, and the United States. Though Japan is still a marginal supplier of LEU compared with the other nations, it has proposed the IAEA Standby Arrangements System for the Assurance of Nuclear Supply.

12. Yuri Yudin, "Multilateralization of the Nuclear Fuel Cycle: Assessing the Existing Proposals" (Geneva: UNIDR, June 2009), p. 32.

13. In April 2009 in Prague, Obama stated, "We should build a new framework for civil nuclear cooperation, including an international fuel bank, so that countries can access peaceful power without increasing the risks of proliferation" (www.whitehouse.gov/the-press-office/remarks-president-barack-obama-prague-delivered).

14. The IUEC was endorsed by the IAEA Board of Governors in November 2009. The IAEA-NTI fuel bank was approved for creation by the IAEA Board of Governors on December 3, 2010. In addition to receiving a contribution from NTI and Warren Buffett (a close NTI adviser), the fuel bank is funded by the European Union and the governments of Kuwait, Norway, the United Arab Emirates, and the United States. See

NTI, "IAEA Board Agrees to Create International Nuclear Fuel Bank, A 'Breakthrough' in Global Cooperation to Reduce Nuclear Dangers," press release, December 3, 2010 (www.nti.org/c_press/release_fuel_bank_120310.pdf).

15. IAEA, "Communication Received from the Resident Representative of the Russian Federation to the IAEA on the Establishment, Structure and Operation of the International Uranium Enrichment Centre," Information Circular 708 (Vienna, June 8, 2007).

16. EURODIF is a joint stock company formed by Belgium, France, Spain, and Sweden in 1973. Sweden withdrew from the company in 1974 and was replaced by Iran and later by SOFIDIF. SOFIDIF, a French-Iranian joint venture, has a 25 percent stake in EURODIF, the owner of the enrichment plant Georges Besse 1. AREVA and the Atomic Energy Organization of Iran (AEOI) have a 60 percent and 40 percent stake in SOFIDIF, respectively. Therefore AEOI holds indirectly 10 percent of the share capital of EURODIF. No Iranian entity other than AEOI has a direct or indirect interest in either SOFIDIF or EURODIF. SOFIDIF is purely a holding company, the sole purpose of which is to hold the shares of EURODIF. SOFIDIF has no activity, no employees, no contract, no role in EURODIF operations, and, in accordance with a bilateral agreement between Iran and France, Iran cannot have access to technology or enriched uranium from Georges Besse. Dividends to the Iranian entity have been frozen since 2007 (see statement from the French Foreign Ministry at www.iranwatch.org/government/France/france-mfa-spokesperson-eurodif-041107.htm).

17. Sweden is the only European country that has a national storage facility, at its CLAB in Oskarshann. Finland is currently building a centralized repository as well.

18. Charles McCombie, Neil Chapman, and Tom Isaacs, "Security Concerns at the Back End of the Nuclear Fuel Cycle," paper presented at International High-Level Radioactive Waste Management Conference, Las Vegas, September 2008.

19. Charles McCombie, "Evaluating Solutions to the Nuclear Waste Problem," *Bulletin of Atomic Scientists* 65 (November/December 2009): 42.

20. Ibid., p. 43. Notwithstanding opposition to such proposals in the past, it should be noted that currently there appears to be renewed interest in promoting lease and take-back arrangements. As this book was going to press, the Obama administration revealed that it is in preliminary discussions about setting up a commercial nuclear fuel leasing arrangement. For more information, see Hannah Northey, "U.S. in Early Talks about Int'l Leasing Arrangements—Official," Greenwire, August 23, 2011 (www.nytimes.com/gwire/2011/08/23/23greenwire-official-us-in-early-talks-about-intl-nuclear-96182.html?pagewanted=all).

21. Charles McCombie and Thomas Isaacs, "The Key Role of the Back End in the Nuclear Fuel Cycle," *Daedalus* (Winter 2010): 36.

22. McCombie, "Evaluating Solutions to the Nuclear Waste Problem," p. 46.

23. Yudin, "Multilateralization of the Nuclear Fuel Cycle," p. 33.

24. These are only two examples of fuel guarantee proposals. Like other MNAs put forth by the questionnaire, these were the foundations of various proposals.

25. World Nuclear Association, "Ensuring Security of Supply in the International Nuclear Fuel Cycle" (London, 2006), p. 3.

26. Ibid., p. 1.

27. Yudin, "Multilateralization of the Nuclear Fuel Cycle," p. 41.

28. Geoffrey Rothwell and Chaim Braun, *The Cost Structure of International Uranium Enrichment Service Supply* (Stanford University, May 23, 2008), pp. 5–7.

29. This was in response to question 7 in part 1 of the survey.

7

Expanding Industry's Nonproliferation Role

MICHAEL MOODIE AND JOHN P. BANKS

A major theme of this volume is that in order to achieve successful nuclear nonproliferation in the decades ahead, the global nuclear industry must become a stronger partner of governments, international organizations, civil society, and other stakeholders in nonproliferation efforts. As a consequence, it is vital for industry not only to support the efforts of others (as important as that is), but also to act proactively and effectively in its own realm. In view of this requirement, the Brookings team sought industry's general views on the current nonproliferation regime, as well as on a variety of multilateral nuclear approaches (MNAs) designed to ensure access to nuclear technologies for peaceful purposes. Equally important, the team also explored industry's perspective on a variety of self-regulatory concepts that have been offered as ways to bolster nonproliferation governance in the nuclear industry itself.[1] These concepts are not new. The Pacific Northwest National Laboratory (PNNL) has been at the forefront of examining the application of self-regulatory approaches in the nuclear industry, as well as of assessing the lessons from other industries. The International Commission on Nuclear Non-Proliferation and Disarmament (ICNND) is also working on ideas to enhance the role of industry in proliferation prevention.[2]

The benefits of a self-regulatory approach across the nuclear industry are summarized in a recent PNNL report:

Because industry is closest to users of the goods and technology that could be illicitly diverted throughout the supply chain, industry information can potentially be more timely and accurate than other sources of information. Industry is in an ideal position to help ensure that such illicit activities are detected. This role could be performed more effectively if companies joined to work together within a particular industry to promote nonproliferation by implementing an industry-wide governance/self-regulation program. Performance measures would be used to ensure their materials and technologies are secure throughout the supply chain and that customers are legitimately using and/or maintaining oversight of these items. This approach is broader than internal compliance programs (ICPs) implemented by individual companies within an industry . . . it includes industry-wide approaches for contributing to nonproliferation.[3]

In soliciting the nuclear industry's response to proposed self-regulatory measures, our goal is to build on existing efforts to continue to chart a clear path forward that companies could support and implement.

Industry Perspectives on Self-regulatory Approaches

Drawing on other research, the Brookings team identified several approaches with the potential to enhance the nuclear industry's contribution to nonproliferation. It then distributed its survey, asking industry to rank the *effectiveness* and *feasibility* of such measures. The approaches offered to industry for evaluation and comment included
    —Code of conduct specifically governing nonproliferation;
    —Whistle-blower policies that help to identify inappropriate action or behavior within industry;
    —Black-box provisions that limit the sharing of proliferation-sensitive technical information;
    —An industry accreditation system that facilitates the sharing of information and capabilities; and
    —A government-industry conference to promote sustained interaction among key stakeholders.[4]
    These approaches are not mutually exclusive. Indeed, any of these specific measures in isolation would probably yield only limited nonproliferation progress. Rather, some combination of a number of them adopted by industry on a widespread, if not global, basis would likely represent an important, robust contribution to the overall nonproliferation regime. Despite this potential, however, no one should be under any illusions as to the difficulties in achieving such a result.
    The findings of the Brookings survey regarding industry's evaluation of the effectiveness and feasibility of various nonproliferation measures are summarized in table 7-1 (p. 194). As earlier in this volume, industry is defined as uranium

mining companies, reactor vendors, enrichment and reprocessing service providers, and nuclear power utilities. In addition to assessing the responses of industry representatives, we also compared them to responses from nonindustry representatives from governments, regulators, and nongovernmental organizations. The following sections provide a more detailed discussion of each measure, and industry's views of and responses to it.

Codes of Conduct

A code of conduct is a set of rules governing corporate practices and behavior. It may be voluntary or involuntary, and it may or may not have legally binding authority. The use of such codes is considered a self-regulatory means of setting basic operating standards that ultimately can be applied industry-wide.

Several organizations in the nuclear industry either have established codes of conduct or are working to develop and share best practices:

The World Nuclear Association (WNA), representing companies throughout the nuclear industry worldwide, has developed a charter of ethics for its members calling for adherence to the "principle and practice of transparency regarding all types of civil nuclear activity," and declaring the "individual and common responsibility to uphold . . . the IAEA statute; safeguards agreements concluded pursuant to the Treaty on the Non-Proliferation of Nuclear Weapons; and regional and bilateral accords providing for IAEA verification."[5]

The International Atomic Energy Agency (IAEA) has several codes of conduct: for example, the Code of Conduct on Safety and Security of Radioactive Sources, Code of Conduct on the Safety of Research Reactors, and the Code of Practice on the International Trans-boundary Movement of Radioactive Waste.

The World Association of Nuclear Operators (WANO) was "created to improve safety at every nuclear power plant in the world" by assisting its members through peer reviews, the sharing of operating experience, technical support and exchange, and professional and technical development. WANO has developed performance indicators, guidelines, and good practices for a variety of areas, such as plant safety, reliability, and personnel safety.[6]

The World Institute for Nuclear Security (WINS) was launched in September 2008 with the mission to "provide an international forum for those accountable for nuclear security to share and promote the implementation of best security practices." Illustrative efforts include the institute's development of best practice guides for managing internal threats and maintaining security equipment.[7]

The Institute of Nuclear Materials Management (INMM) was formed in 1958 to encourage "the advancement of nuclear materials management, including promotion of research, establishment of standards, improvement of the personnel qualifications, and increase and dissemination of information." Leadership is provided primarily by senior members of U.S. national laboratories, and "sustaining members" are a mixture of companies, government agencies, and nongovernmental entities in the United States, with some international organizations, such as the Canadian Nuclear Safety Commission, the Australian Government's Safeguards and Nonproliferation Office, and Sellafield, Limited in the United Kingdom. INMM has a Nonproliferation and Arms Control Technical Division whose goal in part is to "promote and advance the research, development and application of effective technologies to control proliferation risks." Over the years INMM has conducted professional development workshops for industry stakeholders addressing identification, development, and the sharing of global best practices in its principal areas of nuclear materials management: notably international safeguards, material control and accounting, nonproliferation, and waste management.[8]

While these codes touch on nonproliferation, each is formulated either in highly general terms or typically in conjunction with safety and security in the nuclear industry. As a consequence, their contribution to nonproliferation is not consistently the focus or is difficult to define. The nonproliferation community and industry, therefore, have been exploring the concept of a code of conduct that explicitly has proliferation concerns as its centerpiece, with specific practices or processes delineated beyond broad statements of adherence to the international proliferation prevention regime.[9] Accordingly, the Brookings team asked study participants to rank the effectiveness and feasibility of two variants of such a code:

—Proposal 1. A voluntary code of conduct for all commercial entities in the nuclear industry incorporating broad nonproliferation values as well as best-practice guidelines specific to the sector.

—Proposal 2. A code of conduct as in proposal 1 with a binding charter and penalties for noncompliance determined by signatory states.

Industry stakeholders expressed no consensus on the effectiveness of proposal 1, but a majority of respondents viewed it as feasible. Major themes articulated by industry were that this approach would not add much, if any value to strengthening the nonproliferation regime since the existing framework is sufficient, and it could have a negative commercial impact. The following are some illustrative remarks:

—"Industry already complies with nonproliferation constraints of bilateral and international trade relationships. Nonproliferation is too intertwined with commercial/marketing mandates."

—"Many commercial entities in the nuclear industry already have a voluntary code to restrict proliferation and misuse of nuclear materials. This would not add much."

—"A 'voluntary scheme for all commercial entities' would leave loopholes that could render the scheme ineffective for nuclear nonproliferation."

Nevertheless, some comments were supportive, characterizing this approach as "praiseworthy" or a "good" idea, although such views were in the minority.

The level of effort and commitment—not to mention the legally binding nature—of proposal 2 is much more substantial. As a result, industry responses indicated that while this approach could be effective, there was no consensus on feasibility. The general industry view appeared to be that while a legally binding approach was potentially more effective than proposal 1, it may be "almost impossible to enforce" and is "not an improvement over current practice." Several respondents also did not see how proposal 2 differed from existing requirements: "Exports are already [under] NSG controls," and that this concept is "something similar to the NPT and the Additional Protocol." In other words, a binding code of conduct is not necessary since legal obligations are already part of the nonproliferation regime.

Proposals 1 and 2 elicited similar responses from both industry and nonindustry respondents: in general both sets of participants considered proposal 1 less effective but feasible, and proposal 2 potentially effective but unfeasible. Nonindustry responses generally echoed the views of industry in recognizing the benefits and challenges of each approach. For example, one nonindustry respondent stated that proposal 1 is "easily circumvented, hence politically achievable, but quite weak in controlling proliferation," while another indicated that it "could be implemented quickly and will have impact on [the] nuclear industry." Similarly, nonindustry respondents questioned the feasibility of implementing proposal 2: one stated "penalties may not be welcome," and another that it is "better than [proposal] 1, but therefore harder to implement." One government respondent saw the code of conduct approach as a complex challenge:

> Industry can have a more active role in promoting the responsible use of nuclear energy by underlining the importance of full compliance with IAEA safeguards and the Additional Protocol. This could include education, training, peer review, technical advice, and research and development. A code of conduct amongst all commercial entities in the nuclear industry covering all these aspects would be a good thing. It would oblige all companies in the nuclear field to respect high-level non-proliferation standards. All companies would be placed at the same level-playing field in this respect. It will, however, be difficult to convince all companies to be part of the system.

In sum, the responses indicated general agreement that a code of conduct approach to strengthening the nonproliferation regime could be a useful tool. They also suggested, however, that any such tool would have to address in detail, and across the spectrum of companies, questions related to commercial impact, the added value to the existing legal and regulatory regime, and enforcement.

Whistle-Blower Policy

Whistle-blower policies protect employees against retaliatory measures for alerting authorities to improper behavior or any violation of established laws and regulations. Such policies may be in place within individual companies, or they may be adopted on an industry-wide basis.[10] One concept suggests a procedure for reporting suspicious activities to national governments, the IAEA, or other oversight bodies.[11]

The Brookings questionnaire asked participants to assess the following suggestion:

—Proposal 3. A whistle-blower policy among commercial entities in the nuclear industry that explicitly encourages the exposure of actions—either inside or outside of the employee's company—that are deemed to violate nonproliferation standards.

Under this approach, nuclear entities would not only adopt a standard for individual employees to raise proliferation concerns about activities or actions within their own company, but they and their employees would also be encouraged to report to the proper authorities questionable activities and practices *by other firms.*

This proposal generated the least favorable responses from industry in terms of both effectiveness and feasibility. In fact, most respondents ranked its effectiveness as *no impact* and its feasibility as *neutral*, suggesting widespread disregard for the usefulness of this approach and concerns about its potential impacts. For example, one respondent indicated that since whistle-blowers are "alerting industry and governments to things that have already happened . . . they are not a real deterrent." In addition, comments indicated uneasiness about possible unintended results. One participant stated, "Too few people know what nonproliferation is, or what violation looks like. A Pandora's box." Another stated that while the approach "could bring some credibility," it could also result in "false alarms and a lot of antinuclear harassment."

One industry respondent distinguished between whistle-blower policies within an organization, and outside:

> "Within [an] organization . . . in most well-established and reliable corporations in the nuclear industry, whistle-blower policies already exist. Encouraging all companies to do likewise would be beneficial. Whistle-blowing outside the organization to one's national government would make little difference to the risk of nuclear weapons proliferation, for the state would be probably in on the act. Whistle-blowing outside the country, for example to IAEA, could be effective for detecting early signs of nuclear weapons proliferation. However, such an act might constitute high treason, and therefore incur savage penalties from one's host country.

Nonindustry responses were very similar to those of industry. In particular, several nonindustry comments underscored a specific dynamic that complicates this and perhaps several other self-regulatory approaches, as noted in the preceding quotation: namely, the government ownership of many firms in the commercial nuclear fuel cycle. One respondent remarked, "Proliferation problems have not arisen in normal commercial entities." Another thought "proliferation is unlikely to involve purely commercial entities. We envisage that states will control the relevant organizations. What would happen to an Iranian whistle-blower?"

As described in chapter 3, government participation is prevalent throughout the nuclear fuel cycle and includes multinational ownership. It is likely to grow. The implication in both sets of responses is that whistle-blowing to an oversight body outside a country entails a complicated political dynamic for a commercial entity, especially one that is partly or wholly government owned. Furthermore, as one industry respondent observed, another interesting factor to consider in developing an industry-wide whistle-blowing program is that "the concept is not so compatible with many . . . cultures." Given the expected growth in civilian nuclear power worldwide, especially in new nuclear energy states as described in detail in chapter 4, this cultural perspective may prove to be a not insignificant challenge to this approach.

If it is to generate wide support, a whistle-blowing measure requires considerable deliberation and precision as to how it is defined and implemented, especially with regard to commercial, cultural, and political interrelationships. For example, redefining the intent and scope of a whistle-blower approach may generate more support from industry if the emphasis is more on sharing information on suspicious activities rather than on catching someone in a violation of regulations. In addition, it may be necessary to differentiate between the types of industry player; dual-use suppliers are likely to be exposed to more suspect behavior compared with larger fuel cycle companies. Thus a whistle-blower provision for the dual-use companies could not only have more impact on proliferation prevention, but also have more direct influence on day-to-day company operations. In order to ensure buy-in from such dual-use companies, however, they would have to be assured that they were not being singled out as *the* problem in the nonproliferation arena.

Black-Box Provisions

This concept proposes that certain technologies in the fuel cycle be provided to and utilized by operators only on the condition that those operators do not gain access to critical design and technical information supporting those technologies. Some experience exists with this type of arrangement: in July 2006 AREVA and URENCO signed a joint venture in the field of uranium enrichment centrifuge technology. The agreement created the jointly owned, independent Enrichment Technology Company (ETC) comprising all of URENCO's centrifuge enrichment design and manufacturing activities and installations as well as related research and development. The technology is maintained and operated by ETC and is not shared with its customers.[12]

The Brookings survey asked respondents to assess the viability of a more widespread black-box approach:

—Proposal 4. A "black-box" provision ensuring that operators of enrichment and reprocessing facilities have no access to or information on key technical components of the plant.

Most industry respondents ranked this proposal *effective/very effective,* but there was no consensus on feasibility (although half ranked it *feasible/very feasible*). Several industry participants noted that this principle has already demonstrated its viability since it is both already in place and proven, with one company indicating that a black-box approach is "absolutely necessary . . . already in effect." Another stated: "Enrichment and reprocessing technologies are among the most well-guarded process secrets in the world. . . . This [approach] can drastically reduce access to or information on key technical components of the plan, but cannot completely eliminate the risk of eventual leakage of technology."

The caution expressed at the end of this comment was more fully elaborated by several other highly skeptical views, such as "Even with a Black-Box approach, there are still technicians and scientists that have access to the processes," and "Rogue states can take control of facilities." In fact, two industry respondents remained unconvinced of the merits of the approach: "Difficult to see how effective and safe operation can proceed without full technical knowledge of plant," and "Already works for enrichment but can't imagine it would be possible to operate a reprocessing plant under these conditions."

Nonindustry responses were broadly similar to those of industry, as indicated by many stating the approach "has already been done," "would certainly prevent the spread of sensitive nuclear technology," and "is probably in conformity with Article IV of the Non-Proliferation Treaty." Nevertheless, similar doubts also emerged, with one respondent commenting: "This would delay proliferation but could be defeated by determined proliferators who could even use the 'open' plant to learn a lot and would then have to develop only a couple of key steps independently."

The overall responses to the black-box concept indicate a familiarity with the approach and a certain level of acceptance that it has been proven to work for enrichment facilities. As such, it seems to offer an example of how to support an expansion of civilian nuclear power while protecting commercial concerns and ensuring the prevention of proliferation. However, responses indicate that some people—including in industry—remain unconvinced of the effectiveness of this approach. Indeed, even industry is cognizant that there is no ironclad guarantee that a black-boxed technology could not ultimately be accessed or manipulated in some way. Finally, as one respondent suggested, further analysis is needed to establish this proposal's suitability for reprocessing.

Accreditation System

The American Society of Mechanical Engineers has developed an "N-Stamp" program, in which it certifies equipment, components, and activities for nuclear power plants under Section III of the society's Boiler and Pressure Vessel Code.[13] The overall goal is to provide incentives to establish effective quality-control programs and mechanisms that support N-Stamp requirements. N-Stamps are valid for three years, can be applied worldwide, and are specific to a particular facility.

A number of suggestions have been offered to incorporate such an approach in industry's nonproliferation work. PNNL, for example, has promoted the idea of adapting nonproliferation into an International Organization for Standardization (ISO) standard with the idea that companies adopting the standard could gain competitive advantage.[14]

Brookings sought to probe industry's view as to the applicability of such an accreditation approach for components and facilities in the critical areas of enrichment and reprocessing. Specifically, participants were asked to provide their views on the following system:

—Proposal 5. An industry-wide quality management/accreditation system for suppliers of components for sensitive elements of the fuel cycle.

Although there was no consensus on effectiveness, a majority of industry respondents ranked the proposal as feasible. One theme emerging in the comments is that this approach is not necessary: "Suppliers already comply with industry standards, as well as export controls," and "This is fixing something that is not broken. Already regulated." Other respondents, however, indicated that this proposal "could allow for certification of suppliers and regulator monitoring of their compliance to standards of conduct," and that "responsibility inside the supply chain [is an] excellent concept."

Among nonindustry respondents, there was no consensus on effectiveness, while a majority ranked it *feasible/very feasible*. Several comments indicated skepticism ("Doesn't address black market suppliers") and support of existing approaches ("More effective in case of governmental regulation and control").

An accreditation system for suppliers of components for sensitive elements of the fuel cycle received mixed responses on its effectiveness from all participants but is broadly viewed as feasible. In addition, some respondents from both industry and nonindustry did not understand the proposal, perhaps echoing another theme that the nonproliferation framework already attempts to address the transfer of technology. Thus this type of self-regulatory approach would require greater discussion concerning the mechanics of not only how it would work, but also how it complements existing legal obligations.

Government-Industry Conference

This concept is patterned after the Government-Industry Conference against Chemical Weapons (GICCW) that took place in Canberra, Australia, in September 1989 in the midst of the negotiations of the Chemical Weapons Convention (CWC).[15] The meeting provided a framework and forum for governments and the global chemical industry to arrive at an agreement on how to prevent the spread of chemical weapons while taking into consideration industry's legitimate commercial objectives. The conference was preceded by several years of discussions and negotiations between governments and the chemical industry and culminated in industry's commitment to work toward a chemical weapons ban, continue to work with governments, and accept a "self-policing role."

The CWC—which opened for signature in January 1993 and entered into force in April 1997—requires state signatories to destroy all the chemical weapons and production facilities they possess. In addition, the treaty establishes a regime to prevent new proliferation of such weapons. To make such a regime viable, the agreement for the first time in arms control history extended obligations to industry regarding both the reporting and verification of commercial activities (such as levels of production of certain chemicals) that could be linked to chemical weapons production. Because of the relationship that had developed between government negotiators and industry representatives, these provisions were thought to safeguard all of the stakeholders' interests.

With this experience in mind, respondents were asked their views on the following:

—Proposal 6. A periodic high-level international government-industry meeting to review the operation of any agreed system or set of measures.

Industry response to this idea was somewhat mixed: there was no consensus on effectiveness (although half ranked it *effective/very effective*), while the majority ranked it *feasible/very feasible*. There were several positive industry comments, including "Feasible if voluntary," "Good idea if matters are practical and risk informed," and "To be welcomed." For one respondent, government-industry collaboration of this sort greatly enhances the opportunity for any MNA approach to succeed.

Several respondents made highly skeptical remarks, however: "When have high-level international government meetings ever accomplished much?" and "Industry already contributes through host governments and WNA." In addition, one who expressed a positive view also cautioned: "The nuclear industry will be concerned that any multinational approach could disturb a well-functioning market, with potentially harmful economic affects."

Compared with industry participants, those outside industry considered this approach more effective and feasible. One commented that a "high-level government-industry meeting would be a very good thing," and that it could be used to address issues raised in some of the other self-regulatory approaches included in the survey. Another nonindustry respondent suggested using WINS, which "could be very effective."

In sum, nonindustry participants were more enthusiastic about this proposal, with industry expressing guarded views of its effectiveness. Nevertheless, the proposal received the most number of *feasible/very feasible* rankings from all respondents combined, suggesting a foundation for constructing a sustained approach for government-industry dialogue.

Results and a Way Forward

No self-regulatory proposal was overwhelmingly embraced by industry; that is, none gained a favorable consensus with respect to *both* effectiveness and feasibility. The clearest pattern of responses was for proposal 3 (the whistle-blower measure), which received by far the lowest favorable rankings in effectiveness and feasibility.

Overall, industry seems skeptical of self-regulatory approaches, highlighting problems and obstacles (real or theoretical) while not seeing unambiguous potential benefits. This is commensurate with the view expressed in one nonindustry interview that companies are reluctant to draw attention to the proliferation aspect of their business and want to see a benefit in doing so. They also insist on understanding exactly what is being asked of them. That may account in part for industry's concerns about all the proposals, particularly their rationale, how they will be implemented, and their potential impact.

Specifically, responses reveal several common themes (also explored in chapter 5). First, industry considers the current nonproliferation regime to be sufficient, and to the extent that weaknesses exist, commercial entities are not the source. In other words, if industry is not the part of the existing framework that is broken, why fix it? This sentiment was captured in one comment from an industry respondent: "Commercial entities are not where the risk lies. Already highly regulated."

Second, a prevalent view in industry is that nonproliferation is largely a government responsibility. Commercial entities indicated that they can go only so far in taking actions to strengthen proliferation prevention ("government needs to take lead"), or that cooperation already exists ("governments are already close partners").[16]

Third, industry is concerned about the potential commercial impacts of self-regulatory approaches and does not want to disturb the existing framework, whether with respect to its legal obligations or its operating practices. This is the case for several reasons. Commercial entities obviously do not like the unpredictability and instability of changing—or adding to—the established rules of the game for which they have spent resources and developed compliance systems and processes. In addition, industry is concerned that some of these self-regulatory approaches may leave room for loopholes or might assume that all companies have a complete and accurate understanding of the existing regime and what constitutes proliferation. The underlying fear is that by exploiting such loopholes or as a result of limited knowledge, some actors will gain commercial advantage over others. Perhaps more important, this perception is linked to the strongly and commonly held view in industry that one major breach of security anywhere in the world, such as a safety lapse or a proliferation event, will have a major negative impact on the commercial viability of the entire global industry.

Although its skepticism is strong, industry does not necessarily reject self-regulatory approaches across the board (except, as noted, in the case of whistle-blowing). Some encouraging signs and common ground emerge from the responses. Note, too, that nonindustry also shares some of the views just described. For example, many nonindustry respondents cited the challenges of addressing commercial concerns in adopting self-regulatory approaches, thus indicating that governments and international institutions are well aware of this issue. In addition, several proposals garnered broadly favorable assessments from both industry and nonindustry, the most notable being the black-box approach (proposal 4) and the government-industry conference (proposal 6).[17]

Proposal 6 had the most positive responses when industry and nonindustry rankings were combined, that is, the highest *total* number of *effective/very effective* and *feasible/very feasible* rankings. While industry seemed somewhat unsure of the effectiveness of this concept, most participating companies viewed it as *feasible/very feasible*. This is commensurate with industry's responses in part 1 of the survey, in which participants recognized the importance of collaborating with governments and international institutions, as illustrated in several comments:

—"Industry should have greater opportunity to engage with IAEA and governments on nonproliferation regulation."

—"Regular exchanges between the government and the nuclear energy industry providers must take place to ensure that both sides are well informed on the latest development in actions against proliferation."

—"It is very important for industry to be a partner in the discussion of strengthened safeguards."

These sentiments also broadly corroborate the results of other efforts to gauge industry views on the need for government-industry cooperation.[18] Thus industry seems to accept that enhanced government-industry communication is needed, and the concept is likely to continue to gain traction given the changing dynamics described elsewhere in this book. For example, a growing number of new nuclear energy states, the increasing role of governments in the commercial nuclear business, the potential expansion of sensitive fuel cycle technologies, and rising tensions over Article IV of the NPT all challenge the nonproliferation regime. In turn, the pressure to strengthen the existing framework will require the efforts of all stakeholders acting in concert. As one nonindustry respondent commented, a government-industry dialogue "would be in the interest of the industry, [which] wants to further develop its business in a climate of broader acceptance . . . [and a government-industry conference] can be considered as a good starting point. Of course, it will have to be further elaborated."

Certainly those policymakers and analysts aware of the 1989 GICCW generally view it as an important contribution to bringing the negotiations of the CWC to a successful conclusion four years later. It also constituted an important milestone in a government-industry consultative process that both preceded and followed the event itself, a process premised on the recognition that while governments bear the lion's share of the responsibility, industry has to be an active partner in the effort to rid the world of chemical weapons.

The Canberra Conference did not occur in isolation, however. Rather it was one important step in a long international negotiating process to ban the production, use, and stockpiling of chemical weapons. The GICCW could be a useful precedent for involving the nuclear industry in strengthening the nuclear nonproliferation regime. Thus the context, as well as the conference itself and its aftermath, is worth examining.

A Government-Industry Framework

The Geneva Protocol of 1925 banned the use of chemical weapons in warfare, but not their production, stockpiling, or testing. In the 1960s the United Nations began calling for concerted international negotiations to establish a comprehensive framework to ban chemical and biological weapons. The process of negotiating the CWC is usually said to date from 1968, when the responsible multilateral negotiating body—then the Eighteen-Nation Committee on Disarmament, which ultimately became the Conference on Disarmament—placed chemical weapons on its agenda separately from biological weapons for the first time.[19]

The period 1975–90 witnessed a marked change in the urgency and pace of negotiating a universal chemical weapons ban, as well as in the chemical industry's role in doing so. Until the late 1970s and early 1980s, the chemical industry played a relatively passive role in the negotiating process, limited to providing governments with technical inputs. In several countries, increased regulation even created an antagonistic relationship between government and industry.[20] In addition to this significant adversarial relationship, chemical trade associations and individual companies had little to no enthusiasm for participating in an issue that appeared to have little relevance to their business and seemed to be years away in its impact.[21]

Several factors contributed to jump-starting the CWC negotiating process and prompted the chemical industry to play a more proactive role, thus enhancing government-industry cooperation. First, a number of events led to increasing awareness of the industry's activities; chemical accidents at Seveso, Italy, in 1976 and Bhopal, India, in 1984 spurred governments to increase scrutiny of the chemical industry and establish more rigorous environmental standards.[22] In the United States, the chemical industry's association with the use of napalm and the herbicide Agent Orange in the Vietnam War also generated significant public criticism.[23]

The major geopolitical factor, however, was industry's association with production and use, specifically, Iraq's use of chemical weapons in the Iran-Iraq War in the 1980s. Together with concerns over Libya's attempt to acquire chemical weapons, the Iraq experience served as the major factor raising the urgency of drafting a strong and verifiable CWC and encouraging industry to be part of that process. In November 1983 Iran accused Iraq of using chemical weapons, which was subsequently confirmed by a UN investigation. In response, in 1984 the United States submitted a draft CWC to the Conference on Disarmament, marking the beginning of an intensified effort to reach an agreement.

In 1988, while the CWC negotiations continued in Geneva, Iraq used chemical weapons on the Kurdish village of Halabja, which caused an estimated 5,000 deaths. In the wake of the reports of that tragedy, an outraged international community gathered in Canberra in January 1989 for the Conference of State Parties to the 1925 Geneva Protocol and Other Interested States on the Prohibition of Chemical Weapons. More than 100 states reaffirmed support for the Geneva Protocol and urged conclusion of the CWC.[24]

A significant development emerging from the Iraq and Libya cases was the realization that "open commercial sources" had been a predominant feature of the chemical weapons and production facilities in both countries.[25] The chemical industry, already under pressure owing to commercial accidents such as Bhopal, became highly sensitized to the damage such events could inflict on its public image, and hence on its bottom line. As a result, several leaders in the chemical industry began to see the benefit of taking a more proactive role in working with governments to conclude the CWC.

The second major factor generating chemical industry participation in the CWC was commercial concerns. As the process moved forward, it became increasingly clear that the chemical industry needed to be a more active participant in drafting the CWC since many details being discussed by the negotiators would have a direct impact on chemical company operations. Government regulation of the industry was already widespread and intrusive, and it was not difficult to see that the CWC was going in the same direction.[26] The chemical industry, therefore, faced a choice: it could either stand outside the negotiations and seek to block inimical decisions by playing the spoiler, or it could seek to protect its key interests by becoming a partner in the process.

In large part because of the inestimable leadership provided by several key individuals within the chemical industry itself, industry chose the latter course. In January 1988 the U.S. Chemical Manufacturers Association (CMA), CEFIC (the West European industry association), and the Japan Chemical Industry Association identified the industry's priorities in the CWC talks, which revolved around confidentiality, inspection verification procedures, materials to be included in the CWC, and monitoring equipment.[27]

Again as a result of the leadership of key individuals, the chemical industry became increasingly active in the CWC negotiations from the late 1970s up to the time of the conference against chemical weapons in 1989. In the United States, the CMA, representing nearly 200 chemical companies and 90 percent of the country's chemical production capacity, initiated a dialogue on the CWC with representatives of the U.S. Arms Control and Disarmament Agency in 1978, through which strong and invaluable personal relationships were formed between government and industry representatives. In 1987 CMA also formed a chemical weapons working group that met every month and included periodic meetings with U.S. government representatives, reinforcing the personal bonds that had emerged among key players.[28] Similar efforts took place in several other countries with large chemical industries. Primarily at CMA's initiative, representatives of several national chemical industry trade associations met one another, as well as with the Conference on Disarmament delegates, at various meetings, including two in Geneva in July 1987 and July 1988. In addition, the chemical industry in several countries began implementing voluntary, self-regulatory policies—labeled "Responsible Care" programs—designed to curtail abuses in chemical trade.[29]

The GICCW and Its Outcomes

Initially, the chemical industry's increased activity and coordination with governments and with the Conference on Disarmament were informal. But it was generally recognized that implementing the CWC could not succeed without more formal, high-level, and sustained participation of the chemical industry.

The Australian government took the lead and called for a conference to "bring together governments and representatives of chemical industries worldwide, with the aim of raising their awareness about the problems of chemical weapons, and considering ways in which they can work together, in partnership, both internationally and domestically."[30] The conference took place in Canberra on September 18–22, 1989, and was attended by 400 delegates from sixty countries, including four international organizations and industry officials from companies representing 95 percent of the world's chemical production capacity.[31]

The major achievement of the conference was the global chemical industry's formal commitment to support the CWC.[32] Trade associations from the United States, Australia, Canada, Japan, and Western Europe jointly issued a formal statement pledging "to work actively with governments to achieve a global ban on chemical weapons and . . . to contribute additional momentum to the Geneva negotiating process."[33] This was the industry's first formal pledge "to participate in national measures designed to facilitate early implementation" of a treaty.[34] After the GICCW, chemical industry leaders created a new mechanism—the International Chemical Industry Forum—to "provide a formalized vehicle for transferring international industry's views to the Committee on Disarmament."[35]

GICCW as a Precedent

The steps toward government-industry collaboration sparked by the CWC worked: industry's participation is widely viewed as having been vital in concluding the treaty.[36] In reflecting on that experience, Will Carpenter, the leader of the CMA's Chemical Working Group and an individual whose personal contributions to ensuring an effective government-industry process were also vital, identified several key lessons from which other industries confronting a similar situation could draw:

—Issues must be identified early, before they receive attention from Congress, the media, or the general public. Early identification provides time for the stakeholders to find common ground.

—Industry needs to help government determine its objectives and means of achieving them. The chemical industry benefited enormously by becoming a critical resource for government.

—Industry needs to identify its own needs, objectives, and interests.

—It is essential to create multiple and consistent lines of communication, but to do so, each participating entity may have to learn the "tribal language" of the others.[37]

Despite important differences, the experience of the chemical industry in enacting the CWC, and of the GICCW in particular, is instructive for the nuclear industry in suggesting how it can play a more proactive role in strengthening the nuclear nonproliferation regime. Obviously, these industries differ in their overall objectives. The GICCW and subsequent formal cooperation were geared toward *establishing* a new nonproliferation and disarmament regime. For nuclear issues, the goal is *strengthening* the existing nonproliferation regime.[38] This fundamental difference lends itself to various interpretations of implications and lessons.

First, creating a disarmament and nonproliferation regime is by definition more difficult than making incremental improvements that will strengthen an existing framework. Moreover, constraining the spread and use of chemical weapons has been harder owing to widely disseminated technologies, and the fact that, given the less destructive nature of chemical weapons compared with nuclear weapons, a strong consensus to limit their spread did not necessarily exist.[39]

That consensus, however, began to grow stronger in the 1980s, with chemical weapons increasingly delegitimized as a tool of war. That delegitimization, accompanied by public image concerns, played a large role in bringing industry into a more meaningful, elevated, and sustained partnership with government to implement a CWC.[40]

These differences, however, are outweighed by similarities in underlying geopolitical and commercial dynamics in the chemical and nuclear industries. While the nuclear industry fortunately has not witnessed a nuclear event on a par with Iraq's use of chemical weapons, the threats posed by the A. Q. Khan network, North Korea, and Iran have highlighted the urgency of strengthening the nuclear nonproliferation regime. Given the significantly greater destructive capacity of nuclear weapons, any movement toward allowing additional parties to gain access to nuclear weapons is of grave concern. As noted elsewhere, the commercial nuclear industry is very concerned about these developments as well as emerging limitations in the nonproliferation framework and welcomes enhanced dialogue with governments and international institutions. Responses indicate that industry is very much aware of the potential impact on public perceptions, citing the "one-incident-damages-all" concept as foremost in its thinking. Thus the nuclear industry's legitimate and sincere concerns about the strength of the nonproliferation system and its public image are very comparable to those that spurred the chemical industry to action.

A similar commercial concern also exists. As noted, the chemical industry recognized that the CWC negotiations revolved around issues having a direct impact on its business, and it saw proactive participation in the discussions as a way to ensure that its legitimate business concerns were addressed.[41] According to Will Carpenter, "We were able, through very good, effective communications, to bring the diplomats to reality as to what needed to be involved in the treaty for it to be technically sound."[42]

The nuclear industry could now be in much the same place as the chemical industry was in the early 1980s. The changing dynamics described in detail in previous chapters—expanding nuclear capacity, especially in developing countries; an accompanying increase in nuclear commerce, knowledge, and potentially in sensitive technologies; and market trends in the nuclear fuel cycle—are putting increased pressure on an already stressed nonproliferation regime. These dynamics have given rise to numerous MNA and self-regulatory proposals. In a manner broadly similar to the pattern of CWC negotiations, governments and international institutions have suggested various plans and concepts to strengthen the nuclear nonproliferation regime that touch directly on commercial issues.

To be sure, the commercial nuclear industry is already engaged in addressing nonproliferation issues by contributing to the dialogue on the changing market and associated proposals to address both commercial and nonproliferation concerns. When the IAEA conducted a comprehensive review of MNA approaches in 2005, for example, a wide array of industry representatives participated in this effort.[43] In addition, just as the chemical industry established voluntary "Responsible Care" programs in the 1980s, the nuclear industry and nongovernmental entities have taken proactive steps to foster best practices, as illustrated by the WANO and WINS initiatives. Some companies have instituted internal mechanisms and procedures to ensure compliance with the nonproliferation regime at the national and international levels, as explained in the next section.

Nevertheless, government and industry have yet to coordinate their activities in a sustained and structured manner so as to deal specifically with nonproliferation objectives and associated proposals to strengthen the nonproliferation regime. Our research indicates two possible explanations for this. First, the commercial nuclear industry remains by and large skeptical of most MNA and self-regulatory approaches, citing concerns about the lack of detail on how they would function, as well as unknown or potentially deleterious commercial impacts. Perhaps more important, the commercial nuclear industry in general does not see itself as a weak link in the nonproliferation regime and believes that measures to strengthen that regime are mainly the purview of governments and international institutions. The Brookings survey yielded comments from industry participants such as "Industry already complies with nonproliferation constraints," and "Commercial entities are not where the risk lies." This is unlike the chemical industry's recognition that it had played a role in the dissemination and use of chemical weapons in the 1980s and therefore had indeed contributed to chemical weapons proliferation.

Moreover, despite the general support indicated for a government-industry conference and the recognition of the importance of coordinating and partnering with governments in maintaining and strengthening the nonproliferation regime, more work is needed to broaden the acceptance of this approach. Some industry respondents commented that there is "relatively little opportunity for the industry to provide input," and that "industry does not need to be a 'partner'; (inter)national law should regulate the behavior [of companies]." Even in cases in which industry sees the value of enhanced cooperation, the relationship is often viewed as "informal," rather than more structured and sustained. This is illustrated in the following supportive comment from an industry participant:

"An informal partnership approach is essential. Industry and government have the same objectives but different roles. Increased dialogue, voluntary codes of practice, etc. should be encouraged."

Notwithstanding these hurdles, the general support expressed for a government-industry conference may provide an opportunity to allay industry's skepticism of, and pursue agreement on, other self-regulatory approaches as well as MNAs. The experience of the GICCW suggests that an ongoing, structured dialogue between government and industry would not only ensure that industry's commercial concerns are heard but also provide a forum for working out the mechanics of how specific self-regulatory and MNA approaches would work. One industry respondent suggested as much in remarking, "The chance of success of any multinational approach to the fuel cycle will be greatly enhanced if there is high-level international government-industry liaison." Such a "liaison" would also provide a platform from which to consider a variety of approaches together, rather than in isolation, and thus increase the chances of arriving at a workable consensus. Moreover, given the important role of governments and international institutions in the nonproliferation regime, a structured government-industry partnership can help ensure that any industry self-regulatory and MNA approaches are designed to complement and support the existing legal regime rather than inadvertently weaken it.

The ongoing consultative approach instituted between government and industry in the chemical sector was, without doubt, mutually beneficial and bridged significant gaps: "Governments received technical advice . . . and a deeper understanding of its concerns, while industry gained a better appreciation of the limitations imposed on governments by the consensual nature of multilateral diplomacy."[44] This is a precedent directly relevant for the nuclear industry, and the sentiment expressed in this quotation is directly and uncannily analogous to a comment provided by a nonindustry participant in our research: "There needs to be proper dialogue, such that government understands the needs and constraints of industry, and does not impose unnecessary and unreasonable requirements for little gain, and to ensure that industry understands government's needs and the international picture. This would allow effort to be appropriately targeted without unnecessarily restricting competitiveness."

Blueprint for a Government-Industry Dialogue

Industry's cautious and somewhat skeptical view of the MNA and self-regulatory proposals offered in the Brookings survey is not necessarily an obstacle to achieving a commonly agreed approach. Rather it is an opportunity to build further understanding of the concepts and to reach a consensus on the most effective ones.

Drawing on and adapting the lessons Carpenter gleaned from the chemical industry's experience, one can formulate six basic principles to guide the development of self-regulatory proposals and foster government-industry dia-logue, all with the ultimate objective of strengthening the nonproliferation regime:

1. *Personal leadership.* This was critical in the success of the CWC, and one nonindustry participant we interviewed suggested the same was true in the case of establishing WANO. There is every reason to believe that similar personal leadership is required in the nuclear industry to enhance proliferation preven-tion. Governments must look for and work with industry representatives of stat-ure who are highly regarded by their peers and can be champions of greater industry action in the nonproliferation arena.

2. *Building trust and avoiding publicity.* Given the long-standing, often polar-izing views of nuclear power, it is essential to identify issues early, build trust, and find common ground between government and industry in a manner that limits publicity in order to defuse the potential for a highly charged public debate. All of the stakeholders—governments, industry, nongovernmental actors—should look for multiple and alternative ways to foster such trust.

3. *Industry as a resource for government.* The CWC and its impact showed industry to be an important resource for government, especially in determin-ing goals and shaping workable solutions. The nuclear industry can perform a similar service, even beyond the contributions it has already made in this regard.

4. *Developing an industry consensus.* The chemical industry was able to iden-tify its own needs, goals, and interests, thus providing for a more efficient and productive dialogue, and making a final agreement possible. Nuclear industry can do no less, especially in view of the multifaceted nature of "the industry."

5. *Establishing multiple lines of communication.* Communication must take place along more than a single line, because the dialogue needs to incorporate all views.

6. *Communicating and specifying benefits and steps.* Industry needs to under-stand what it is being asked to do, and the benefits of doing it.

Although many details of the way a sustained dialogue would function need to be ironed out by the parties themselves, the following broad blueprint could pro-mote a sustained partnership that strengthens the nuclear nonproliferation regime.

1. Develop a Formal, Ongoing Mechanism to Shepherd the Government-Industry Partnership Forward

Industry's responses to proposed self-regulatory approaches indicate that, despite its skepticism, sufficient interest and familiarity with the approaches exist to develop solutions through a structured dialogue within industry and between it and governments and international organizations. Moreover, some specific concepts—including ones currently being implemented among some of the larger industry stakeholders—could form the basis for "best practices" to be shared and implemented more broadly. They could prove especially useful if applied to smaller—and newer—actors in the industry. For example, black-box and accreditation mechanisms have the advantage of being generally familiar to the nuclear industry. Indeed, industry representatives highlighted each of these in our outreach. The development and dissemination of best practices can be a valuable tool, as illustrated by the activities of institutions such as WANO, WINS, and the Institute of Nuclear Power Operations in the United States in enhancing safety and security of nuclear power facilities.[45]

In the area of internal compliance—explicit corporate policies and governance processes developed to ensure compliance with the nonproliferation regime—it is generally acknowledged that such practices are not widely implemented across the industry.[46] Although the survey's feedback in this area was limited, several companies reported that they handle proliferation as a distinct function at a structurally high level: it is either addressed by the chief executive officer as a formal responsibility or by a separate department that reports to him or her. In addition, distinct organizational units handle export controls, safeguards, and physical protection requirements, and internal training programs related to nonproliferation have been developed that are applicable to all employees. In some cases, a broad commitment to nonproliferation is incorporated into a mission or values statement.

Companies that have implemented internal training programs, developed written policies or practices, and structured and staffed their organizations to ensure compliance with the nonproliferation regime offer practical lessons for other firms, and their efforts could form the basis for developing best practices. These procedures and policies can be especially valuable for smaller firms that may not yet have focused on proliferation issues in detail, as well as for new entrants in the sector.

Industry and government clearly need to communicate better their concerns about MNA approaches. From the specific responses to our survey (assessed in chapter 6), it appears that broadly speaking the industry is highly dubious of the feasibility of MNA proposals, whereas people outside the industry find some of them potentially effective. This indicates that considerable room for dialogue exists to explain the respective concerns, narrow the options to the most practicable solutions, and work out detailed mechanics of how to implement them. Industry's concerns about the fuel bank concept provide a case in point. Many industry respondents saw potential problems in specific aspects of implementing a fuel bank, such as establishing a location, financing, fabricating fuel, and replenishing stocks. An ongoing government-industry dialogue would provide an effective means of addressing those concerns by bringing their joint skills and experience to bear on the issues.

Institutionally, an ongoing dialogue could be structured in several ways, for example, by using existing industry institutions, establishing a new nongovernmental organization, or forming smaller industry groups.[47] Responses in this study indicate that several existing organizations may be capable of providing the forum or leadership needed to move forward on self-regulatory approaches and keep alive the discussions pursuant to a government-industry conference on nuclear power (GICNP), discussed in the next section. Two that were specifically mentioned by respondents were WINS and the INMM.

The idea of using established entities has at least three advantages. First, it obviates the need to spend time and resources in establishing an additional body with a particular mandate. Second, such institutions can provide a ready-made arena and focal point for industry-wide discussions, and potentially serve as the industry's representative voice in a GICNP, as well as in follow-up discussions. Third, they may be ideally suited to coordinate with commercial entities in agreeing and sharing best practices, since this is a large part of their current respective missions.

On the negative side, existing institutions already have well-defined programs and limited resources that may make them reluctant to assume new responsibilities, particularly when they are not yet fully agreed or precisely defined. One institution indicated to us, for example, that it is not interested in taking on the role described here.[48] This, of course, may not be the final word on the subject, but it does highlight the challenges to making quick progress in this area.

Using the CWC process as a model, an international nuclear industry forum (INIF) could be established to represent the commercial nuclear industry on nonproliferation issues, both publicly and in more private interactions with governments and international organizations such as the IAEA. The details of who would participate and how the forum would function should be worked out by industry. Participation is an important issue. The "nuclear industry" in reality comprises many different entities engaged in a wide range of disparate activities and functions. Should they all be included in an INIF? Some reason exists for arguing that they should. Certain reactions to our survey suggest considerable attention must be directed at smaller companies such as component manufacturers who face much stronger pressures to make a sale and have fewer resources with which to resist cutting corners to do so. A government representative argued during our research, for example, that the "mainstream nuclear industry is not [a] major problem; . . . the problem is more with component manufacturers, where too many companies are prepared to turn a blind eye to make a sale." Relative to larger firms in the nuclear fuel cycle that were the focus of our research, dual-use suppliers are generally more numerous, smaller in size, and more limited in their resources; appear to be more directly and frequently confronted with "suspicious" activities; and are generally more apprehensive of dealing with governments.[49] All of these factors make bringing them into the government-industry dialogue both more challenging and perhaps more necessary. Including all the different parts of the industry could clearly cause operational and other problems. At the same time, not having a component of industry at the table could foster difficulties as the evolution of the industry continues.

A second issue relates to leadership. An INIF along the lines of the International Chemical Industry Forum established after the GICCW could include major nuclear industry trade associations at national, regional, or international levels. A lead implementing organization could be named or created, or several of the larger commercial nuclear companies could lead the forum's organization and implementation.

Regardless of who leads, the objective is to provide a sustained forum for collaboration among industry entities, as well as to serve as a single voice and point of contact for governments and international organizations. The INIF could work out self-regulatory and governance approaches as well as specific MNA approaches. With regard to timing, the INIF process could be established in the short term, before a more formal, high-level conference takes place, in order to build consensus within the industry and find common ground with nonindustry actors.

The INIF could directly complement and provide important input to preparations for the next Nuclear Nonproliferation Treaty Review Conference in 2015. This formalized dialogue would address one of the conclusions emanating from the most recent NPT Review Conference concluded in May 2010:

> The Conference underlines the importance of continuing to discuss in a non-discriminatory and transparent manner under the auspices of IAEA or regional forums, the development of multilateral approaches to the nuclear fuel cycle, including the possibilities to create mechanisms for assurance of nuclear fuel supply, as well as possible schemes dealing with the back-end of the fuel cycle, without affecting rights under the Treaty and without prejudice to national fuel cycle policies, while tackling the technical, legal and economic complexities surrounding these issues, including in this regard the requirement of IAEA full scope safeguards.[50]

The INIF could provide the structured mechanism enabling industry to contribute to these continued discussions.

2. ESTABLISH AND IMPLEMENT A GOVERNMENT-INDUSTRY CONFERENCE AGAINST NUCLEAR PROLIFERATION (GICNP)

A conference within the context of the INIF would provide a catalyst for transforming INIF discussions of issues into a concrete action plan. As in the GICCW, the main objective of a GICNP would be to establish a structured forum for governments and industry to discuss specific issues of concern to all parties. Broad questions to address could include the following:

—What does each party view as the principal challenges to the nonproliferation regime?

—What are the best approaches, concepts, and proposals for meeting the challenges? Who would take the lead in their implementation, and what other stakeholders should be involved?

—For the major MNA and self-regulatory approaches being considered, what are the respective detailed concerns of industry, governments, and others?

—What is the best way forward for agreeing on a common approach and timetable?

—What are expected outcomes for stakeholders, and in particular, what are the benefits for industry?

This GICNP would not be a one-time event. Rather, it would be a periodic focal point at which each party could convey its perspectives, hear the views of others, and support an ongoing dialogue on specific proposals with the aim of developing solutions by consensus. The conference could be repeated every few years, with the understanding that regular discussions would be held between conferences (in part through the INIF).

Most important, despite the challenges inherent in the two-part approach outlined here, it is imperative to widen and deepen industry's awareness of non-proliferation risks and its responsibilities as a partner in managing those risks. Industry representatives themselves told us that the level of awareness in their sector was far too low. This problem is only likely to get worse as a nuclear renaissance proceeds, particularly if it moves forward rapidly and robustly. A sustained awareness-raising program conducted by and for industry is essential regardless of who emerges as an industry leader in promoting best practices and other nonproliferation measures.

Conclusion

An INIF and a GICNP would help to clarify roles and responsibilities for both government and industry, promote joint assessments of key risks and appropriate responses, and foster international "buy-in" to key decisions. Specifically, this process would provide a platform from which to devise a strategy for achieving international consensus on multilateral control of sensitive elements of nuclear fuel cycle facilities, work out mutually acceptable best practices, advance awareness of the need for self-regulation, and provide a foundation for creating them.

In addition, this recommended process for sustained dialogue would enable industry to become more proactive, as it has stated it wants to be, and realize the benefits of self-regulatory approaches. These benefits directly address the major commercial concerns raised in our survey. Voluntary industry initiatives could help harmonize and standardize corporate nonproliferation practices, enhance efficiency, improve performance, and close the gap between leading performers and those lagging behind. Moreover, self-regulatory measures can demonstrate

to the public and shareholders alike that industry is taking steps on nonproliferation that are bringing commercial benefits and comparative advantage.[51] In
short, the measures we recommend can help a broader segment of the nuclear
business community work together and with nonindustry actors to do more to
prevent a serious incident from occurring. This makes more business sense than
being passive or simply letting government lead.

The nuclear industry is anything but an uninterested bystander where
strengthening the nuclear nonproliferation regime is concerned. Indeed, the
industry must do more. An important step would be to launch an INIF and
GICNP, both useful mechanisms for this purpose. Groundwork could be laid
for a new set of arrangements or new "rules of the road" that would have a significant impact on how the nuclear industry does business in the future. Political
disagreements may prevent that from happening. But even if no agreements are
reached, the attempt to do so could have beneficial repercussions for the nuclear
industry as it would contribute, perhaps substantially, to the tenor of the global
nuclear commercial environment in the years ahead.

The nuclear industry believes that the expansion of civilian nuclear power per
se does not increase proliferation risks. Industry also has relevant observations on
proposals for managing the fuel cycle. Its views may help governments achieve
workable solutions. But because the debate on these issues is highly political,
industry and government can only arrive at such solutions through a sustained
dialogue with a view to sharing information, building consensus, and understanding each other's expectations, both in terms of objectives and benefits.
An INIF and a GICNP mechanism should be initiated as soon as possible to
advance this partnership and ensure the strengthening of the nuclear nonproliferation regime.

Table 7-1. *Responses to Self-Regulatory Proposals and Selected Comments*[a]

Proposal	Industry	Nonindustry
1. A voluntary code of conduct for all commercial entities in the nuclear industry incorporating broad nonproliferation values as well as best-practice guidelines specific to the sector.	No consensus on effectiveness; majority viewed it as feasible. *Major themes* Good idea, but . . . . Would not add value; existing regime is sufficient. Could have negative commercial impact. "The legal obligations of the industry have to be established by the governments." "Already highly regulated. Voluntary code would not add anything significant." "Certainly good idea to [promote] such a collegial pledge to excellence."	No consensus on effectiveness; majority viewed it as feasible. *Major themes* Weak in proliferation prevention. "Difficult to convince all companies to be part of the system." "Easily circumvented, hence politically achievable, but quite weak in controlling proliferation." "Could be implemented quickly and will have impact on nuclear industry."
2. A code of conduct such as that described in proposal 1 with a binding charter and penalties for noncompliance determined by signatory states.	Majority ranked it *effective/very effective;* no consensus on feasibility. *Major themes* Difficult to enforce. Measures already in place through NSG and Additional Protocol. Commercial concerns. "Almost impossible to enforce. Exports already controlled by NSG controls, etc." "Something similar to the NPT and its additional protocol. Not an improvement over current practice." "A binding code would be more effective, but simultaneously more difficult to impose. If penalties determined by signatory states were dissimilar and affected commercial entities to larger or smaller extent, this could unfairly affect the competitive position of those companies in the world market."	Majority ranked it *effective/very effective;* no consensus on feasibility. *Major themes* Difficult to enforce. Measures already in place. "System exists under INFCIRC/153 NNWS." "A code of conduct with binding charter and with penalties for non-compliance would be a good thing." "Better than [Proposal 1] . . . but therefore harder to implement."

3. A whistle-blower policy among commercial entities in the nuclear industry that explicitly encourages the exposure of actions—either inside or outside of the employee's company—that are deemed to violate preapproved nonproliferation standards.	No consensus on effectiveness (most ranked it *no impact*); majority ranked it *neutral*. *Major themes* Could work but . . . . Needs more definition on implementation. Could have commercial and political complications. "Whistle-blowers alert the industry and governments that things have already happened. They are not a real deterrent." "Too few people know what nonproliferation is, or what violation looks like. A Pandora's box." "Commercial entities are not where the risk lies." "Could bring some credibility also false alarms and a lot of antinuclear harassment."	No consensus on effectiveness (most ranked it *no impact*); no consensus on feasibility (most ranked it *neutral*). *Major themes* "Proliferation problems have not arisen in normal commercial entities." "Would give no real added value to existing rules." "Proliferation is unlikely to involve purely commercial entities. We envisage that states will control the relevant organizations. What would happen to an Iranian whistleblower?" "Should be implemented anyway."
4. A "black-box" provision ensuring that operators of enrichment and reprocessing facilities have no access to or information on key technical components of the plant.	Majority ranked it *effective/very effective*; no consensus on feasibility (half ranked it *feasible/very feasible*). *Major themes* In effect and working. Still won't prevent determined actors from gaining access. "This can drastically reduce access to or information on key technical components of the plan, but cannot completely eliminate the risk of eventual leakage of technology." "Absolutely necessary . . . already in effect." "Difficult to see how effective and safe operation can proceed without full technical knowledge of plant." "Even with black-box approach, there are still technicians and scientists that have access to the processes."	Majority ranked it *effective/very effective*, and *feasible/very feasible*. *Major themes* In effect and working. Still won't prevent determined actors from gaining access. "Principle exists already for commercial reasons." "A black-box approach would certainly prevent the spread of sensitive nuclear technology. It is probably in conformity with Article IV of the NPT." "This would delay proliferation but could be defeated by determined proliferators who could even use the "open" plant to learn a lot and would then have to develop only a couple of key steps independently."

(continued)

Table 7-1 (*continued*)

Proposal	Industry	Nonindustry
5. An industry-wide quality management/ accreditation system for suppliers of components for sensitive elements of the fuel cycle.	No consensus on effectiveness; majority ranked it *feasible/very feasible*. *Major themes* Familiar concept makes it feasible. Largely unnecessary, regime already addresses. Some did not understand concept as presented. "Suppliers already comply with industry standards, and export controls." "This approach could allow for certification of suppliers and regular monitoring of their compliance to standards of conduct." "How would this prevent proliferation?? This is fixing something that is not broken. Already regulated." "Responsibility inside supply chain = excellent concept . . . takes time, not so easy to control."	No consensus on effectiveness; majority ranked it *feasible/very feasible*. *Major themes* Largely unnecessary, regime already addresses. Existing similar controls not fully adequate. Some did not understand concept as presented. "Doesn't address black market suppliers." "Commercial database exists, supported by companies." "This didn't work very well for centrifuges, among other examples." "More effective in case of governmental regulation and control." "Limiting the transfer is better."
6. A periodic high-level international government-industry meeting to review the operation of any agreed system or set of measures.	No consensus on effectiveness (half ranked it *effective/very effective*); majority ranked it *feasible/very feasible*. *Major themes* An idea that could work, with some skepticism on effectiveness. Collaboration with governments already happening. "Feasible if voluntary." "When have high-level international government meetings ever accomplished much? They are the grandstands for countries to profess their support without actually doing anything." "Industry already contributes through host governments and WNA. More effective engagement is welcome. Industry should be effectively engaged by governments and IAEA to inform their development of safeguards." "Good idea if matters are practical and risk informed . . . no NGOs, no media, as low as reasonably possible."	Majority ranked it *effective/very effective* and *feasible/very feasible*. *Major themes* Nonindustry viewed it as more effective and feasible, Should be pursued and would be valuable, with some skepticism on effectiveness. "A periodic high-level international government-industry meeting would be a very good thing." "This could simply become a talking shop, and not be effective." "Need to make reference to WINS which . . . could be very effective."

a. "Effectiveness" refers to the ability to strengthen the nuclear nonproliferation regime; "feasibility" refers to the ease of logistical and political implementation; "no consensus" means no majority in ranking a proposal either favorably (*effective/very effective* or *feasible/very feasible*) or unfavorably (*ineffective/very ineffective*, or *unfeasible/very unfeasible*).

Notes

1. We use the term "self-regulation" broadly to refer to actions initiated and implemented by industry that bolster its role in working with governments and international organizations to prevent proliferation. We assume that these measures involve interaction with governments and others but are voluntarily proposed and implemented by industry, and that they are not mandated by nonindustry actors. More generally, we use the term to convey the sense that industry is adopting a positive, proactive partnership posture toward addressing the risks associated with nuclear proliferation.

2. See especially Gretchen Hund and Oksana Elkhamri, "Industry Self-Regulation as a Means to Promote Nonproliferation," PNNL-15355 (Richland, Wash.: Pacific Northwest Center for Global Security, Pacific Northwest National Laboratory, October 2005); Gretchen Hund and Amy Seward, "Broadening Industry Governance to Include Nonproliferation," PNNL-17521 (Richland, Wash.: Pacific Northwest Center for Global Security, Pacific Northwest National Laboratory, November 11, 2008); and Martine Letts and Fiona Cunningham, "The Role of the Civil Nuclear Industry in Preventing Proliferation and in Managing the Second Nuclear Age" (Canberra, Australia: International Commission on Nuclear Nonproliferation and Disarmament, February 2009).

3. Hund and Seward, "Broadening Industry Governance to Include Nonproliferation," p. 2.

4. The range of concepts put forth here is based on Hund and Seward, "Broadening Industry Governance to Include Nonproliferation," p. 23; and Letts and Cunningham, "The Role of the Civil Nuclear Industry in Preventing Proliferation."

5. World Nuclear Association (WNA), "Charter of Ethics" (www.world-nuclear.org/about/ethics.html).

6. World Association of Nuclear Operators, "What Is WANO" (www.wano.org.uk/WANO_Documents/What_is_Wano.asp).

7. From the World Institute for Nuclear Security (www.wins.org/index.aspx).

8. From the Institute of Nuclear Materials Management (www.inmm.org).

9. Pacific Northwest National Laboratory, the Carnegie Endowment for International Peace, the Stimson Center, and the International Commission on Nuclear Nonproliferation and Disarmament have all promoted or are working on concepts for a code of conduct.

10. For the U.S. nuclear industry, for example, Title II, Section 211 of the Energy Reorganization Act of 1974 contains whistle-blower protections for industry employees. For more information, see www.nrc.gov/reading-rm/doc-collections/nuregs/staff/sr0980/rev1/vol-1-sec-2-to-5.pdf.

11. Hund and Seward, "Broadening Industry Governance to Include Nonproliferation," p. 17; and Letts and Cunningham, "The Role of the Civil Nuclear Industry in Preventing Proliferation," p. 19.

12. Other examples include Louisiana Energy Services (owned by URENCO) and AREVA each constructing a centrifuge enrichment facility in the United States under black-box conditions; Russian enrichment technology being used in China is also thought to be operating under black-box conditions. See James E. Goodby, "Internationalizing

the Nuclear Fuel Cycle" (Stanford University, Hoover Institution, May 2008) (http://web.mit.edu/stgs/pdfs/Goodby--Internationalizing%20the%20nuclear%20fuel%20cycle.pdf).

13. The certifications (N-Stamps) include N (nuclear vessels, pumps, valves, piping systems, storage tanks, core support structures, concrete containments, and transport packaging); NA (field installation and shop assembly); NPT (fabrication, with or without design responsibility, for nuclear appurtenances and supports); NS (nuclear supports); NV (pressure relief valves); and N3 (containment for spent fuel and radioactive waste). From Brian Schimmoller, "Stamp of Approval," *Power Engineering* 113 (October 27, 2008).

14. Hund and Seward, "Broadening Industry Governance to Include Nonproliferation," p. 3.

15. Letts and Cunningham, "The Role of the Civil Nuclear Industry in Preventing Proliferation," pp. 22–26.

16. These comments are responses to question 5 in part 1 of our survey (What is your view of the need for industry to be a partner with government in managing proliferation risks?).

17. These two proposals received the most number of *effective/very effective*, and *feasible/very feasible* rankings from industry and nonindustry combined.

18. Gretchen Hund, Amy Seward, and Oksana Elkhamri, "A Role for Industry in Promoting Nuclear Security and Nonproliferation," *Nuclear News*, November 2009, p. 59. Based on PNNL's survey of fourteen companies that provide dual-use items: "According to the survey results, a strong industry/government partnership would be the most effective means of stemming illicit trade."

19. Timothy L. H. McCormack, "Some Australian Efforts to Promote Chemical Weapons Non-Proliferation and Disarmament," *Australian Year Book of International Law*, 1992. In the 1960s the negotiating body was originally called the Eighteen-Nation Disarmament Committee, and after several iterations, in 1979 it was finally called the Conference on Disarmament.

20. Daniel Feakes and Ian R. Kenyon, *The Creation of the Organization for the Prohibition of Chemical Weapons: A Case Study in the Birth of an Intergovernmental Organization* (The Hague: TMC Asser Press, 2007), pp. 180–81.

21. Will D. Carpenter and Michael Moodie, "Industry and Arms Control," in *Biological Warfare: Modern Offense and Defense,* edited by Raymond A. Zilinskas (Boulder, Colo.: Lynne Rienner, 2000), p. 178.

22. See Feakes and Kenyon, *The Creation of the Organization for the Prohibition of Chemical Weapons.*

23. Office of Technology Assessment (OTA), "The Chemical Weapons Convention: Effects on the U.S. Chemical Industry," OTA-BP-ISC-106 (Washington: Government Printing Office, August 1993).

24. See McCormack, "Some Australian Efforts to Promote Chemical Weapons Non-Proliferation and Disarmament."

25. See Feakes and Kenyon, *The Creation of the Organization for the Prohibition of Chemical Weapons.*

26. Carpenter and Moodie, "Industry and Arms Control," p. 179.

27. The CMA is now the International Council of Chemical Associations. CMA is used throughout this section to refer to the entity's activities in that period; Carpenter and Moodie, "Industry and Arms Control," p. 179.

28. OTA, "The Chemical Weapons Convention."

29. Julian Perry Robinson, "The Canberra Conference," *Chemical Weapons Convention Bulletin* 6 (November 1989); see also Hund and Elkhamri, "Industry Self-Regulation as a Means to Promote Nonproliferation," p. 7.

30. Ibid.

31. See OTA, "The Chemical Weapons Convention." The following industry trade associations attended: the U.S. Chemical Manufacturers Association, the Council of European Chemical Industry Federations, Japan Chemical Industry Association, the Canadian Chemical Producers Association, the Chemical Confederation of Australia, and the U.K. Chemical Industries Association.

32. See Robinson, "The Canberra Conference."

33. Department of Foreign Affairs and Trade, "Government-Industry Conference against Chemical Weapons," September 18–22, 1989, National Convention Centre, Canberra, Australia.

34. Ibid.

35. See Robinson, "The Canberra Conference."

36. The CWC was concluded in 1993, entered into force in 1997, and now has 183 signatory states. See Mary Beth Nikitin, Paul Kerr, and Steven A. Hildreth, "Proliferation Control Regimes: Background and Status," Congressional Research Service, January 31, 2008, p. 30.

37. Carpenter and Moodie, "Industry and Arms Control," pp. 178–80.

38. Although nuclear weapons disarmament is a cornerstone of the Nuclear Nonproliferation Treaty (that is, all existing weapons states are expected to work toward disarmament), this issue is beyond the scope of this analysis.

39. See Nikitin and others, "Proliferation Control Regimes: Background and Status."

40. On the other hand, nuclear weapons continue to be viewed—principally by the weapons states—as a legitimate deterrent. See Jonathan Tucker, "Verifying a Multilateral Ban on Nuclear Weapons: Lessons from the CWC," *Non-proliferation Review* (Winter 1998).

41. This reveals another similarity: the dual-use nature of the industries. Chemicals and nuclear technology both have legitimate, peaceful uses that can be diverted for military purposes. Thus both industries, while highly conscious of this fact, seek to ensure that peaceful uses are protected. See Tucker, "Verifying a Multilateral Ban on Nuclear Weapons."

42. See OTA, "The Chemical Weapons Convention."

43. International Atomic Energy Agency (IAEA), "Multilateral Approaches to the Nuclear Fuel Cycle: Expert Group Report submitted to the Director General of the International Atomic Energy Agency," INFCIRC/640 (Vienna, February 22, 2005).

44. See Feakes and Kenyon, *The Creation of the Organization for the Prohibition of Chemical Weapons,* p. 182.

45. The Institute of Nuclear Power Operations (INPO) is a U.S.-based entity founded in 1979 with a mission "to promote the highest levels of safety and reliability . . . in the operation of commercial nuclear power plants," through, in part, "establishing performance objectives, criteria and guidelines for the nuclear power industry" (www.inpo.info/AboutUs.htm).

46. For a summary of more specific types of governance mechanisms that could be implemented, see Hund and Elkhamri, "Industry Self-Regulation as a Means to Promote Nonproliferation," pp. 12–16. Also, David Albright, *Peddling Peril: How the Secret Nuclear Trade Arms America's Enemies* (New York: Free Press, 2010).

47. For a discussion of institutional approaches, see Hund and Seward, "Broadening Industry Governance to Include Nonproliferation," pp. 11–12.

48. Pacific Northwest National Laboratory found in its research that WANO, WNA, and INMM were not likely candidates; see Hund and Elkhamri, "Industry Self-Regulation as a Means to Promote Nonproliferation."

49. We are grateful to Gretchen Hund at Pacific Northwest National Laboratory for these insights.

50. United Nations, "2010 Review Conference of the Parties to the Treaty on the Non-Proliferation of Nuclear Weapons Final Document," vol. 1 (New York, 2010).

51. See Hund and Seward, "Broadening Industry Governance to Include Nonproliferation," pp. 1–3; and Letts and Cunningham, "The Role of the Civil Nuclear Industry in Preventing Proliferation," p. 17.

Appendix:
The Brookings Survey

Overview and Methodology

The Brookings research effort consisted of reaching out to stakeholders in the civilian nuclear energy community, with a focus on industry and nonindustry entities and individuals. These are defined as follows, and these definitions are used throughout this volume:

—*Industry:* commercial entities, including uranium mining companies, reactor vendors, enrichment and reprocessing service providers, and nuclear power utilities. This includes privately owned companies, as well as those either wholly or partly government owned. It also includes umbrella organizations representing companies.

—*Nonindustry:* nongovernmental organizations (NGOs), government agencies, nuclear regulators.

We targeted the larger commercial entities in the fuel cycle for several reasons: (1) they account for a significant portion of the overall market share of the civilian nuclear energy industry globally, and thus are leaders in their respective stages of the fuel cycle; (2) they often work at the highest levels of corporate-government relations and are increasingly at the nexus of discussions with international organizations, regulators, governments, and NGOs on approaches to strengthen the nonproliferation regime; and (3) they are increasingly globally engaged in a wide variety of high-profile commercial arrangements, investments, partnerships, and other activities.

We did not target dual-use technology providers and other industry participants, such as brokers, freight forwarders, and engineering, procurement, and construction entities; the number of players in this realm did not permit including them in this effort. In addition, this sector of the industry has been the focus of several other organizations, especially since the extent of the A. Q. Khan network was exposed. For example, the work of the Pacific Northwest Center for Global Security, the Institute for Science and International Security, the Henry L. Stimson Center, and the Wisconsin Project on Nuclear Arms Control have been closely monitoring or assessing the dual-use supplier market.

The outreach was conducted by the authors of this volume with support from the staff of the Energy Security Initiative at Brookings from the late fall of 2009 through August 2010. It was implemented in two ways: through discussions and interviews with stakeholders in the civilian nuclear energy community and the dissemination of a written survey. All responses are nonattributable; that is, we do not identify the source of any of the comments forming the basis of our analysis.

As noted in chapter 1, the written survey consisted of two parts. Part 1 asked participants their general views on the nonproliferation regime; part 2 asked participants to evaluate the *effectiveness* and *feasibility* of ten MNA approaches to varying aspects of the nuclear fuel cycle, and six proposals on industry self-regulation. *Effectiveness* refers to the ability of the proposal to strengthen the nonproliferation regime; *feasibility* refers to the logistical and political ease of implementation. The written survey and the ranking scale are provided later in the appendix.

Note that our survey was not intended as a formal, complete accounting of the many stakeholders throughout the civilian nuclear energy community. Rather it was distributed informally through our network of contacts with the intention of garnering a sufficient sample of responses that would reveal broad trends and patterns on major issues of the day affecting the development and expansion of nuclear power.

Results and Analysis

The written survey was distributed to ninety-two entities, with the following results:
  —Thirty-two responded (35 percent).
  —Nine declined to respond (10 percent).
  —Fifty-one did not respond (55 percent).
Our outreach was global, but most responses were from the United States and Europe, with twenty-two from industry and ten from nonindustry. As noted, a number of entities, mostly companies, actively declined to respond for a variety of reasons, and many simply did not respond. In some cases, discussions were

held with entities that also completed the survey, and follow-up questions were submitted to several survey participants.

Responses to part 1 questions are summarized and assessed in chapter 5, and part 2 responses are addressed in chapter 6 (on Multilateral Nuclear Approaches, MNAs) and chapter 7 (on self-regulation). Given that part 2 of the survey was structured to gather responses according to a specific scale to rank the effectiveness and feasibility of the proposals put forth, we are able to summarize the responses in a more quantitative manner across all respondents. The breakdown of responses from industry and nonindustry survey participants is provided in the following pages. For part 2 of the survey, ten industry responses were provided in a form that could not be aggregated in this quantitative presentation, and thus these responses are not included in the total number of industry responses. However, the information in those ten responses did inform the overall assessment of trends and patterns in the industry responses. In addition, in several other instances various participants in both categories did not provide answers to all questions.

Our analysis of part 2 responses attempts to identify broad trends and patterns. We examine industry and nonindustry responses individually, and then compare them. Specifically, we seek to identify where a majority of respondents ranked a proposal favorably (*effective/very effective* or *feasible/very feasible*) or unfavorably (*ineffective/very ineffective*, or *unfeasible/very unfeasible*). A "majority" is more than half of total respondents in a particular category; "no consensus" indicates that there was no majority in ranking a proposal in a particular category.

Brookings Nuclear Nonproliferation and Industry Study: Questions Guideline

Part 1: Overview Questions. Views of the nonproliferation regime, its current status and future strengthening opportunities

Part 2: Survey Questions. Views on specific proposals or ideas for strengthening the nonproliferation regime

NOTE: all responses will be nonattributable

Part 1: Overview Questions

1. What does your company/organization consider to be the biggest current nuclear proliferation risks?
2. To what extent does the projected expansion of the nuclear energy sector (in new and existing countries) represent a threat to the current nonproliferation regime?
3. What are the weaknesses and institutional gaps of the current nonproliferation regime? What mistakes can we learn from? In what ways has the nonproliferation regime been successfully strengthened to date?
4. How could the current Nonproliferation Treaty (NPT) be modified to better address the threats of nuclear proliferation? Which articles?
5. What is your view of the need for industry to be a partner with government in managing proliferation risks? How strong is the incentive for engagement? Beyond regulation, what should be the relationship between government and industry in such a partnership?
6. Which elements of the fuel cycle pose the greatest nonproliferation challenge?
7. What are your views on the proposed multinational agreements (MNAs) for the management of the fuel cycle? Would fuel-cycle-related MNAs strengthen/weaken the current nonproliferation regime? Which fuel cycle MNA model do you think would work best?
8. To what extent do new technologies increase/decrease proliferation risk?
9. In making nuclear power more safe, secure, and proliferation-resistant, how would you prioritize technical vs. institutional approaches?
10. What could the IAEA do to better address the challenges of nonproliferation in the twenty-first century?

Part 2: Survey Questions

Please rate the effectiveness and feasibility of the following proposals for strengthening the nuclear nonproliferation regime. Please give each proposal a number ranking from 1 to 5 for effectiveness in strengthening the nonproliferation regime, as well as a letter ranking of A to E for logistical and political feasibility of implementation.

Proposal	Effectiveness (1–5)	Logistical and political feasibility (A–E)	Comments (if any)
Multinational approaches to fuel cycle			
1. An IAEA-administered international enriched uranium fuel bank accessible to all countries			
2. An IAEA-administered international enriched uranium fuel bank accessible to all countries in compliance with NPT regulations			
3. An IAEA-administered international enrichment facility			
4. Conversion of all existing nuclear enrichment and reprocessing facilities currently under national control and IAEA safeguards into multinational facilities			
5. Commercial fuel leasing and take-back offers by internationally owned/operated bodies			
6. Commercial interim storage and disposal of spent fuel by internationally owned/operated bodies			
7. A long-term spent fuel repository under regional, multinational supervision			
8. Internationally supervised guarantees of supplies of nuclear fuel to states that forswear enrichment and reprocessing outside of formal "fuel bank" system			
9. Guarantees of internationally supervised supplies of nuclear fuel to states that do not forswear enrichment and reprocessing capabilities			
10. An internationally subsidized mechanism to increase supply of nuclear fuel to a level at which it becomes uneconomic for countries to engage in enrichment activities			

1 = very effective; 2 = effective; 3 = no impact; 4 = not effective; 5 = very ineffective;
A = very feasible; B = feasible; C = neutral; D = unfeasible; E = very unfeasible.

Proposal	Effectiveness (1–5)	Logistical and political feasibility (A–E)	Comments (if any)
Industry regulation/ compliance			
1. A voluntary code of conduct for all commercial entities in the nuclear industry incorporating broad nonproliferation values as well as best-practice guidelines specific to the sector			
2. A code of conduct such as that described above with a binding charter and penalties for noncompliance determined by signatory states			
3. A whistle-blower policy among commercial entities in the nuclear industry that explicitly encourages the exposure of actions—either inside or outside of the employee's company—that are deemed to violate preapproved nonproliferation standards			
4. A "black-box" provision ensuring that operators of enrichment and reprocessing facilities have no access to or information on key technical components of the plant			
5. An industry-wide quality management/accreditation system for suppliers of components for sensitive elements of the fuel cycle			
6. A periodic high-level international government-industry meeting to review the operation of any agreed system or set of measures			

1 = very effective; 2 = effective; 3 = no impact; 4 = not effective; 5 = very ineffective;
A = very feasible; B = feasible; C = neutral; D = unfeasible; E = very unfeasible.

Overall Survey Responses

Ranking of Effectiveness *of MNA Proposals*

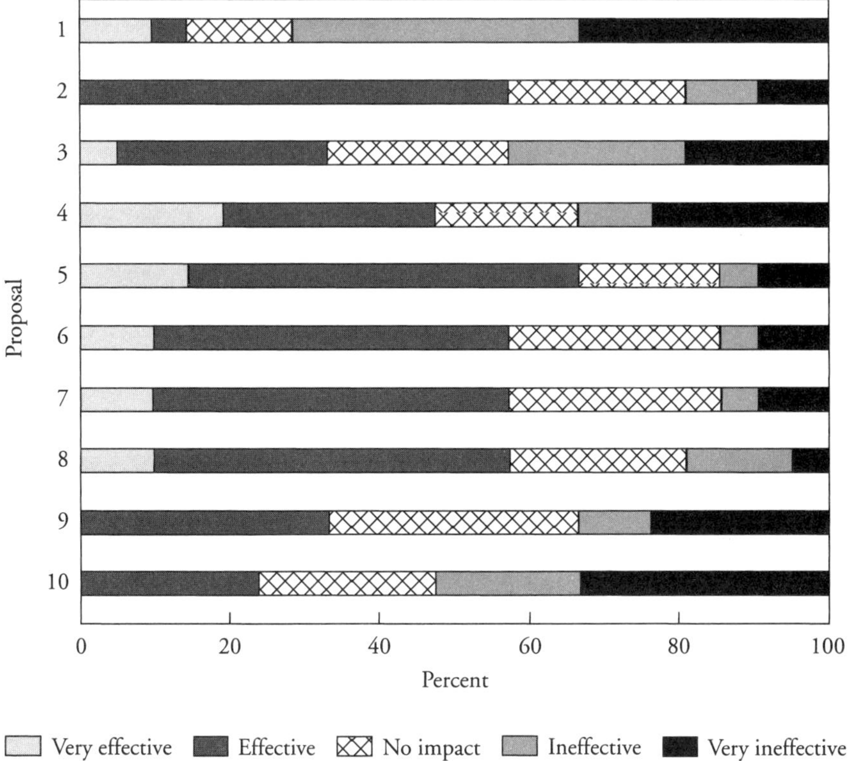

Proposal (number of responses: 21 for each proposal):

1. An IAEA-administered international enriched uranium fuel bank accessible to all countries
2. An IAEA-administered international enriched uranium fuel bank accessible to all countries in compliance with NPT regulations
3. An IAEA-administered international enrichment facility
4. Conversion of all existing nuclear enrichment and reprocessing facilities currently under national control and IAEA safeguards into multinational facilities
5. Commercial fuel leasing and take-back offers by internationally owned/operated bodies
6. Commercial interim storage and disposal of spent fuel by internationally owned/operated bodies
7. A long-term spent fuel repository under regional, multinational supervision
8. Internationally supervised guarantees of supplies of nuclear fuel to states that forswear enrichment and reprocessing outside of formal "fuel bank" system
9. Guarantees of internationally supervised supplies of nuclear fuel to states that do not forswear enrichment and reprocessing capabilities
10. An internationally subsidized mechanism to increase supply of nuclear fuel to a level at which it becomes uneconomic for countries to engage in enrichment activities

Ranking of Feasibility *of MNA Proposals*

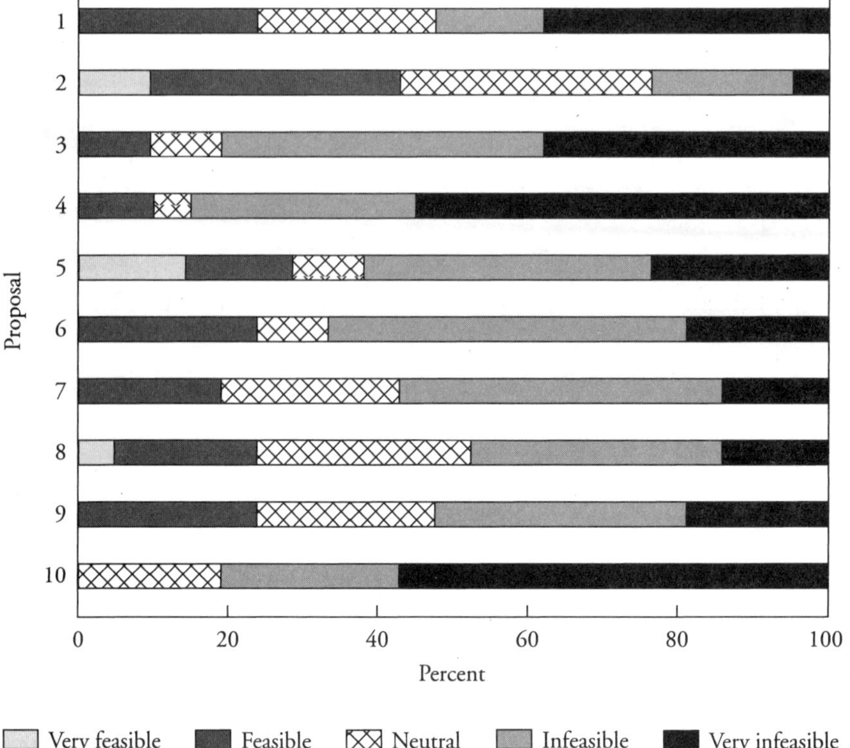

Proposals (number of responses: 21 for each proposal, except Proposal 4 [20]):

1. An IAEA-administered international enriched uranium fuel bank accessible to all countries

2. An IAEA-administered international enriched uranium fuel bank accessible to all countries in compliance with NPT regulations

3. An IAEA-administered international enrichment facility

4. Conversion of all existing nuclear enrichment and reprocessing facilities currently under national control and IAEA safeguards into multinational facilities

5. Commercial fuel leasing and take-back offers by internationally owned/operated bodies

6. Commercial interim storage and disposal of spent fuel by internationally owned/operated bodies

7. A long-term spent fuel repository under regional, multinational supervision

8. Internationally supervised guarantees of supplies of nuclear fuel to states that forswear enrichment and reprocessing outside of formal "fuel bank" system

9. Guarantees Of internationally supervised supplies of nuclear fuel to states that do not forswear enrichment and reprocessing capabilities

10. An internationally subsidized mechanism to increase supply of nuclear fuel to a level at which it becomes uneconomic for countries to engage in enrichment activities

Ranking of Effectiveness *of Self-Regulatory Proposals*

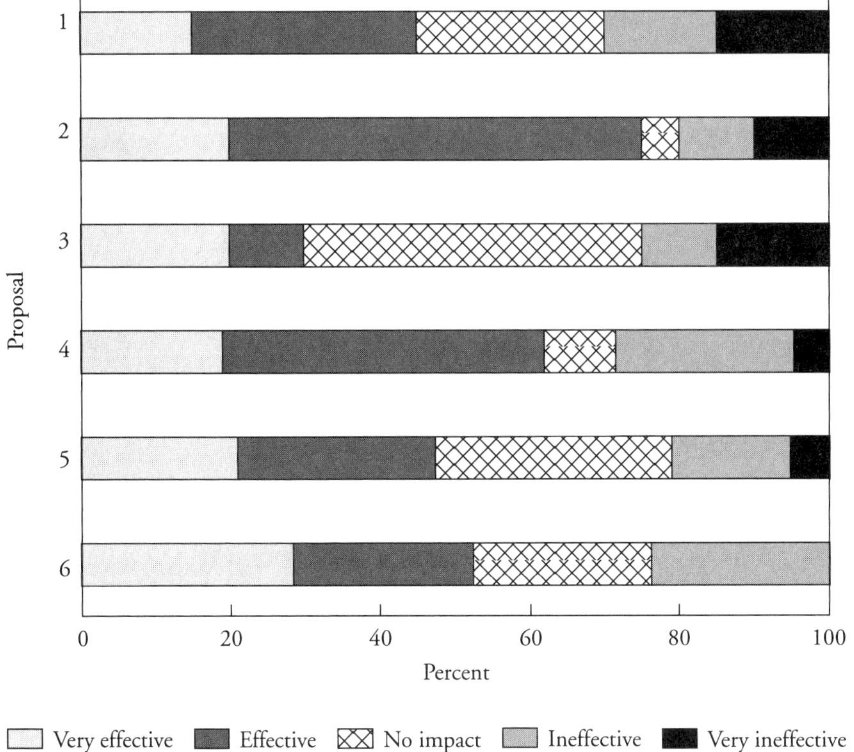

Proposals (number of responses: for Proposals 1, 2, and 3 [20]; for Proposals 4 and 6 [21]; for Proposal 5 [19]):

1. A voluntary code of conduct for all commercial entities in the nuclear industry incorporating broad nonproliferation values as well as best-practice guidelines specific to the sector
2. A code of conduct such as that described above with a binding charter and penalties for noncompliance determined by signatory states
3. A whistle-blower policy among commercial entities in the nuclear industry that explicitly encourages the exposure of actions—either inside or outside of the employee's company—that are deemed to violate preapproved nonproliferation standards
4. A "black-box" provision ensuring that operators of enrichment and reprocessing facilities have no access to or information on key technical components of the plant
5. An industry-wide quality management/accreditation system for suppliers of components for sensitive elements of the fuel cycle
6. A periodic high-level international government-industry meeting to review the operation of any agreed system or set of measures

Ranking of Feasibility *of Self-Regulatory Proposals*

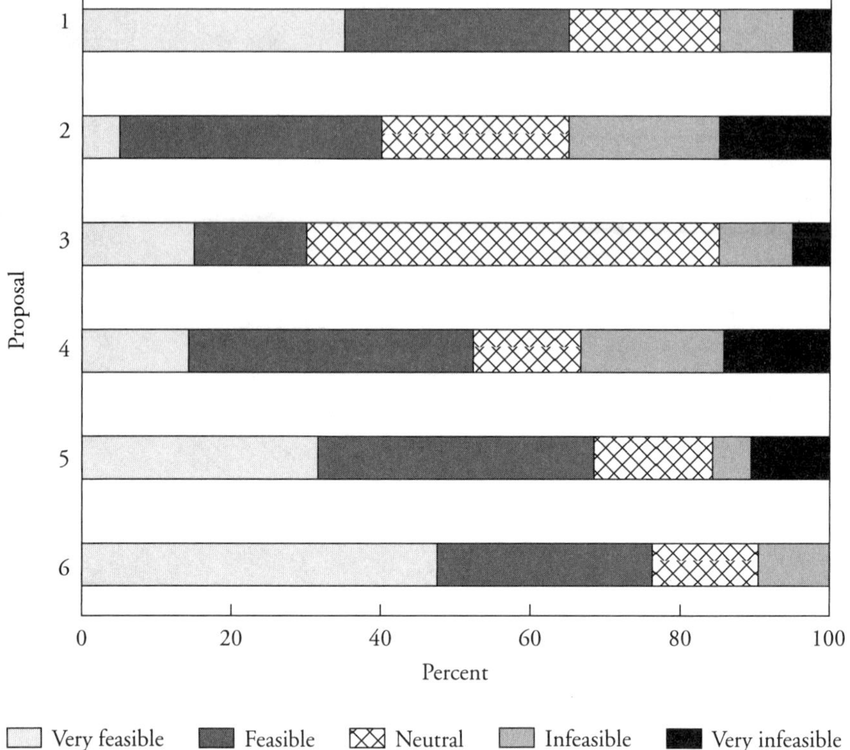

Proposals (number of responses: for Proposals 1, 2, and 3 [20]; for Proposals 4 and 6 [21];
for Proposal 5 [19]):

1. A voluntary code of conduct for all commercial entities in the nuclear industry incorpo-
    rating broad nonproliferation values as well as best-practice guidelines specific to the
    sector
2. A code of conduct such as that described above with a binding charter and penalties for
    noncompliance determined by signatory states
3. A whistle-blower policy among commercial entities in the nuclear industry that explicitly
    encourages the exposure of actions—either inside or outside of the employee's
    company—that are deemed to violate preapproved nonproliferation standards
4. A "black-box" provision ensuring that operators of enrichment and reprocessing facilities
    have no access to or information on key technical components of the plant
5. An industry-wide quality management/accreditation system for suppliers of components
    for sensitive elements of the fuel cycle
6. A periodic high-level international government-industry meeting to review the operation
    of any agreed system or set of measures

Industry Survey Responses

Ranking of Effectiveness of MNA Proposals

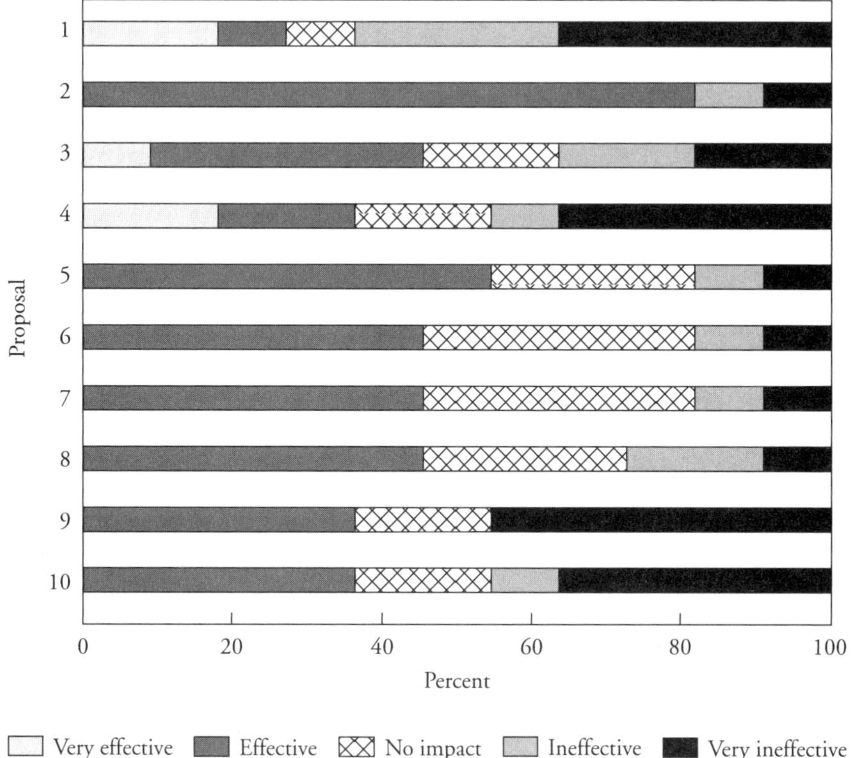

Proposals (number of responses: 11 for each proposal):

1. An IAEA-administered international enriched uranium fuel bank accessible to all countries
2. An IAEA-administered international enriched uranium fuel bank accessible to all countries in compliance with NPT regulations
3. An IAEA-administered international enrichment facility
4. Conversion of all existing nuclear enrichment and reprocessing facilities currently under national control and IAEA safeguards into multinational facilities
5. Commercial fuel leasing and take-back offers by internationally owned/operated bodies
6. Commercial interim storage and disposal of spent fuel by internationally owned/operated bodies
7. A long-term spent fuel repository under regional, multinational supervision
8. Internationally supervised guarantees of supplies of nuclear fuel to states that forswear enrichment and reprocessing outside of formal "fuel bank" system
9. Guarantees of internationally supervised supplies of nuclear fuel to states that do not forswear enrichment and reprocessing capabilities
10. An internationally subsidized mechanism to increase supply of nuclear fuel to a level at which it becomes uneconomic for countries to engage in enrichment activities

Ranking of Feasibility of MNA Proposals

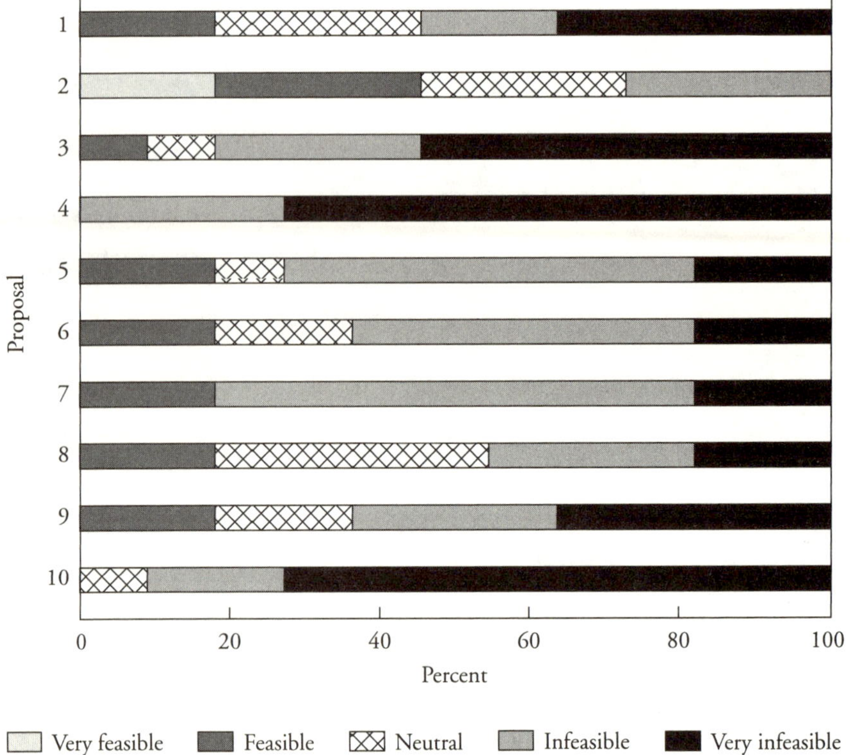

Proposals (number of responses: 11 for each proposal):

1. An IAEA-administered international enriched uranium fuel bank accessible to all countries
2. An IAEA-administered international enriched uranium fuel bank accessible to all countries in compliance with NPT regulations
3. An IAEA-administered international enrichment facility
4. Conversion of all existing nuclear enrichment and reprocessing facilities currently under national control and IAEA safeguards into multinational facilities
5. Commercial fuel leasing and take-back offers by internationally owned/operated bodies
6. Commercial interim storage and disposal of spent fuel by internationally owned/operated bodies
7. A long-term spent fuel repository under regional, multinational supervision
8. Internationally supervised guarantees of supplies of nuclear fuel to states that forswear enrichment and reprocessing outside of formal "fuel bank" system
9. Guarantees of internationally supervised supplies of nuclear fuel to states that do not forswear enrichment and reprocessing capabilities
10. An internationally subsidized mechanism to increase supply of nuclear fuel to a level at which it becomes uneconomic for countries to engage in enrichment activities

Ranking of Effectiveness of Self-Regulatory Proposals

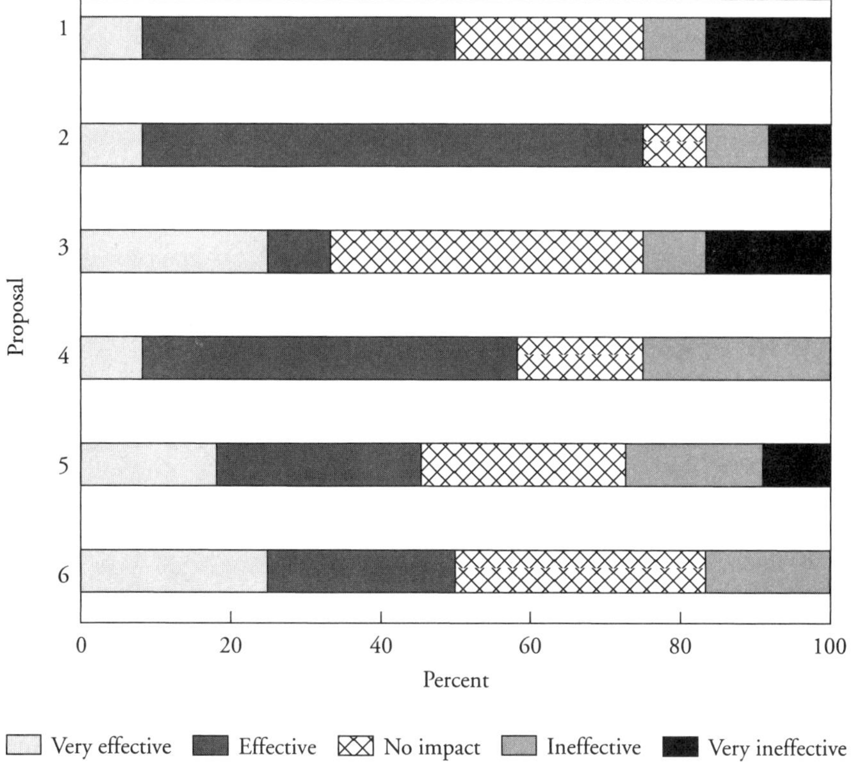

Proposals (number of responses: 12 for each proposal, except Proposal 5 [11]):

1. A voluntary code of conduct for all commercial entities in the nuclear industry incorporating broad nonproliferation values as well as best-practice guidelines specific to the sector
2. A code of conduct such as that described above with a binding charter and penalties for noncompliance determined by signatory states
3. A whistle-blower policy among commercial entities in the nuclear industry that explicitly encourages the exposure of actions—either inside or outside of the employee's company—that are deemed to violate preapproved nonproliferation standards
4. A "black-box" provision ensuring that operators of enrichment and reprocessing facilities have no access to or information on key technical components of the plant
5. An industry-wide quality management/ accreditation system for suppliers of components for sensitive elements of the fuel cycle
6. A periodic high-level international government-industry meeting to review the operation of any agreed system or set of measures

Ranking of Feasibility of Self-Regulatory Proposals

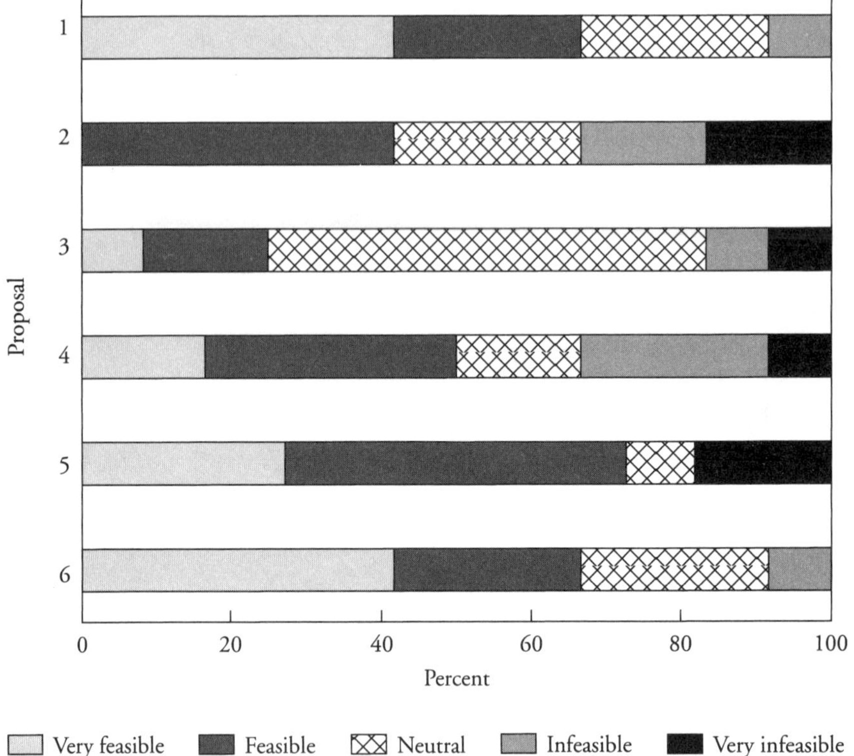

Proposals (number of responses: 12 for each proposal, except Proposal 5 [11]):

1. A voluntary code of conduct for all commercial entities in the nuclear industry incorporating broad nonproliferation values as well as best-practice guidelines specific to the sector
2. A code of conduct such as that described above with a binding charter and penalties for noncompliance determined by signatory states
3. A whistle-blower policy among commercial entities in the nuclear industry that explicitly encourages the exposure of actions—either inside or outside of the employee's company—that are deemed to violate preapproved nonproliferation standards
4. A "black-box" provision ensuring that operators of enrichment and reprocessing facilities have no access to or information on key technical components of the plant
5. An industry-wide quality management/accreditation system for suppliers of components for sensitive elements of the fuel cycle
6. A periodic high-level international government-industry meeting to review the operation of any agreed system or set of measures

Nonindustry Survey Responses

Ranking of Effectiveness of MNA Proposals

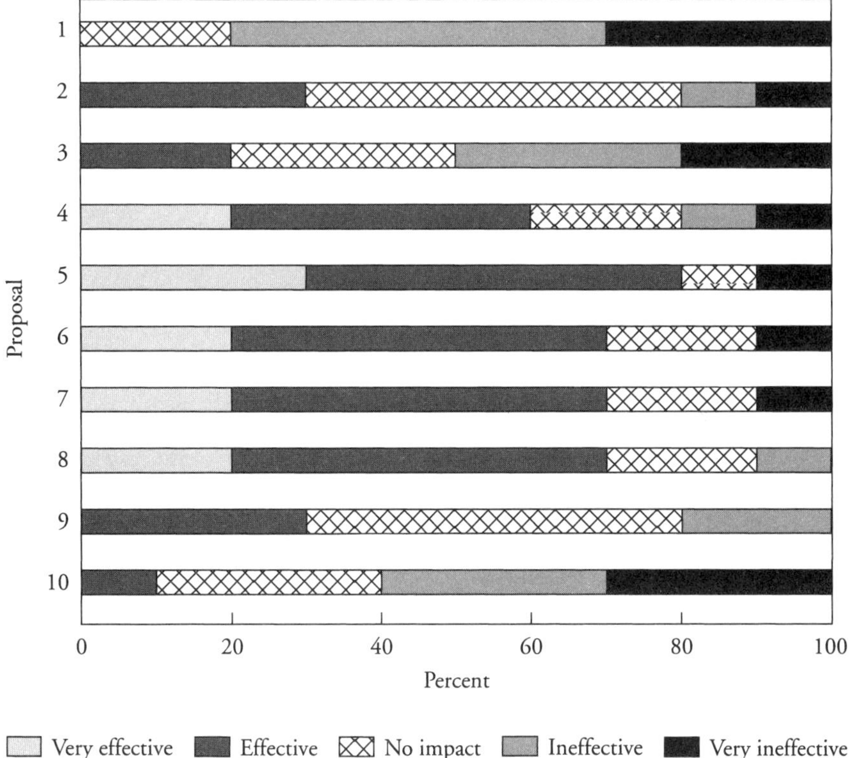

Proposal (number of responses: 10 for each proposal):

1. An IAEA-administered international enriched uranium fuel bank accessible to all countries
2. An IAEA-administered international enriched uranium fuel bank accessible to all countries in compliance with NPT regulations
3. An IAEA-administered international enrichment facility
4. Conversion of all existing nuclear enrichment and reprocessing facilities currently under national control and IAEA safeguards into multinational facilities
5. Commercial fuel leasing and take-back offers by internationally owned/operated bodies
6. Commercial interim storage and disposal of spent fuel by internationally owned/operated bodies
7. A long-term spent fuel repository under regional, multinational supervision
8. Internationally supervised guarantees of supplies of nuclear fuel to states that forswear enrichment and reprocessing outside of formal "fuel bank" system
9. Guarantees of internationally supervised supplies of nuclear fuel to states that do not forswear enrichment and reprocessing capabilities
10. An internationally subsidized mechanism to increase supply of nuclear fuel to a level at which it becomes uneconomic for countries to engage in enrichment activities

Ranking of Feasibility of MNA Proposals

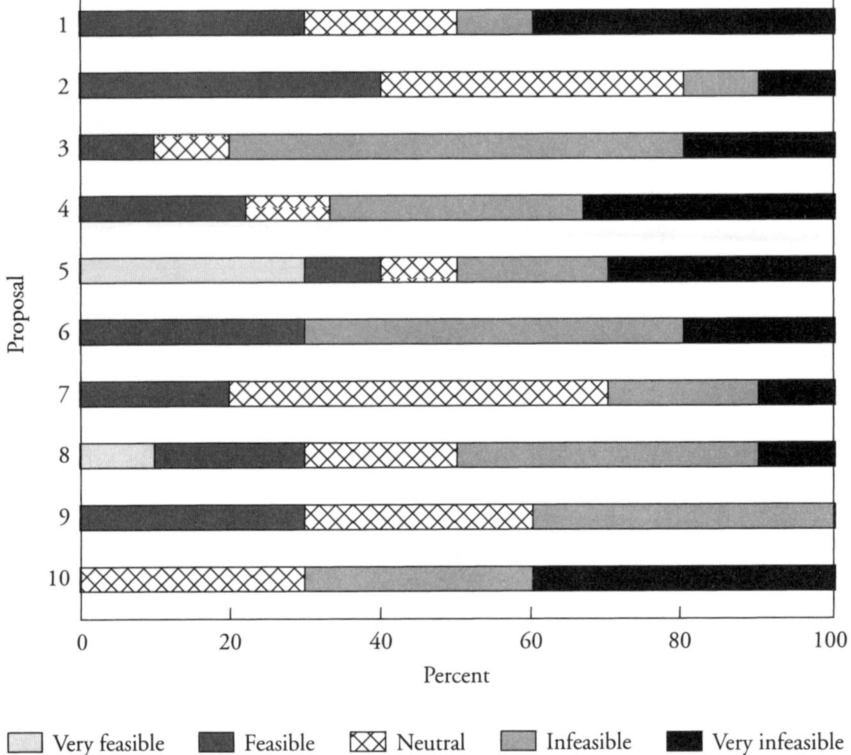

Proposals (number of responses: 10 for each proposal, except Proposal 4 [9]):

1. An IAEA-administered international enriched uranium fuel bank accessible to all countries
2. An IAEA-administered international enriched uranium fuel bank accessible to all countries in compliance with NPT regulations
3. An IAEA-administered international enrichment facility
4. Conversion of all existing nuclear enrichment and reprocessing facilities currently under national control and IAEA safeguards into multinational facilities
5. Commercial fuel leasing and take-back offers by internationally owned/operated bodies
6. Commercial interim storage and disposal of spent fuel by internationally owned/operated bodies
7. A long-term spent fuel repository under regional, multinational supervision
8. Internationally supervised guarantees of supplies of nuclear fuel to states that forswear enrichment and reprocessing outside of formal "fuel bank" system
9. Guarantees of internationally supervised supplies of nuclear fuel to states that do not forswear enrichment and reprocessing capabilities
10. An internationally subsidized mechanism to increase supply of nuclear fuel to a level at which it becomes uneconomic for countries to engage in enrichment activities

Ranking of Effectiveness of Self-Regulatory Proposals

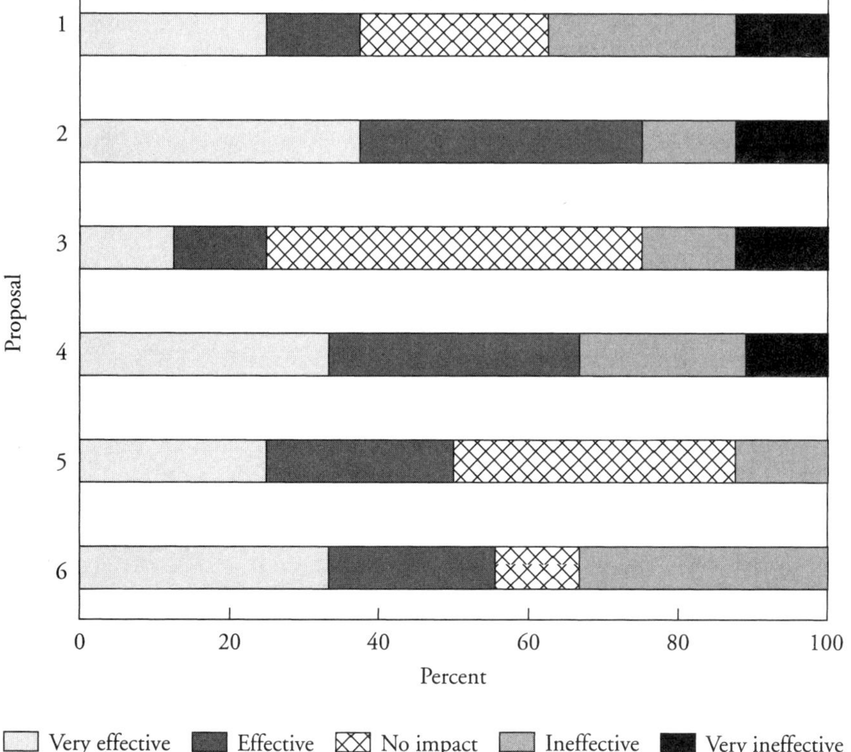

Proposals (number of responses: for Proposals 1, 2, 3, and 5 [8]; for Proposals 4 and 6 [9]):

1. A voluntary code of conduct for all commercial entities in the nuclear industry incorporating broad nonproliferation values as well as best-practice guidelines specific to the sector
2. A code of conduct such as that described above with a binding charter and penalties for noncompliance determined by signatory states
3. A whistle-blower policy among commercial entities in the nuclear industry that explicitly encourages the exposure of actions—either inside or outside of the employee's company—that are deemed to violate preapproved nonproliferation standards
4. A "black-box" provision ensuring that operators of enrichment and reprocessing facilities have no access to or information on key technical components of the plant
5. An industry-wide quality management/accreditation system for suppliers of components for sensitive elements of the fuel cycle
6. A periodic high-level international government-industry meeting to review the operation of any agreed system or set of measures

Ranking of Feasibility of Self-Regulatory Proposals

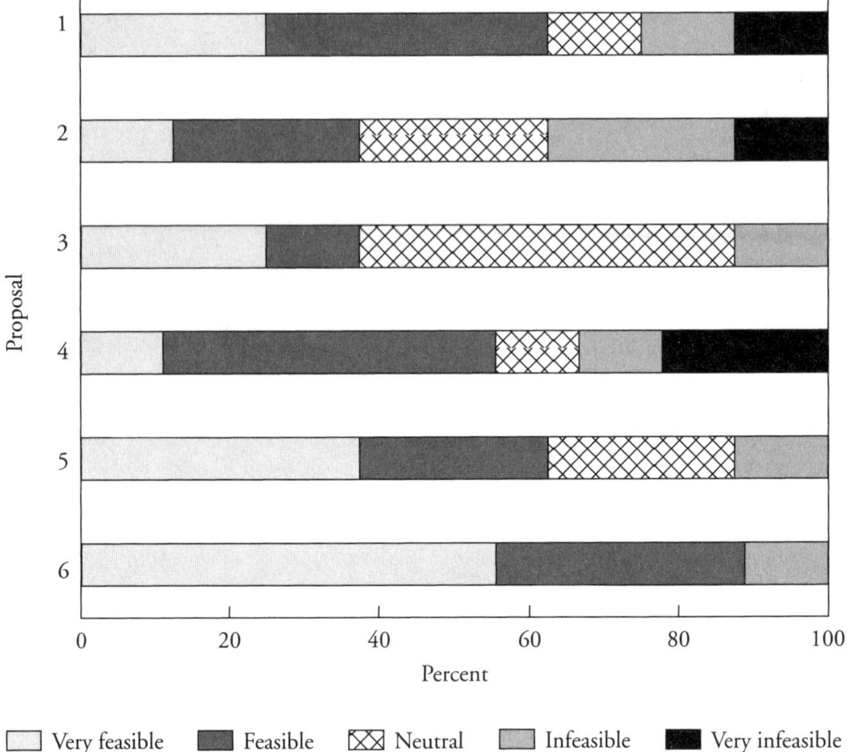

Proposals (number of responses: for Proposals 1, 2, 3, and 5 [8]; for Proposals 4 and 6 [9]):

1. A voluntary code of conduct for all commercial entities in the nuclear industry incorporating broad nonproliferation values as well as best-practice guidelines specific to the sector
2. A code of conduct such as that described above with a binding charter and penalties for noncompliance determined by signatory states
3. A whistle-blower policy among commercial entities in the nuclear industry that explicitly encourages the exposure of actions—either inside or outside of the employee's company—that are deemed to violate preapproved nonproliferation standards
4. A "black-box" provision ensuring that operators of enrichment and reprocessing facilities have no access to or information on key technical components of the plant
5. An industry-wide quality management/ accreditation system for suppliers of components for sensitive elements of the fuel cycle
6. A periodic high-level international government-industry meeting to review the operation of any agreed system or set of measures

About the Authors

Govinda Avasarala is a Research Assistant with the Energy Security Initiative at the Brookings Institution.

John P. Banks is a Nonresident Fellow with the Energy Security Initiative at the Brookings Institution and an adjunct professor at the Johns Hopkins School of Advanced International Studies.

Charles K. Ebinger is a Senior Fellow and Director of the Energy Security Initiative at the Brookings Institution.

Michael Moodie is Assistant Director of Foreign Affairs, Defense, and Trade at the Congressional Research Service.

Lawrence Scheinman is Distinguished Professor at the Center for Nonproliferation Studies, Monterey Institute of International Studies, and an adjunct professor at the Johns Hopkins School of Advanced International Studies.

Sharon Squassoni is a Senior Fellow and Director of the Proliferation Prevention Program at the Center for Strategic and International Studies.

Index